ELEANOR ROOSEVELT'S
My Day

ELEANOR ROOSEVELT'S
My Day

VOLUME II: THE POST-WAR YEARS

Her Acclaimed Columns,

1945–1952

EDITED BY DAVID EMBLIDGE
INTRODUCTION BY PAMELA C. HARRIMAN

PHAROS BOOKS
A SCRIPPS HOWARD COMPANY
NEW YORK

973.917 - Roosevelt
Vol. 2.

Frontispiece: This portrait study of Mrs. Roosevelt was made during a press conference in Copenhagen, at the residence of the U.S. Ambassador to Denmark, one of the many stops on her 1950 tour of Europe. *(UPI/Bettmann)*

Copyright © 1990 by Pharos Books
Introduction © 1990 by Pamela Harriman

First published in 1990.

Library of Congress Cataloging-in-Publication Data

(Revised for vol. 2)
Roosevelt, Eleanor, 1884–1962.
  Eleanor Roosevelt's My day.

  Includes index.
  Contents: v. 1. Her acclaimed colums, 1936–1945 —
v. 2. The Post-war years, 1945–1952.
  1. Roosevelt, Eleanor, 1884–1962—Political and
social views.   2. Roosevelt, Eleanor, 1884–1962—Friends
and associates.   3. United States—Politics and
government—1933–1945.   I. Chadakoff, Rochelle.
II. Title.
E807.1.R48A3   1989   973.917'092'4   88-28821
ISBN 0-88687-407-6 (v. 1)

Book design by Bea Jackson

Printed in the United States of America

Pharos Books
A Scripps Howard Company
200 Park Avenue
New York, N.Y. 10166

10 9 8 7 6 5 4 3 2 1

Contents

Preface

It is often easy to see, with the clear view afforded by hindsight, where leaders of the past made mistakes. In the case of Eleanor Roosevelt, this common if unforgiving historical process has generally reversed itself: if anything, as the years pass Mrs. Roosevelt rises higher and higher in the public's estimation as the country's pre-eminent First Lady. Historian James MacGregor Burns, in his magisterial three-volume *The American Experiment* (1989), singled out Eleanor Roosevelt as his one hero—notably in fact a heroine—of social change. Burns praises her for her political wisdom, her concern for the downtrodden, her internationalism, and her crusading for women's rights.

This is of course not to say that other First Ladies have not made substantial contributions to the nation's cultural and political life. But whether we look way back in American history or scan the recent list of President's wives, it is arguably impossible to find another who comes close to matching Eleanor Roosevelt's sheer energy and diversity of interests. She was a dynamo.

As these selections from her syndicated newspaper column, "My Day," amply show, no activity or work or subject was too humble to gain Eleanor Roosevelt's attention. No glittering gala event with royalty from foreign lands or famous entertainers from her own country was too sophisticated for her tastes. From one day to the next her readers watched Eleanor shift, for example, from the joys of gardening at her beloved Hyde Park, New York, residence to the painstaking negotiations required of her as chair of the United Nations Committee on Human Rights in hammering out an acceptable Universal Declaration of Human Rights. She was a woman who could find fascination in the details of child rearing related to any of her multitudinous family or just as much fascination in visiting a foreign capital where everyday life may not have been to her liking but where the people's struggle to survive with dignity would engage her imagination and her heart.

This volume covers the period from April 1945 (just after President Roosevelt died) through the end of 1952. (A third volume completing the coverage of Eleanor Roosevelt's newspaper columns through the year she died, 1962, will follow.) In Volume II we see Mrs. Roosevelt recovering from the shock of the President's death and, with surprising quickness, finding her own way as a widow and a working woman. Soon after the war President Harry Truman asked her to serve as a delegate to the first United Nations sessions, and she eventually goes on to chair the Committee on Human Rights. By 1952, when Truman leaves the White House, Eleanor Roosevelt's official standing at the UN is over (although in subsequent years her work as an interested citizen in support of the UN occupies a large share of her time). The year 1952 marks the end of the long Democratic control of the Executive Branch when Adlai Stevenson's first campaign for the presidency fails, despite Mrs. Roosevelt's active support. That year also saw the beginning of the painfully slow truce negotiations in the Korean conflict, and by this time, though a good deal more Red-baiting was still to come, much of the worst of McCarthyism—including the Senate's own condemnation of the fiery anti-Communist senator, was over.

During the Depression and throughout most of World War II, when FDR was in the White House, Eleanor Roosevelt often functioned as his ears and eyes by traveling all across the country and around the world on the President's behalf. She also spoke frequently at public gatherings and wrote everything from newspaper articles to magazine journalism to the first volume of an autobiography. Her position as the President's wife nevertheless required that she be circumspect in expressing her opinions, letting her loyalty to the President's programs override her natural tendency to play the role of gadfly. Once the President was gone, however, Eleanor Roosevelt took off the padded gloves and became the indefatigable, outspoken fighter for a whole rainbow of causes, many of them far from popular. She was, like most brave reformers, well ahead of her time. The selections from "My Day" in this volume bear this out.

Mrs. Roosevelt produced five hundred words per column and often more, six days per week, with virtually no interruptions, for nearly twenty-six years (1936–1962). I have selected the best and most important of the columns with an eye to representing the full range of her interests during the 1945–1952 period. Not a great prose stylist, she required the help of her endlessly loyal secretaries to get the daily columns cleaned up, typed, and transmitted by wire or phone to the United Feature Syndicate in New York. Eleanor Roosevelt had the good fortune to be blessed with a high energy metabolism and a touch of chronic insomnia: She often wrote her "My Day" columns or her other material for publication in bed at the end of a packed sixteen-hour day.

For their help in preparing this volume I want to thank my editor at Pharos Books, Eileen Schlesinger, and our copy editor, H. L. Kirk; the archivists in the F.D.R. Presidential Library at Hyde Park; Sheila Buff who introduced me to this editing project and provided hospitality on my visits to Hyde Park; the reference librarians at the Berkshire Athenaeum, Pittsfield, Massachusetts; and the many people, young and old—Roosevelt lovers and Roosevelt haters—whose spontaneously offered stories about this great lady confirmed for me the fact that among American women, Eleanor Roosevelt indeed ranks first.

DAVID EMBLIDGE

Introduction

Writing in the week that the American Revolution took new steps forward and the Communist Revolution fell further into disarray, I can't help thinking how much these events would have pleased Eleanor Roosevelt. On Election Day, November 7, 1989 (the twenty-seventh anniversary of her death), Americans voted without regard for race; on the same day (the seventy-second anniversary of the Russian Revolution), Soviets and East Germans were protesting openly against repression. Thus, in the west *and* the east, people demonstrated the civic courage that would have confirmed Eleanor Roosevelt's faith in the decency of ordinary men and women and in the strength of democracy's appeal. Suffusing the columns collected here from the first seven years of her widowhood, her convictions transform her daily journalism from period pieces to a lasting testament.

To readers meeting her for the first time in this volume, Mrs. Roosevelt may seem something of a period piece herself. As a former First Lady who put up her own fruits and vegetables, who got around alone on the New York subway, who read Kipling aloud to her grandchildren, who sang childhood hymns to lure her straying dog back, who found A *Streetcar Named Desire* and *Death of a Salesman* unsatisfying theater, she might appear only an odd bird or historical curiosity. Those who dismiss her in such terms miss a major significance of her life: In feminine and feminist form, Mrs. Roosevelt embodied the transition of an elitist Victorian social consciousness into the politics of the mass society and the global village.

"An incorrigible doer of good deeds" former White House aide Rexford Tugwell called her in his memoirs of the New Deal. Outside

5

the White House and at the United Nations in the years covered by these "My Day" columns she took "a role of democratic leadership, has promoted extensive international understanding and cooperation, and has earned for herself a reputation as one of the outstanding women of the world," wrote Samuel Rosenman, FDR's former speechwriter. But, Rosenman added, "Only those who were privileged to know her personally . . . can appreciate her feminine grace, charm, simplicity and tolerant understanding. No act of kindness and courtesy ever seemed too trivial for her personal attention. No act of helpfulness and encouragement seemed too difficult for her to undertake."

Neither a victim of what is now called "liberal guilt" nor a caricature of noblesse oblige, Mrs. Roosevelt was an American aristocrat for whom high moral standards dictated a commitment to the betterment of her world. Like her contemporaries John Dewey and George Santayana, she took her ethics from the Sermon on the Mount and insisted on their immediate relevance to both personal and public conduct in the midst of twentieth-century relativism.

Like her husband, she was heir to the muscular faith preached by the rector of Groton, Endicott Peabody, who taught FDR and presided at his marriage to Eleanor. A formidable figure, the rector struck one new student, Averell Harriman, in 1904 as someone who "would be an awful bully if he weren't such a terrific Christian."

Averell's irreverent youthful verdict on his headmaster offers a valid, if incomplete, description of Eleanor Roosevelt as well. Her own words, in the May 7, 1945, column (the second in this volume) flesh out the portrait of a moral activist: "Young or old, in order to be useful, we must stand for the things we feel are right, and we must work for those things wherever we find ourselves." And in her November 10, 1952, column the credo takes on broader meaning: "[I]t would be a good thing for governments to realize that a man's philosophy, when it is given practical demonstration through what he does at home for the people of his own country, can be vastly important to the people of other nations."

The idea of Americans as both moral and pragmatic exemplars to the world is hardly unique to Mrs. Roosevelt. It runs from John

Winthrop's "City upon a hill" sermon in 1630 aboard the ship *Arabella* to the frequent use of the theme by President Ronald Reagan—a onetime New Deal Democrat. For Eleanor Roosevelt, however, the concept was a compelling one, not a rhetorical device. It guided her not just as an author published daily in seventy-five to ninety newspapers in the years 1945–1952 but also in her nonstop public and private lives.

As she wrote in a 1945, sixty-first-birthday column that is excerpted in the preceding volume, her friends did not believe she would ever "sit by the fire with a little lace cap on my head and a shawl about my shoulders and knit baby things. . . . The day will come, however, and when it does, I think it will be rather pleasant." That day never came; she staved it off with relentless activity.

Her public life did not fully resume until President Harry Truman sent her at the end of 1945 as the only U.S. woman delegate to the first meeting of the United Nations General Assembly in London. She arrived full of hope for postwar unity, for "building . . . a united force which will control all individual force throughout the world." Repeated frustrating encounters with Soviet obstructionism, however, made her a realist in fairly short order. In "My Day" for June 10, 1947, she boiled East–West tension down to a single sentence: "If the Russian Government still hopes for world revolution brought about by representatives in other countries guided from Russia, it cannot be honest in trying to work cooperatively with other governments as they now exist."

The way to frustrate Soviet designs, she saw, was to feed both the flesh and the spirit of democracy. "Starving people," she wrote in her April 9, 1947, column opposing moves to bar food aid to Poland and Yugoslavia, "are [not] going to be better democrats. What we are doing is building up enemies." But the danger lay in Communism abroad, not subversion at home: "Only here and in other free democracies can we criticize our Government and have the freedom to think independently. [A] very precious freedom, it requires of us something more than apathetic citizenship. We must really believe in democracy and in our objectives. . . .

"Proposals to outlaw the Communist Party seem to be another

7

evidence of a feeling of insecurity. I can imagine nothing stupider than to believe that the mass of people of this country would really find Communism a greater advantage." (March 27, 1947)

While she excoriated what was to become McCarthyism in the United States, she led the nobler effort in the United Nations to define universal human rights and make respect for them a cornerstone of international cooperation. Presiding over the drafting of the 1948 Declaration of Human Rights, she outdebated and outwitted the Soviets at every turn. The columns in this collection tell only a fragment of that story and next to nothing of her own role. Yet "never," commented a State Department adviser, "have I seen naïveté and cunning so gracefully blended."

In a 1958 work she wrote for the UN, *The Great Question*, Mrs. Roosevelt looked back ten years to her triumph and found it significant only insofar as human rights were applied "close to home," in neighborhoods, schools, factories, farms, and offices, "where every man, woman and child seeks equal justice, equal opportunity, equal dignity without discrimination. Unless these rights have meaning there, they have little meaning anywhere. Without concerned citizen action to uphold them close to home, we shall look in vain for progress in the larger world."

That theme of responsible citizenship is a steady leitmotiv of these columns. It surfaces in straightforward endorsements of various charities, in calls for greater public participation in politics, and with rising indignation in her battle against racism in the United States. What may surprise a modern reader is the number of issues to which she turned her attention and her pen—health care costs, Middle East peace, drug addiction, school prayer, historic preservation—that still trouble Americans today.

What is reassuring is how sensible her prescriptions for these various problems still sound. Not a doctrinaire liberal or a reflexive advocate for bigger government, she constantly puts the burden of action on individual conscience and community self-interest. And in the face of all difficulties, she radiates an inspiring optimism. As her friend Adlai Stevenson said on the day she died, "She would rather light candles than curse the darkness, and her glow has warmed the world."

Only once in this volume will the reader hear her despairing, and it is over a dilemma that has only grown worse since she first faced it. Her May 15, 1948, column recounts her anguish a few nights earlier at finding a man unconscious—"drunk, ill or asleep" on the sidewalk in the Greenwich Village section of New York City. Uncertain what to do, she reported his plight to "the first policeman we met" and walked on to the lecture she had planned to attend. But the problem haunted her:

"The story of the Good Samaritan kept running through my head, and I wondered whether it was possible in a big city to feel the same responsibility for your fellow man as you would feel on a country road. I don't suppose the man was worthy, and I doubt if you can take a man you see lying in the street and have him carried into an apartment house. But leaving him there seemed heartless and senseless and inhuman, and I don't think I like the way we live in these days."

Her mission was always to make her own days better ones. They were incredibly full ones and, in the years after her husband's death, as exhausting as they had been in the White House. In both periods, Eleanor Roosevelt was (there should be such a word) an omnipresence. She was always writing, a monthly magazine column as well as "My Day" and her copious private correspondence; always in public, on her own television program as well as at countless lecterns; always on the go.

And so even without knowing her personally, I could feel, as most of the world did, that she was a friend and a source of support. Once at a dinner in London after the war, Clare Boothe Luce, a very different public woman from Mrs. Roosevelt, announced that her success as a playwright, as a two-term Republican Member of Congress from Connecticut, and as an authority on the world had made her think of running for president. No one laughed outright at her presumption; her tongue dripped acid, and her husband, Harry Luce, was the powerful publisher of *Time* and *Life*. But Lord

Beaverbrook, publisher of the *Daily Express* and a former minister in Churchill's Cabinet, had the temerity to venture a small joke. The idea seemed splendid, he said, and if she won the White House, "Harry could write 'My Day.'"

Mrs. Luce was not amused. But, as you are about to discover in the pages that follow, she should have been flattered. The great lady who did write "My Day" set a high standard of engaged journalism and responsible opinion. Her columns are not just worth reading. They are inspiring.

PAMELA C. HARRIMAN

1945

ranklin Delano Roosevelt took the oath of office for President in 1932 as the country was reeling from the continuing shock of economic collapse. When he died on April 12, 1945, of a cerebral hemorrhage while vacationing and seeking rest for a generally weakened condition at Warm Springs, Georgia, the nation still had not had the chance to recover fully from the economic trials of the thirties. The trauma of World War II had occupied the President's and the nation's attention day in and day out since the conflict broke out in Europe in 1939. Through all of this—the struggle to bring the country back to economic health with the New Deal and the struggle to save Western civilization from material and moral destruction at the hands of totalitarian and racist imperialists in both Europe and the Far East—Eleanor Roosevelt stood steadfastly by her husband's side.

She was not, by either training or personality, a woman to wallow in grief. Perhaps there was also an underlying belief in her that industry is indeed the best enemy of melancholy. Allowing herself only a few days' rest after the President's death, Mrs. Roosevelt resumed her writing of the "My Day" column. (It did not appear from April 12 to April 16.) At first she wrote of her activities in the transition from wife to widow, from First Lady to private citizen. But soon the great unresolved issues of the war, the impending economic recovery, and the future of the hundreds of thousands of refugees and displaced persons and homeward-bound servicemen and -women began to occupy Eleanor Roosevelt's attention.

Vice President Harry S. Truman took up the cause where FDR

left off. Within days after FDR's death, Truman addressed Congress and the people to assure them of a smooth transition and continuance of the dead President's military and economic policies. By late April, U.S. and Soviet troops, fighting as allies, met for the first time in Germany. At the same time, in San Francisco, representatives of fifty nations gathered to work out a document that would become the Charter of the United Nations, an organization whose peaceful principles symbolized a ray of hope for a war-weary civilization. On May 7 Germany surrendered to the Allied command at Reims, France; Gen. Dwight D. Eisenhower accepted on behalf of the victorious Allies. President Truman declared the following day V-E Day, and the country rejoiced.

War in the Pacific Theater dragged on, however, with the Japanese still resolutely believing they would prevail. While the Big Four (the United States, Britain, France, the Soviet Union) met to divide Berlin and Germany into spheres of control (laying the groundwork unwittingly for the still-divided Germany of the late 1980s), Allied troops on land and sea in the Pacific scored numerous victories but in so doing lost thousands of lives as well. Japan surrendered Okinawa to the Allies by the end of June, and Gen. Douglas MacArthur recaptured the Philippine Islands one week later. With no comprehensive surrender by the Japanese in sight, the United States proceeded to test a new weapon: On July 16, 1945, the first atomic bomb was successfully exploded in the New Mexico desert, and the nuclear age began.

Eager to bring the war in the East to an end, and convinced there were no other more humane alternatives, President Truman approved the dropping of atomic bombs on Hiroshima and then Nagasaki on August 6 and 9. The extent of the material destruction and loss of human life surprised even the scientists who had developed the bomb. By September 2 Japan had surrendered unconditionally, bringing WW II to a bloody, costly end.

The work of adjusting the world to postwar life began. The Allies divided Korea at the 38th Parallel, with Soviet troops occupying the north and American troops the south, unwittingly setting the stage for later conflict. President Truman urged the British, now in control of Palestine, to accept 100,000 Soviet Jewish refugees. At home, Truman and Congress began dismantling wartime economic controls—a subject about which Eleanor Roosevelt would have much to say. Among the first commodities from which rationing was lifted were shoes, electricity, meat, butter, and tires.

And there were signs of new political life in America too. The President proposed compulsory national health insurance for the first time in November 1945, initiating a contest of opinions and wills among interest groups, politicians, and patients. Gen. Dwight Eisenhower, considered by many the greatest American hero of the war, was named army chief of staff, one more step on his own climb toward the presidency. Perhaps the best stateside evidence that things were quickly getting back to normal was the outbreak of a major, protracted labor-management dispute when the United Auto Workers went on strike in late November.

The last eight months of 1945 were a roller coaster for Americans, with many highs and lows, with rapid and disorienting changes swirling about them. What Eleanor Roosevelt said about each of the great issues of the time touched the lives and influenced the thinking of countless thousands of her readers.

~ ~ ~

Less than a fortnight after the President's death Mrs. Roosevelt, her immediate family, and her secretary, Malvina Thompson [Scheider], returned to Hyde Park. Many a family would have given itself a rest before diving again into the affairs of business or the sensitive issues of inheritance and distribution of memorabilia, but not the Roosevelts. A sense of obligation and responsibility always seemed to outweigh any of the more self-serving inclinations difficult times might have brought to Eleanor Roosevelt's doorstep. Her husband had been an enthusiastic collector of everything historical from miniature books to model boats, and as president he had received scores of gifts from other nations and from admiring private citizens all around the world. Assigning each piece of presidential and private property to an

13

appropriate new home was a monumental job that took Mrs. Roosevelt months to complete.

HYDE PARK, APRIL 24—We came back to Hyde Park yesterday morning, just one week from the time we all gathered here for the committal service in our hedge-surrounded garden. My sons and I went to look at the grave. If two soldiers had not been on guard, and the beautiful orchids flown up from the South had not covered the spot where the sod had been put back so carefully, we would hardly have known that the lawn was not as it had always been.

Before very long, the simple stone which my husband described very carefully for us will be in place. But in the meantime the children and the dogs will be quite unconscious that here a short time ago a solemn military funeral was held, and they will think of it as a place where flowers grow and where the hedge protects them from the wind and makes the sun shine down more warmly. And that is as my husband would have it. He liked children and dogs and sunshine and flowers, and they are all around him now.

We drove over the boundaries of the place yesterday afternoon trying to ascertain, from the maps we had, exactly what the memorandums meant which my husband so carefully wrote out for us. If you have ever tried to reconcile a map and the actual roads through the woods with the descriptions in a memorandum, no matter how accurate it is, you will understand how difficult we found it. Many a time we stopped where two trails ran into each other and wondered just exactly where this road really was on the map.

It was a wonderful day, but very windly and much colder than when we were here two weeks ago. We have had open fires in our living rooms all the afternoon and evening. But the house as a whole is very cold, and I don't dare turn up our heat because we have a very limited amount of oil.

Miss Thompson looks with despair on three clothes-baskets filled with mail, and so, dear readers, if you don't get any answers to your letters, you will know that eventually they will all be read. Meanwhile, it is physically impossible to do more than thank you here for your kindness and your real understanding and sympathy.

Today our heavier tasks begin, as trucks arrive from Washington and things are unpacked and made available for the further business of settling an estate. I foresee that we have many long days of work in the big house before it is presentable for government visitors, and many long evenings ahead of us just opening and reading this incoming mail. Some day, however, we will actually find ourselves sitting down to read a book without that guilty feeling which weighs upon one when the job you should be doing is ignored.

~ ~ ~

In the wake of the death of someone close, the impulse to philosophize about the meaning of our mortality is often irresistible.

NEW YORK, MAY 7—A friend of mine has just sent me a prayer by John Oxenham, a British poet. It is a very beautiful prayer for older people, or for people who have spent themselves so greatly that they fear not to be able to give their best in their remaining years on earth:

"Lord, when Thou see'st that my work is done, Let me not linger here With failing powers, A workless worker in a world of work; But with a word, Just bid me Home And I will come, Right gladly will I come, Yea—Right gladly will I come—"

I have always felt that one could have a certain sense of resignation when people die who have lived long and fruitful lives. My rebellion has always been over the deaths of young people; and that is why I think so many of us feel particularly frustrated by war, where youth so largely pays the price. It seems as though youth was so much needed to carry the burdens of peace.

A friend of mine, however, not long ago said something to me which may be comforting to many other women. In speaking of her young son, she remarked that what she wanted for him was that he should feel that he had fulfilled his mission in life; that if he had not spent himself during this war fighting for the things in which he believed, he would feel empty. If he died and was here to carry on in peacetime, she would still not rebel. She would know that to have denied him participation in the great adventure of fighting against the forces of evil, so that the forces of good might have an opportunity in the future to grow, would have left him warped and unable to carry on the battle for a better world in peace.

Of one thing I am sure: Young or old, in order to be useful we must stand for the things we feel are right, and we must work for those things whereover we find ourselves. It does very little good to believe something unless you tell your friends and associates of your beliefs. Those who fight down in the marketplace are bound to be confused now and then. Sometimes they will be deceived, and sometimes the dirt that they touch will cling to them. But if their hearts are pure and their purposes are unswerving, they will win through to the end of their mission on earth, untarnished.

~ ~ ~

There were ticker-tape parades; there was dancing in the streets; church bells rang and factory whistles tooted the joyful news all across America: The war was finally over in Europe. V-E Day brought relief and smiles to a country yearning to see an end to its greatest sustained loss of life and materiel in a military conflict. Yet Mrs. Roosevelt brought a sobering perspective to the celebration. As war raged on in the Far East against the third member of the Axis, Japan, she called on all jubilant Americans to recognize that until this war was fully won and over, true victory could not really be declared.

NEW YORK, MAY 9—All day yesterday, as I went about New York City, the words "V-E Day" were on everybody's lips. Part of the time, paper fluttered through the air until the gutters of the streets were filled with it. At Times Square crowds gathered—but that first report the other night had taken the edge off this celebration. No word came through from Washington and everybody still waited for official confirmation. Today it has come.

Over the radio this morning President Truman, Prime Minister Churchill and Marshal Stalin have all spoken—the war in Europe is over. Unconditional surrender has been accepted by the Germans. I can almost hear my husband's voice make that announcement, for I heard him repeat it so often. The German leaders were not willing to accept defeat, even when they knew it was inevitable, until they had made their people drink the last dregs in the cup of complete conquest by the Allies.

Europe is in ruins and the weary work of reconstruction must now begin. There must be joy, of course, in the hearts of the peoples whom the Nazis conquered and who are now free again. Freedom without bread, however, has little meaning. My husband always said that freedom from want and freedom from aggression were twin freedoms which had to go hand in hand.

The necessity to share with our brothers, even though it means hardship for ourselves, will now face all of us who live in the fortunate countries which war has not devastated.

I cannot feel a spirit of celebration today. I am glad that our men are no longer going to be shot at and killed in Europe, but the war in the Pacific still goes on. Men are dying there, even as I write. It is far more a day of dedication for us, a day on which to promise that we will do our utmost to end war and build peace. Some of my own sons, with millions of others, are still in danger.

I can but pray that the Japanese leaders will not force their people to complete destruction too. The ultimate end is sure, but in the hands of the Japanese leaders lies the decision of how many people will have to suffer before ultimate peace comes.

What are our ultimate objectives now? Do we want our Allies in Europe, and later in the Far East, to have the opportunity to rebuild quickly? Looked at selfishly, we will probably gain materially if they do. That cannot be our only responsibility, however. The men who fought this war are entitled to a chance to build a lasting peace. What we do in the next months may give them that chance or lose it for them. If we give people bread, we may build friendship among the peoples of the world; and we will never have peace without friendship

17

around the world. This is the time for a long look ahead. This is the time for us all to decide where we go from here.

~ ~ ~

Eleanor Roosevelt had a seesaw relationship with the idea of an Equal Rights Amendment to the Constitution as a way to guarantee more explicitly that women would not be the object of discrimination. Her most frequent tendency was to question the wisdom of any proposed constitutional amendment, on the grounds that she felt the original Constitution to be an eminently workable document that failed to meet the country's needs far less often than the intricate web of state and local laws that had evolved over time. Not until the early years of the civil rights movement did Mrs. Roosevelt begin to recognize the need for more positive steps at the federal and constitutional levels to protect women's rights, driven to that change of opinion only by years of resistance on the part of state legislatures to calls for legal reform on behalf of the women's cause.

HYDE PARK, MAY 14—I have been getting a good many letters of late about the Equal Rights amendment, which has been reported out favorably to the House by the House Judiciary Committee. Some of the women who write me seem to think that if this amendment is passed there will be no further possibility of discrimination against women. They feel that the time has come to declare that women shall be treated in all things on an equal basis with men. I hardly think it is necessary to declare this, since as a theory it is fairly well accepted today by both men and women. But in practice it is not accepted, and I doubt very much whether it ever will be.

Other women of my acquaintance are writing me in great anxiety, for they are afraid that the dangers of the amendment are not being properly considered. The majority of these women are employed in the industrial field. Their fear is that labor standards safeguarded in the past by legislation will be wrecked, and that the amendment will curtail and impair for all time the powers of both state and federal government to enact any legislation that may be necessary and desirable to protect the health and safety of women in industry.

I do not know which group is right, but I feel that if we work to remove from our statute books those laws which discriminate against women today we might accomplish more and do it in a shorter time than will be possible through the passage of this amendment.

~ ~ ~

A. J. Liebling once quipped that freedom of the press belongs to those who own one, but Eleanor Roosevelt would not have appreciated that observer's cynical joke. She was consistently quick to aid in the defense of any reporters or publishers whose implicit right to keep their information sources confidential might be challenged. Ironically, in this case involving the reporter Albert Deutsch and his stories about the veterans' hospitals, veterans' benefits—one of Mrs. Roosevelt's favorite causes—was lost in the shuffle, a fact that did not sit well with the former First Lady.

HYDE PARK, MAY 22—I was shocked on Saturday to read about the hearing before the House Veterans Legislation Committee in which Albert Deutsch, of the newspaper "PM," was questioned.

I imagine that most people are interested, as I am, in making sure that our returned veterans, if they need treatment at a veterans' hospital, receive the best medical care possible. At this hearing, however, the discussion did not seem to center on an effort to find out whether that care was good or bad. It seemed to be primarily directed at trying to discredit a man who had written some critical articles. He was cited for contempt because he would not give the names of a few employees of the Veterans Administration who, in confidence and on condition that their names be not used, gave him some information.

I certainly am conscious of the wisdom of asking newspapers and their writers to show that their information has come from good sources. Plenty of things have been written about me which had no foundation in fact whatsoever. Yet in this particular case the writer had given plentiful evidence as to his sources. To force him to give a few names of people from whom he had obtained confidential information would mean that in the future no employees of any government or private group would dare to give such information. That would mean, in many cases, that investigations would not be started, because no one would know that anything was wrong. Few people can afford to risk their jobs in order to bring to light things which they may know should be remedied.

If good sources of information had not been given, there would then be valid criticism of a writer or a newspaper. But this was not the case in the present instance, and therefore the procedure of holding Mr. Deutsch in contempt endangers the public interest. I hope that all who have any interest in our veterans or in good government will write to Representative John Rankin, chairman of the committee, as well as to their own congressmen, and protest the action. If this procedure is not changed, future sources of information will be intimidated, and that is dangerous to the public good.

I am sure that the men who took this action did so without thinking through what the implications were, and how it might harm not only the veterans, but the public. If our veterans do not receive the best medical care, they will not return to a self-supporting basis. These men are young men, and the cost to the public of good care which returns them to normal living will be far less than poor care which leaves them a burden on the public for the rest of their lives. Beyond that, the public is entitled to know the truth as a reputable journalist sees it.

~   ~   ~

Throughout the Depression, when almost the entire American agricul-tural community was either unemployed or unable to get fair prices for its crops, Mrs. Roosevelt spoke out vigorously in support of the New Deal's various programs to help farmers. She visited farm communities many times, in rich and poor areas alike. These close and repeated contacts lay behind her concern for the most dispossessed of all agricultural people, the migrant farm laborers.

HYDE PARK, JUNE 7—For a long time I have been concerned about our migratory farm workers, who move from place to place following the crops wherever there is need for their labor. I read in the paper the other day a report on conditions in some of the camps for these workers in New York State, and I must say, when I have seen some of the places in which families are expected to live, or even just the barracks where we expect the workers themselves to be housed, I am filled with shame.

Now and then you see something really good, and then you find contented workers. Their comments are appreciative, but at the same time show surprise at the good conditions. These workers are essential. Without them our big growers of vegetables and small fruits and other seasonal crops could not possibly operate, and yet we have given very little thought to their problems.

If these workers have children, how do those children get an education? It would really make sense if schools were organized to move with them. As it is now, many of these children, if they go to school at all, go sporadically for a few months here and a few there, and there is no continuity in what they learn. It is from their ranks that we recruit a goodly number of our illiterates.

You have but to read our draft records to know that we are not people who are universally able to read and write, and in a democracy those are two requisites to good citizenship. It is entirely true that intelligence cannot be judged by whether you are able to read and write; in many cases, this is only a question of whether you have had the opportunity to learn. But in our country, when we find illiterate people, it is an indication that as citizens we have not faced our responsibilities and tackled the difficult problem of seeing that everyone has an opportunity for an education.

Since the war, in order to get the emergency seasonal work done on our farms, we have imported labor through arrangements entered into with nearby countries. I was ashamed to read some of the things which Mexico felt it had to write into our labor contracts in order to protect those of its citizens who came to work on our farms and ranches. But I was glad, nevertheless, that the workers were protected.

~ ~ ~

A significant development for Mrs. Roosevelt as she moved toward her eventual appointment as delegate to the United Nations was her increasing outspokenness about foreign affairs. While she was First Lady, there were good policy reasons for her to reign in some of her more colorful opinions; after FDR's death she could speak more freely. As the preliminary negotiations concerning the establishment of the UN went forward, Mrs. Roosevelt commented several times in her "My Day" column that the Soviets and the Communists in America were obstructing this important progress. Her later experience in the UN would show her that dealing with the Soviet Communists could severely tax her patience. And she came to see, in due time, during the worst years of McCarthyism, that cooperation with Soviet or American Communists would be politically difficult at best.

Nevertheless, in 1945 we see Eleanor Roosevelt trying to maintain a policy of cooperation and reconciliation that she thought held the greatest promise for world peace. Shortly before the next two columns appeared, in late June, 1945, Mrs. Roosevelt had written a column advocating cooperation with the Soviet Communists—despite their severe ideological differences with America. By that time there were many voices in the State Department and in the press advocating exactly the opposite: that America should refuse to entangle itself in any way with the Soviets, despite the fact the two had become allies by the end of the war. Those who believed Communism of any kind to be unworthy of respect or recognition often took Mrs. Roosevelt to task when she expressed her opinion: Working with the Soviets would be far better than pretending peace could be maintained in an atmosphere of alienation between the great powers of the east and the west.

HYDE PARK, JUNE 22—I want to make it absolutely clear that my

22

whole desire in writing that column on the American Communists was to show how it is possible to work with the USSR and the people of that great country, and why we need have no fear of them. Those of us who take the trouble to understand it know what Communism in Russia is. We also know that any leader, no matter how powerful, has to listen to the people with whom he works. While for obvious reasons the people of Russia are still largely dictated to by their leaders, they have objectives and opportunities for growth in freedom, just as we had when we wrote our Constitution.

I, for one, think democracy better than Communism if the people exercise their power. Nevertheless, I feel we can cooperate with the USSR and its people, just as we do with other nations.

But because I have experienced the deception of the American Communists, I will not trust them. That is what I meant when I said that I did not think the people of this country would tolerate the type of American Communists who say one thing and do another.

HYDE PARK, JUNE 26—I know very well that there are dangers in cooperation, but I know, too, what the dangers are when you have no cooperation. That has been made clear to many, many families in this country and throughout the world. I think I speak for the average man and woman when I say that we might as well take a chance and try something new, having faith in our fellow men because they have suffered just as we have suffered and must want peace as much as we do.

I don't believe that greed and selfishness have gone out of the human race. I am quite prepared to be considerably disappointed many times in the course of cooperation. I shall probably be disappointed in myself as much as in other people, but I want to try for a peaceful world. The ratification of the charter as soon as possible, in compliance with President Truman's wishes, will, I think, make easier every step we take in the future. It will inspire our people to prepare for the real work of building understanding and peace throughout the world.

~ ~ ~

Legislative ombudsman describes a role Mrs. Roosevelt liked to play
in her "My Day" columns. Frequently she identified for her readers
specific pieces of legislation she liked or disliked, spelling out the pros
and cons almost in debate format. Congressmen and senators knew
that once the salient points of their proposed bills appeared in one of
Mrs. Roosevelt's articles, they could expect at least a minor flood of
mail and telephone calls or wires from the citizenry. Senator Pepper
of Florida must have been pleased in the case of his bill concerning a
frequent theme in the women's rights debate: equal pay for equal work.*

HYDE PARK, JULY 10—There are two labor situations to which I
want to draw attention at the present time. One is embodied in a bill
introduced in the Senate by Senator Claude Pepper and referred to
the Committee on Education and Labor. As far as I know it has not
yet been introduced in the House, though I imagine Congresswoman
Mary Norton will eventually introduce it.

It is Senate bill 1178, and it provides "equal pay for equal work for
women and for other purposes." The first section presents the
situation very well: "The Congress hereby finds that the existence in
industry of differentials based on sex is an inequity in compensation
standards which constitutes an unfair wage practice and (1) leads to
labor disputes; (2) depresses wages and living standards of employees,
male and female; (3) interferes with and prevents an adequate
standard of living of such workers and the families depending on
them for support; (4) in particular, has serious detrimental effects on
the standard of living of families of deceased or disabled veterans;
(5) prevents the maximum utilization of our labor resources and
plant capacity essential for full production, in war and in peace;
(6) endangers the national security and general welfare and thereby
burdens and obstructs commerce."

That puts the whole thing in a nutshell. But basically there is no
excuse for not paying an equal wage for equal work, and there never
has been. This principle holds good, I think, in the professional field

24

as well as in the field of industry, and it certainly should hold good in all the service fields.

~ ~ ~

In a life filled with appointments and dinners and correspondence, a walk in the woods at Hyde Park with her beloved Scottie Fala was a tonic to Mrs. Roosevelt's mind and soul. And, like many intellectuals whose real work is the art of abstract thinking and communicating about complex problems, Mrs. Roosevelt thought the concreteness of gardening and the activity of putting food by for the winter were tremendously refreshing kinds of labor. The millions of housewife readers who were loyal to the "My Day" column found something to identify with in Mrs. Roosevelt's sharing of domestic chitchat.

HYDE PARK, JULY 26—The rain has been wonderful for the woods. As I walk every morning with Fala, I realize that it is a long time since I have seen our little planted pines make such a growth, or found such luxuriance of foliage everywhere. It is a grand year for mosquitoes, too. Sometimes I think I'll never walk past some of our swamps again till autumn, but then the beauty of the ferns draws me back.

Fala, too, has such a wonderful time hunting whatever may be the hidden things in that particular part of the woods that I can't bear not to take him there. Occasionally he gets a scent and disappears entirely. I can't stand and wait for him, because the mosquitoes then settle on me with too much ease. So I walk on just as fast as possible, meanwhile singing in unmusical fashion and as loudly as possible all the hymns I can remember from my childhood days. That seems to bring Fala back more quickly than calling him by name.

Our garden has done pretty well and we are getting vegetables in great quantity, but my family has been so large all summer that I have not had a chance to put as much into the freezer as I otherwise might have done. In August, however, I shall have to be away from here for a time, and I am counting on putting many things up for the winter months. My freezer, which is a new acquisition, makes it possible to plan for the future and use one's surplus.

This is a quiet life we lead up here, but it seems nevertheless to be a busy one. People are coming to tea today, and late this afternoon Postmaster General and Mrs. Hannegan, Paul Fitzpatrick and Miss Doris Byrne, chairman and vice-chairman respectively of the Democratic State Committee, are all coming to spend the night. Tomorrow we attend the ceremonies at the post office when the stamp issued in memory of my husband, showing the Hyde Park house, is first put on sale.

~   ~   ~

It has become a commonplace to cite August 6, 1945, as the date on which the atomic age began. In hindsight, we see this day for what it really was: the day the U.S. Air Force dropped the first atomic bomb on Hiroshima, Japan. But at the time many people—politicians and military experts among them—did not recognize the gravity of the decisions first to develop and then to use the atomic bomb. Mrs. Roosevelt seems to have grasped almost immediately not only the strategic military implications of the new weapon but also its long-term political meaning. For the rest of her life she campaigned for peaceful applications of atomic (or nuclear) power.

We see in her column dated August 8 and in an undated one (presumably written just after August 14, when the fighting in the Far East officially stopped) that she was immediately sensitive to the political issues soon to divide the Allies and fuel the cold war: How long could the secret of the bomb be kept, who should share it, and how could this new terror be controlled so as eventually to become the servant and not the enemy of mankind?

NEW YORK, AUGUST 8—The news which came to us yesterday afternoon of the first use of the atomic bomb in the war with Japan may have surprised a good many people, but scientists—both British and American—have been working feverishly to make this discovery before our enemies, the Germans, could make it and thereby possibly win the war.

This discovery may be of great commercial value someday. If wisely used, it may serve the purposes of peace. But for the moment we are chiefly concerned with its destructive power. That power can be multiplied indefinitely, so that not only whole cities but large areas may be destroyed at one fell swoop. If you face this possibility and realize that, having once discovered a principle, it is very easy to take further steps to magnify its power, you soon face the unpleasant fact that in the next war whole peoples may be destroyed.

The only safe counter weapon to this new power is the firm decision of mankind that it shall be used for constructive purposes only. This discovery must spell the end of war. We have been paying an ever-increasing price for indulging ourselves in this uncivilized way of settling our difficulties. We can no longer indulge in the slaughter of our young men. The price will be too high and will be paid not just by young men, but by whole populations.

In the past we have given lip service to the desire for peace. Now we meet the test of really working to achieve something basically new in the world. Religious groups have been telling us for a long time that peace could be achieved only by a basic change in the nature of man. I am inclined to think that this is true. But if we give human beings sufficient incentive, they may find good reasons for reshaping their characteristics.

Good will among men was preached by the angels as they announced to the world the birth of the child Jesus. He exemplified it in His life and preached it Himself and sent forth His disciples, who have spread that gospel of love and human understanding throughout the world ever since. Yet the minds and hearts of men seemed closed.

Now, however, an absolute need exists for facing a nonescapable situation. This new discovery cannot be ignored. We have only two alternative choices: destruction and death—or construction and life! If we desire our civilization to survive, then we must accept the responsibility of constructive work and of the wise use of a knowledge greater than any ever achieved by man before.

NEW YORK (undated)—When word was flashed that peace had come to the world again, I found myself filled with very curious sensations. I had no desire to go out and celebrate. I remembered the way the people demonstrated when the last war ended, but I felt this time that the weight of suffering which has engulfed the world during so many years could not so quickly be wiped out. There is a quiet rejoicing that men are no longer bringing death to each other throughout the world. There is great happiness, too, in the knowledge that some day, soon, many of those we love will be at home again to give all they have to the rebuilding of a peaceful world.

One cannot forget, however, the many, many people to whom this day will bring only a keener sense of loss, for, as others come home, their loved ones will not return.

In every community, if we have eyes to see and hearts to feel, we will for many years see evidences of the period of war which we have been through. There will be men among us who all their lives, both physically and mentally, will carry the marks of war; and there will be women who mourn all the days of their lives. Yet there must be an undercurrent of deep joy in every human heart, and great thankfulness that we have world peace again.

These first days of peace require great statesmanship in our leaders. They are not easy days, for now we face the full results of the costs of war and must set ourselves to find the ways of building a peaceful world. The new atomic discovery has changed the whole aspect of the world in which we live. It has been primarily thought of in the light of its destructive power. Now we have to think of it in terms of how it may serve mankind in the days of peace.

This great discovery was not found by men of any one race or any one religion and its development and control should be under international auspices. All the world has a right to share in the beneficence which may grow from its proper development.

Great Britain and Canada and ourselves hold the secret today— and quite rightly, since we used its destructive force to bring the war to an end. But if we allow ourselves to think that any nations or any group of commercial interests should profit by something so great, we will eventually be the sufferers. God has shown great confidence in mankind when he allowed them wisdom and intelligence to discover this new secret. It is a challenge to us—the peoples who control the discovery—for unless we develop spiritual greatness commensurate with this new gift, we may bring economic war into the world and chaos instead of peace.

The greatest opportunity the world has ever had lies before us. God grant we have enough understanding of the divine love to live in the future as "one world" and "one people."

~ ~ ~

The painful experience of interrupted family income during the Depression and World War II, coupled with the escalating cost of ever more scientifically sophisticated medicine, undoubtedly lay behind the rising tide of public favor in the 1940s for some kind of national health insurance. Americans were waking up to the cruel truth that sickness and injury strike when they want to and not necessarily when one is prepared to pay for their consequences.

Blessed, as she says, with good health and with financial resources, Mrs. Roosevelt recognized the vulnerability of middle- and lower-income people without health insurance and was a continuous campaigner for all reasonable proposals for reform in what was otherwise a sink-or-swim financial dilemma for most Americans.

Senator Robert Wagner of New York was a likely candidate to sponsor such reforms: in cooperation with FDR's brain trust, (Cabinet and other advisers), Wagner had introduced several successful pieces of social legislation during the New Deal, including the National Industrial Recovery Act (1933), the Social Security Act and the National Labor Relations Act (in 1935), and a major housing act (1937). President Truman contributed his own proposal in November 1945 for a national compulsory health insurance program.

HYDE PARK, SEPTEMBER 7—I happen to be one of the fortunate people of the world on whom any health insurance, carried by any company, would have certainly paid dividends to the company. However, I have enough friends and neighbors to know that one of the things which brings distress and completely unbalanced budgets into many homes is the illness which was not expected.

Most people who have even moderate incomes prepare for the advent of a baby and lay the money aside. If there are no great complications, that does not cause a complete dislocation of the family budget. It has meant a great deal to many young wives of men in the service to be taken care of under the EMIC plan, and I have had a number of them say rather wistfully that they wished such a plan could continue functioning in peacetime.

Of course, something similar should function. Above everything else, under whatever plan is undertaken, I think two things should not suffer. One is research, which we know should go on at all times and should be completely free. I was shocked to be told that years ago we might have had many of the things which have saved lives during the war, if the cost had not seemed too high for development from the commercial point of view.

Secondly, no matter what we do, the training of doctors and our schools of medicine must be properly financed and kept to the highest standards of efficiency. Young men who seem good material and are willing to put in the time for this arduous training should receive every assistance during their training years, regardless of what they themselves can pay toward their education. Research and training are two things which are essential to the health of the nation. They should not depend upon private funds alone.

It seems to me the government might well guarantee that these two phases of the health of the nation shall go forward unhampered and properly financed.

The Senate health bill, as proposed, puts much responsibility on the states. But it does leave supervision in the hands of the Surgeon General, and I think the advisory committee gives the kind of safeguard which should make sure that there will be no hampering of either research or education in the future.

Federal assistance should be available for the building of hospitals and clinics. This, of course, is essential, since many communities can meet the running expenses but are unable to make the first capital investment for buildings and equipment.

On the whole, the Wagner-Murray-Dingle health bill seems to me to give us more hope than we have ever had for health in our communities throughout the nation.

~ ~ ~

Mrs. Roosevelt's feelings could run both hot and cold. The next two columns show the warmth of her appreciation for her fellow citizens and then the angry chill behind her feelings about the Germans. For a woman who had a nearly unparalleled ability to bring disparate people together for both productive work and convivial socializing (witness her roles as hostess of the White House and, soon, as chairperson of the UN Commission on Human Rights), she nonetheless could also fix on the disagreeable qualities of the enemy. For years after World War II it was the Germans. During the Cold War she added key Soviet UN diplomats to her list of least tolerable people.

HYDE PARK, SEPTEMBER 10—In the last few weeks I have been much in and out of New York City, and I found myself rather frequently on the subways. It has warmed my heart to discover how many people would stop and speak to me as they left the train, often murmuring only: "We loved your husband."

I always like that because, like the elephant's child in Kipling's story, I have an insatiable curiosity about people in general. The glimpses one gets into people's lives from casual conversations are often very valuable in helping one to understand the general ideas and feelings of the country as a whole.

HYDE PARK, OCTOBER 13—Today I want to talk to you about something which came to me from a member of a USO entertainment group that had been in both Italy and Germany very recently.

These entertainers are young. They have perhaps a better opportunity than even the officers have for reaching conclusions about the

31

situation as it really exists for our soldiers overseas. They see both officers and enlisted men informally. They hear much talk among the men which would never occur when officers were within earshot, and some talk among the officers which would perhaps not be as free if enlisted men were present.

The conclusions which this individual reached were that both officers and servicemen in Germany were the victims of a well-organized underground propaganda carried on through the German girls. For instance, it is quite usual for a German girl to throw herself upon the sympathy of the Americans because "she is a refugee from Russian-held territory." In subtle ways, she sows seeds of hate against the Russians; against the Jews; against all our allies. She points out that "only the Germans have plumbing comparable to what you have in America." She asks, "How could we look with anything but contempt on the French? In France, dirt and decadence reign." She is not quite so bitter about the British. But, of course, "you Americans are better than the British," and so it goes until we almost forget that we fought the war with allies whom we found to be loyal and honest and good soldiers.

We liberated people who, because of the Germans, have sunk to physical conditions of dirt and malnutrition which would lower anyone's morale and will take years to wipe out. We almost forget that the Germans are our enemies; that they brought about all this destruction and horror and death that we see in Europe, as well as the losses among our own men. Of course, say our boys, "the girls are not responsible, because we know our girls at home would not be responsible for bringing about a war."

Last but not least, our economic advisers—looking primarily to the interests of the industrialists of this country, backed by a similar group of industrialists in England—are saying that we should re-establish the industries of Germany so that Germany may live.

Anyone who looks at the German people knows that they have suffered less than any people in Europe. What are we doing? Are we planning to make them strong again so we can have another war? Small wonder the Russians and some of the other European people are frightened by our attitude. Will we never learn the lessons of history? Not the Russians, but the Germans have brought about the past two world wars.

~ ~ ~

The Daughters of the American Revolution was never one of Mrs. Roosevelt's favorite organizations. While they always seemed to see the world through conservative glasses, Eleanor Roosevelt's lens was clearly liberal. It would have been easy for her to take acerbic potshots at the DAR and at other groups whose segregationist policies excluded blacks from full participation in the nation's social and cultural life. But Mrs. Roosevelt chose a different tack, one that, over the years leading up to the civil rights struggle of the 1950s and 1960s, made a quiet but important contribution to the liberal cause. Her point was often that racism is not merely personal but rather built into the system of laws and social values.

HYDE PARK, OCTOBER 15—In this recent controversy centering, again, around the granting of the use of the hall owned in the District of Columbia by the Daughters of the American Revolution for a concert by the gifted pianist, Mrs. Hazel Scott Powell, I do not think one can hold the Daughters of the American Revolution alone responsible. There is an agreement among all theater owners in the District of Columbia as to how their theaters shall be used. Only the public can make the theater owners change that agreement.

It is sad that in our nation's capital, where the eyes of the world are upon us, we should allow discrimination which impedes the progress and sears the souls of human beings whose only fault is that God, Who made us all, gave their skin a darker color.

~ ~ ~

Conservation of our natural resources and preservation of such national treasures as the White House (or, in this case, Fort Clinton in New York City) were among Eleanor Roosevelt's favorite causes. Mrs. Roosevelt knew she was taking on a formidable adversary in criticizing

Robert Moses, the controversial New York City Parks Commissioner and Chairman of the New York State Council of Parks, who wanted to remove the old fort in Battery Park at Manhattan's southern tip.

Moses used his official posts (which he held through several mayors' tenures, from 1934 to 1960) to lobby for several enormous projects, many of which Eleanor Roosevelt would have gladly supported. Known around City Hall as a power broker, Robert Moses insinuated himself onto the boards of other city agencies. Among the monuments in the Moses legacy are dozens of state and city parks, including Jones Beach on Long Island; 416 miles of highways; the Whitestone, Triborough, Throgs Neck, and Verrazano–Narrows bridges; the Queens Midtown Tunnel; numerous housing projects; and both Lincoln Center and the United Nations complex on Manhattan's East River.

Still, in the face of such power, Eleanor Roosevelt did not hesitate to speak her mind.

New York, October 23—All over our country we destroy old historic buildings when we should preserve them, and here in New York City I understand that the war is on again between our very efficient Parks Commissioner, Robert Moses, and such people in the city as really care about preserving old landmarks. The issue this time is Fort Clinton, which was designed by John McComb, the architect of our City Hall.

The fort should be preserved as one of New York City's historic spots. Heaven knows, I am not one of the people who object to change when it is really necessary to bring about improvements. But there are very few of these old landmarks left. The walls of Fort Clinton are nine feet thick, it speaks of years gone by when forts really could defend New York, and it might serve as a landmark to teach many children the history of their city.

In 1941 the Board of Estimate authorized Mr. Moses to destroy the fort. A short time ago, President Nathan of the Borough of Manhattan moved to rescind that vote. But Mr. Moses is a powerful antagonist, and while under ordinary circumstances the Board of Estimate might be willing to let the old fort stand, and feel rather happy about it, they certainly would not be happy to antagonize Mr. Moses.

I am sure I am not the only older person in New York who has associations with this building. I have been there with my children. I have an affection for the Battery, and I can remember when a very old and charming cousin, who once danced with Lafayette, told me how the high society of her day promenaded on the Battery. I like to see it all in my mind's eye when I go back and walk there.

I don't want to give up my modern comforts and live as my ancestors did. I like central heating and running water—but that doesn't seem to enter into this controversy, since no one is going to have to live in the fort.

In Washington, I found that all young people who visited the White House seemed to be impressed by the fact that it still had the same walls which were in the original house before it was burned when the City of Washington was captured in the War of 1812. For that reason, I think in a completely reconditioned Battery Park with all of the old landmarks removed there will be nothing to tie the imagination to the history of the past.

Down at Williamsburg, Virginia, much money and research and architectural skill have been put into rebuilding many buildings that had almost disappeared, so that we can see how people once lived and how they carried on their local government in the earliest days of our country. Thousands of people go there to see a reconstructed town. Why, then, do we have to destroy such things as we have still intact from the past?

~ ~ ~

When the end of the war in Europe came there was enormous thankfulness that at last the fighting had stopped. Most military personnel and civilians involved in the war were able to return to their native countries and to the business of re-establishing their normal lives. But there were certain groups of displaced persons who had become refugees during the war and for whom there was no clear plan, in some cases not even a clear hope, about where they could settle to

start life anew. The United Nations Relief and Rehabilitation Admin-
istration (UNRRA) took on the daunting task of trying to find
appropriate homes for hundreds of thousands of people without citi-
zenship status, whose financial and medical conditions were all
dubious at best. Mrs. Roosevelt had seen much the same problem in
the years after World War I, and this time she was determined to help
pave the way toward solutions. She believed the UN relief agency held
the most promise. She did not realize, however, how difficult the
problem would become for those displaced European Jews who wanted
most of all to go to Palestine—a territory easily identifiable as their
ancestral homeland that was rapidly becoming a political hot potato
in the rapidly shifting balance of power in the Middle East.

HYDE PARK, NOVEMBER 7—There is in Europe at the present time a
group of 100,000 displaced persons—the miserable, tortured, terror-
ized Jews who have seen members of their families murdered and
their homes ruined, and who are stateless people, since they hate the
Germans and no longer wish to live in the countries where they have
been despoiled of all that makes life worth living. Naturally they want
to go to Palestine, the one place where they will have a status, where
they will feel again that sense of belonging to a community which
gives most of us security.

President Truman has asked Great Britain for consideration of
their condition and permission for their admittance to Palestine.
Prime Minister Attlee is said to be coming over the end of this month
to discuss this and other matters with the President.

It seems to me urgent that these people be given permission to go
to the home of their choice. They are the greatest victims of this war.
We might as well face the fact that we may be asked to assume some
responsibility; and, if so, we should be prepared to do it. Our
consciences can hardly be clear when we read about and see the
pictures of these emaciated, miserable people who suffer while we sit
comfortably and let them die at the rate of 50 per day—which is what
is happening now, I am told.

It seems to me imperative, also, that the Senate pass the UNRRA
appropriation as rapidly as possible. The House passed it but attached

some restrictions, which seems to me an untenable position for us to take in view of the fact that this is a contribution to a fund in which we are only one of many contributors, and the rules for which are laid down by the group as a whole. We authorized our appropriation some time ago. The need is great. Other nations have paid their full share for the first year and even made their appropriations for the second year. We have not yet made available the whole of our first year's appropriation, and we want to tie strings to it!

The Senate, it seems to me, has a grave responsibility to the American people to see that their good name is protected in the family of nations. This is not the way to create good will and respect towards us who are the strongest people, from the material standpoint, in the world today.

~ ~ ~

After the President's death, Mrs. Roosevelt became more active than ever as a representative of the New Deal's commitment to education and equal rights. She was invited again and again to accept gifts and awards, deservedly hers as well as the late President's, from black organizations and institutions. George Washington Carver was a very likely hero for the Roosevelts because of his scientific and business achievements. The son of slave parents, he had risen on his own initiative to the highest stature in the academic world and also retained an eminently practical streak. Carver promoted crop diversification among Southern tenant farmers, especially the adoption of peanuts and soybeans as cash crops. He had developed more than 300 derivative products from peanuts and 118 from sweet potatoes before his death in 1943.

NEW YORK, NOVEMBER 9—In the afternoon, a group presented me with the second sheet of seals being sold for the Carver Memorial Fund. Dr. George Washington Carver, the outstanding scientist of Tuskegee Institute, will always remain to me one of the most impressive people I have ever known. He had a beautiful face, and a serenity and dignity which I have rarely seen equaled in any human being. His memorial should be a tribute by the whole of the American people to one of their great men.

~ ~ ~

What is socialized medicine? We are still somewhat unsure in late twentieth-century America, and the confusion was even greater in the 1940s when President Truman proposed national health insurance. Mrs. Roosevelt took on the dual tasks of supporting the legislation that would bring such insurance into effect and of explaining to the public—repeatedly—that socialized does not mean the same thing as socialist.

HYDE PARK, NOVEMBER 24—I have signed today an endorsement of President Truman's health message. There is only one point that seems to me not quite to coincide with our practice in other things. For instance, you do not pay school taxes only up to a certain percentage of your income. You pay taxes according to the size of your income. Furthermore, no matter what your income may be, you can send your children to public school, and it seems to me that the same should apply in the case of these new health services. The proposed tax is to be 4 percent on incomes up to $3600 a year. No matter how much income we have, only that amount, apparently, is taxed for this plan; and only people with that income, or less, are expected to make use of it.

This does not seem to me to have anything whatever to do with socialized medicine; and I am particularly glad that the proposed plan recognizes the need for giving help to our medical schools, since research and education are essential to keeping up the standards of medical care. This may make it possible for young doctors to work in rural communities, where medical care has been very inadequate in the past.

~ ~ ~

Eleanor Roosevelt always admired pioneers, and Frances Perkins, America's first (and for some time only) woman Cabinet member was surely a pathmaker. Freshly returned from a meeting of the International Labor Organization, Miss Perkins here receives Mrs. Roosevelt's high praise and is used by the former First Lady as a symbol of a broader point: that women can do as well as men at anything. As Secretary of Labor throughout the New Deal years (1933–1945), Perkins became especially well known as FDR's main advocate for the Fair Labor Standards Act.

NEW YORK, NOVEMBER 29—Yesterday Miss Frances Perkins came back full of optimism and hope for the success of the ILO and its work. Her return made me reflect on many things. No Secretary of Labor has stood up under more press attacks than did Miss Perkins during the latter part of her public service. Even the women of the country failed, in many cases, to stand by this member of their own sex. You would hear people say: "We need a man, a strong man who will prevent strikes," or "We need someone who will knock the heads of the leaders in the labor movement together, and make them see the light," or "A strong man would make labor and management agree."

Well, we have the strong man, and everyone will agree that Secretary of Labor Schwellenbach has done as good a job as any man could do with the difficulties which face his department at the present time. I think it is not unfair to point out, however, that we have not done away with strikes, nor have we reconciled the warring elements in labor. Congress is no more cooperative than it was before, and though Secretary Schwellenbach on the whole has a better press, I don't believe he has any fewer worries.

If we look back over Miss Perkins' whole record we will find that she accomplished a great deal. In view of that record, I hope many women now recognize the fact that, before condemning one of their own sex in office, they should really know the truth about the situations which the particular officeholder has to handle.

A woman will always have to be better than a man in any job she undertakes. There is no woman in the Cabinet today, but there will be again in the future. When there is, I hope she will get more support from the women of her own political party than has been the case in the past.

~   ~   ~

As the year ended and the evidence of Eleanor Roosevelt's value to the country continued to grow, President Truman made an astute political move. In choosing the former First Lady as an official delegate to the United Nations General Assembly, he accomplished several things at one stroke. He reinforced an already-known fact: Eleanor Roosevelt was not about to quiet down and retire. He gave a huge vote of confidence to women as national spokespeople and leaders. And he secured for America's benefit an absolutely untiring worker in the UN cause. In October 1945 Mrs. Roosevelt had turned sixty-one, and a decision on her part to seclude herself at Hyde Park, to occupy herself henceforth with her social life and her knitting needles undoubtedly would have been forgiven by a loving nation. Instead, with this artful push from Harry Truman, Eleanor Roosevelt was about to go back to work, to harder work than ever before.

NEW YORK, DECEMBER 22—Now that I have been confirmed by the Senate, I can say how deeply honored I feel that President Truman has named me one of the delegates to the General Assembly of the United Nations Organization. It is an honor, but also a very great responsibility. I know it has come to me largely because my husband laid the foundation for this Organization through which we all hope to build world peace.

In many ways I am sure I will find much to learn; but all of life is a constant education. Some things I can take to this first meeting—a sincere desire to understand the problems of the rest of the world and our relationship to them; a real good will for all peoples throughout the world; a hope that I shall be able to build a sense of personal trust and friendship with my co-workers, for without that type of understanding our work would be doubly difficult.

This first meeting, I imagine, will be largely concerned with organization and the choice of a site within this country as a permanent home.

. Being the only woman delegate from this country, I feel a great responsibility, also, to the women of my own country. In other lands women have gone with their men into the fighting forces. Here we have more nearly followed the traditional pattern of working and waiting at home.

1946

*A*merica had entered the war reluctantly (and not until after the Japanese attack on Pearl Harbor) and struggled alongside its allies until both brilliant fighting and the atomic bomb had forced a decisive conclusion to the destruction. How would the United States react to the outbreak of peace? If the signs were unclear in the last months of 1945, the new year was to provide plenty of answers. While muddling through the economic complications of converting the domestic economy back to peacetime activity, the country began quickly to assert itself as a confident global power, fully aware of its new responsibility to take the lead in charting the path toward worldwide reconstruction.

The United Nations held its first formal meetings in 1946, in London and then in New York—where philanthropist John D. Rockefeller, Jr., had provided an $8.5-million gift to buy a Manhattan building site for its yet-to-be-designed headquarters. It created UNESCO (the UN's Educational, Scientific and Cultural wing), which the United States joined at midyear. The General Assembly also set up the UN Atomic Energy Commission in the hope it could steer the development of atomic power into civil control rather than military and thus toward peaceful applications. The United States followed suit, establishing a few months later its own Atomic Energy Commission on similar principles. Never shy of contradictions in policy, the Truman White House authorized more military testing of the bomb on tiny Bikini in the Pacific's Marshall Islands.

July 4, 1946 saw President Truman declare the Philippines a republic; August saw Congress pass the Fulbright Act, creating for the first time a structure for the exchange of international students and professors on the assumption that the better we know our neighbors around the globe, the better our trade and political relations will become. Contrasting with such bright spots in the year's foreign policy events were two distinctly foreboding statements the future importance of which would have been hard to recognize at the time: Winston Churchill coined the phrase *iron curtain* to describe the way "police governments" were taking control of and closing off Eastern Europe. And Undersecretary of State Dean Acheson asserted unequivocally that the United States would not leave Korea until that nation was reunited and politically free. No one could foresee at the time that it would take still another war to bring the Korean unification question to a head and that even after the war unification would not be achieved.

On the domestic front, the country clamored for relief from wartime economic controls, but Mrs. Roosevelt urged caution. Early in the year the President appointed Chester Bowles (an Eleanor Roosevelt favorite) director of the new Office of Economic Stabilization. By year's end most price controls on consumer goods were lifted. Farm prices reached a twenty-five-year high in April. But wages were the central issue in workers' minds: 1946 witnessed a rash of strikes, some wildcat, many well-planned and of long duration, as pent-up frustration over wartime wage controls boiled over. At one time or another in 1946 telephone mechanics, steelworkers, autoworkers, railroad men, and many other unions went out on strike. John L. Lewis, elected vice president of the AF of L, was climbing steadily toward a position of enormous power in the world of labor and hence in the economy, a fact that brought no cheer to Mrs. Roosevelt's heart.

The Republicans swept both houses of Congress in the November elections, but Truman forged ahead confidently with the shaping of his postwar program, the Fair Deal. Mrs. Roosevelt gave him respectful support. Further evidence of the growing recognition of women's power came symbolically in 1946 when Emily Green Balch, head of the Women's International League for Peace and Freedom, was awarded the Nobel Peace Prize. And a happy publishing event caught the attention of thousands of expectant and new parents: Dr. Benjamin Spock's *The Commonsense Book of Baby and Child Care,* destined to become the nation's bible in the crib room, appeared.

~ ~ ~

At times Eleanor Roosevelt's prose style reached for the elevated heights of the essay, even the sermon, especially when she was writing about the importance of the United Nations. Both Mrs. Roosevelt and the UN were just starting out in their joint efforts for peace. As yet neither political gridlock within the organization nor willful refusal to cooperate in its mandates by countries operating independently of it had had time to develop, and the former First Lady was all idealism.

ENROUTE TO LONDON, JANUARY 5—I have been thinking of the grave responsibility which lies not only on the delegates to the United Nations Organization but on the nation as a whole as we gather for our first meeting of the UNO Assembly.

On the success or failure of the United Nations Organization may depend the preservation and continuance of our civilization.

We have learned how to destroy ourselves. Mankind can be wiped off the face of the earth by the action of any comparatively small group of people. So it would seem that if we care to survive we must progress in our social and economic development far more rapidly than we have done in the past.

We must, of course, lay proper stress in building this organization on the united force which will control all individual force throughout the world. At the same time, our real hope for the future lies in the development of a united economic, cultural and social pattern.

This must increase the well-being of the peoples of the world. Otherwise it will not win their loyalty and their constant, active participation and work as citizens. This is the only way in which we can hope to create the leadership needed in this organization to bring about the changes which can keep the world at peace.

The greed, suspicion and fear which have created wars in the past will create them again unless, through education and understanding, human beings can be brought to see that their own best interests lie along new lines of development. If we hope to prosper, others must prosper too, and if we hope to be trusted, we must trust others.

Above all, we must remember some of our ancient teachings which told us that a man could not guarantee the degree of development any other man might attain; but if he rose to his own greatest heights, willy-nilly, those around him would strive to achieve more than they would have without a great challenge.

The building of this organization is the greatest challenge that civilized man ever has faced. From earliest days he has fought for self-preservation, but always through destruction. Now for the first time, he has reached a point where destruction can be so complete that he must find new ways to fight for self-preservation.

The building of a United Nations Organization is the way that lies before us today. Nothing else except security for all the peoples of the world will bring freedom from fear of destruction.

Security requires both control of the use of force and the elimination of want. No people are secure unless they have the things needed not only to preserve existence, but to make life worth living. These needs may differ widely now. They may change for all, from time to time. But all peoples throughout the world must know that there is an organization where their interests can be considered and where justice and security will be sought for all.

~ ~ ~

The pomp and circumstance afforded the delegates by the British prime minister at a gala dinner soon after their arrival in London provided Mrs. Roosevelt an opportunity to take her American readers behind the scenes where royalty and diplomats entertained themselves.

LONDON, JANUARY 19—The dinner which Prime Minister Attlee gave for the delegates the other evening, in the Painted Hall of the Royal Naval College, was one of the most beautiful occasions of this kind that I've ever attended. Since I was the only woman delegate attending the dinner, Mrs. Attlee did not wish me to feel isolated, so she acted as hostess and it was not a completely stag party.

Historically, the Royal Naval College is extremely interesting. It stands on the site of the palace where both Henry VIII and Queen Elizabeth [I] were born. From the palace windows, Elizabeth watched Martin Frobisher set out in search of the Northwest Passage and, when Francis Drake returned from his trip around the world in the "Golden Hind," it was here that she welcomed him—as she did Walter Raleigh when he returned from America.

The Painted Hall in which we dined was designed by Sir Christopher Wren and was originally used as a dining room for Naval pensioners. Its wall and ceiling paintings were executed by Sir James Thornhill. The ceiling has portraits of King William and Queen Mary in center, with allegorical paintings representing all their virtues covering the rest of the ceiling.

Since a historian had been kind enough to bring me a description of all this, I tried very hard to bend my head backward and examine the ceiling with care, but one really should lie on the floor! I always wonder how painters of ceilings ever do their work.

One little thing at the table struck me. Each of us had a small silver ashtray. I examined mine and found that it bore an inscription of presentation by a Chinese cadet trained in the Royal Naval College during the first World War. Every ashtray carried a different Chinese name. I thought it was a charming way for these young Chinese to commemorate the opportunity which was given them to study at this historic college—and characteristic of the thoughtful generosity of the Chinese people.

It may seem absurd, but the person who impresses me most at these state dinners in Great Britain is the master of ceremonies who announces the toasts and speeches. He stands behind each speaker and intones: "Your Royal Highnesses, Your Grace, my Lords, Ladies and Gentlemen . . ." It always seems to me that he is much more important than anyone else present!

The Archbishop of Canterbury, whom I met for the first time and whom I found entirely delightful, said grace at the beginning and end of the meal. The last grace was just three words long, which caused a ripple of laughter as he finished.

Even formal dinners in Great Britain are still held down to three courses—soup, the main course of fish or chicken, and dessert.

~ ~ ~

A certain degree of frustration and impatience on Mrs. Roosevelt's part with her own country's citizens' frequent complaints about inadequate supplies of consumer goods under wartime rationing comes through in the next column. Or it may simply have been out of compassion for the British, whom she loved and admired, that she chose to tell her readers in detail about the deprivations still being suffered by the British and by other Europeans, deprivations that far outstripped anything Americans had to deal with because of the war.

LONDON, JANUARY 22—As to the clothes situation, utility clothes are still the main garments that can be purchased by the average woman. They were just coming in when I was here before. They are made to Government specification, are under rigid price control, and are not subject to a purchase tax.

They are cheap, whereas uncontrolled luxury garments, with a high purchase tax, are very expensive. And even if you have the money to buy them, you may not have the points. No matter who you are, you have only 24 clothing coupons for a period of eight months.

A dress takes 11 coupons, a slip five, a girdle (when you can find one) five points, a pair of stockings (and they are hard to find) three. A winter coat takes 18 points, gloves two, a tailored suit 18, a blouse five.

It is easy to see from this list that to get one outfit a year would probably cost you more than your allotment of points. So the British women look as though they had worn their clothes for some time and I don't believe they enjoy it any more than American women would.

Towels, curtain material, all materials by the yard and knitting wool all cost points. A young married couple have an advantage in that they are given extra points, because it is presumed that they are starting from scratch.

In America, my mother-in-law's generation bought in greater quantities than we do at present because they often had more space in which to keep things. Over and over again, since I have been here, I have hoped that the older generation of British people also laid up stores of goods because, without such things put away years ago, I don't see how they have managed to get along during these past few years.

Even in our hotel, I notice that the old man-sized bath towels are cut in half, and all the linen is worn!

~ ~ ~

Eleanor Roosevelt was a natural-born optimist, even an idealist. In addition she genuinely thrived on hard work and was therefore enormously productive. There was little that could bring Mrs. Roosevelt up short, leaving her lost in space and time with unsettling philosophical or practical questions. She almost always felt that she knew what to think and what to do next. The anger, sorrow, grief, and shame she experienced at a Jewish displaced-persons camp in Germany in the wake of the Holocaust left her, if not speechless, at least emotionally stunned.

BERLIN, FEBRUARY 16—My visit to Frankfurt was packed so full of emotions it is hard to give you an adequate idea of what I saw and how I felt. Yesterday morning, we visited the Zeilsheim Jewish displaced-persons camp. It is one of the best, since the people are living in houses previously occupied by Germans.

In these houses, each little family has a room to itself. Often a family must cross a room occupied by another in order to enter or leave the house, but there are doors and walls to separate them. If they like, they may bring food from the camp kitchen to their rooms and eat in what they call "home."

They made me a speech at a monument they have erected to the six million dead Jewish people. I answered from an aching heart.

49

When will our consciences grow so tender that we will act to prevent human misery rather than avenge it?

Someone asked a man, who looked old but couldn't have been really old, about his family. This was his answer: "They were made into soap." They had been burned to death in a concentration camp.

Outside the school, the children greeted me. They told me a little boy of ten was the camp singer. He looked six. He had wandered into camp one day with his brother, all alone, so he was the head of his family. He sang for me—a song of his people—a song of freedom. Your heart cried out that there was no freedom—and where was hope, without which human beings cannot live?

There is a feeling of desperation and sorrow in this camp which seems beyond expression. An old woman knelt on the ground, grasping my knees. I lifted her up but could not speak. What could one say at the end of a life which had brought her such complete despair?

~ ~ ~

Re-educating the German people for participation in a democratic government based on acceptance of all races and religions was a task demanding the highest priority in Eleanor Roosevelt's mind. Mrs. Roosevelt and many others at the time believed that re-education was the only way to ensure that the appeal of racist totalitarianism would be eradicated from German consciousness forever. Here Mrs. Roosevelt combines her idealistic faith in the power of education and a free press to shape (or reshape) national character with her virulent disapproval of the Nazi worldview.

NEW YORK, FEBRUARY 27—I want to tell you a little today about one branch of the work our Army is doing in Germany which I think we know little about over here. In the American zone, Brigadier General Robert A. McClure, a Regular Army officer, is in charge of the policies and operations of the information-control division of our Military Government. He seems to be fully aware of the issues at stake and very well qualified for his job. I talked to a number of the men working under him and gained an insight into some of their problems. Hitler and Goebbels did a wonderful job, from their own point of view, on the thinking processes of the German people!

We began, of course, in the period of psychological warfare, to study the warped German mentality and the propaganda techniques used by the Nazis to bring it about. We are now carrying on a re-education and a reorientation program. This must not be relaxed for a minute or the consequences will be very serious, for the Nazi poison has gone deep into the hearts and minds of young and old in Germany.

Their Führer gave them some material things which they could appreciate—full employment (even if it was in preparation for war), better houses, radios, the little three-wheeled cars. They closed their eyes to the concentration camp which lay over the hill and which, as human beings, they had to forget in order to be able to enjoy life. The job before us is a long-term job.

One of the things going on now is an effort to re-establish a free press. None has existed in Germany for many years. It is not wholly free today, for it is not allowed to criticize the Military Government or Allied policy. However, the papers are staffed by German editors and German reporters, and are subject only to postpublication scrutiny. They are being encouraged to develop high modern standards based on the high ideals of American journalism, but they may not propagate ideas of racism, Nazism or militarism. The same general policy applies to radio news.

This is one of the most important undertakings by our Military Government, and everyone should be watching it with interest and should insist that it be carried on until the roots of Nazism are wiped out.

~ ~ ~

A steady stream of mail, sometimes accumulating into a near tidal wave of correspondence, came to Eleanor Roosevelt from all across the country. Through her "My Day" columns and other journalism she invited the public to tell her about social and even personal problems that might be of interest to others. The contents of someone's letter to

Mrs. Roosevelt could become the text of her newspaper column if the point it brought out was general enough. Offensive instances of ethnic discrimination always caught Mrs. Roosevelt's attention.

NEW YORK, MARCH 8—I had a sad letter the other day—one which points out one of the big problems that the people of the United States are facing today. I am quoting from it for that reason:

"In 1944, I married a young Chinese woman who had come to the United States in 1938 with her A.B. from Yenching University seeking higher education. She received her M.A. from Mills College in 1940, and it was in the fall of that year that I met her when she came to the University of California to work for a Ph.D. in educational psychology. She is a most beautiful young woman, beloved by all who know her. After a great deal of soul-searching, we were finally married—while I was a junior medical student.

"... When we were married, we were entirely conscious of the shape of general social reaction in the United States, most particularly in the West, against mixed marriages. Indeed, California has a statute against miscegenation which made it necessary for us to be married in Washington. Nevertheless, until recently, we have not encountered any direct evidence of this traditional hostility.

"Our recent encounter has been in the field of housing accommodations. Recently I have taken a position in the Donner Laboratory of Medical Physics at this university. . . . In order to function effectively in this new job, it was necessary for us to move to Berkeley. I arranged for an exchange of apartments from San Francisco to Berkeley, and we moved in.

"I did not tell the manager that my wife was Chinese. I did not and do not feel that I had any moral obligation to give such information. By present rental and housing rules of the OPA, we are quite secure in our new home. The unpleasant experience that precipitates my writing was a conversation with the manager and his wife, just held after a month's tenancy, in which I was reproached for not informing them of the fact of my wife's nationality.

"... I am writing for my many Oriental friends, whom I know through my marriage and through residence at the Berkeley International House, where I met my wife, for my Negro friends, for my Filipino and Mexican friends, and for the host of all these races whom I can only know as they are symbolized in my friends."

If this sort of prejudice exists in our land, it seems to me that we deny the spirit of the various religions to which we all belong, for all religions recognize the equality of human beings before God. We deny the spirit of our Constitution and Government which our forefathers fought to establish. We make future good will and peace an impossibility, for no United Nations organization can succeed when peoples of one race approach those of other races in a spirit of contempt.

~ ~ ~

True to form, Mrs. Roosevelt admired the production of Jean Anouilh's Antigone *she saw on Broadway. The story concerns a young woman forced to make an impossible choice between adherence to the law and a filial love contradicting that law. Antigone represents woman at her strongest and most independent: that is, woman as Eleanor Roosevelt saw all women in the best sense. Katharine Cornell, the famous actress and a friend of Mrs. Roosevelt, had a gift for playing such characters. Another of her many standout performances was in George Bernard Shaw's similarly political drama,* Saint Joan.

NEW YORK, MARCH 9—Night before last was an unforgettable evening. I went to see the play "Antigone" with a friend who fortunately appreciated it as much as I did. It would be presumptuous of me to try to praise adequately the work done by Miss Katharine Cornell and Sir Cedric Hardwicke in the principal roles. Everything they did was beautifully done, and I can only express deep gratitude that it was possible for me to see something as moving and as beautiful as this play.

It is not the play that Sophocles wrote, and yet the essence of what he wanted to convey is all there. It is an adaptation by Lewis Galantière from a French play by Jean Anouilh. I wish that I could have seen it given in French before the German censors in occupied

France. M. Anouilh must have done a very interesting piece of writing to get the story past the censors, and yet give the French, who were subtle enough to understand it, the lift of seeing their masters condemned for their crimes against France. Apparently, the Germans were unaware of what was being conveyed through the drama!

The English adaptation is very beautiful and I thought that Mr. Braham as the chorus was remarkable. I am tremendously proud that something as fine as this is on our New York stage and that it has a good audience.

When the curtain went down, it took me a minute to realize that the play was over and that I was not in ancient Thebes, but in the modern city of New York, where the same old fight is going on between the things of the flesh and the things of the spirit! We certainly need a modern Antigone, but I don't know just where we are going to find her!

~ ~ ~

Fala, the Roosevelts' Scots terrier, was so popular that he even received his own fan mail. His antics provided the "peg" for many a "My Day" column. Many of the columns included brief comments on two or more subjects that had come up in the course of Mrs. Roosevelt's busy schedule. In this one we again find her commenting on the meaning of the term socialistic.

NEW YORK, APRIL 4—Next week is "Be Kind to Animals Week" and, having a little dog, I always feel it incumbent upon me to remember this week with gratitude. Anyone who really enjoys the companionship of some animal always wants to remind people of the obligation that human beings have to the dumb creatures who cannot talk in our language, but who, in their own way, show so many qualities that add to the joy of our lives.

Fala's wagging tail and warm greeting is always a pleasure. When he runs away in the country to go a-hunting and leaves me calling him for hours with no response, I feel like spanking him, but I never quite have the heart to do it when he returns. He enters with a sheepish expression of knowing he has misbehaved, or with an expression of triumph if he has run his prey to earth, and I find myself so glad to see him that he gets a pat instead of a spank!

I see by the papers that Senator Robert Taft and Senator James Murray, in a committee meeting, had a slight difference of opinion as to whether the new national health bill was socialistic or not. It seems to me that Senator Taft might remember that the postal service is one of the most socialistic things we have in this country, and yet I hardly think he wants to do away with that.

Labeling something socialistic may, from his point of view, be detrimental to the endeavor, but my experience is that, when people really want something, the label you put on it makes very little difference. And there is no doubt in my mind that the people want, in the words of President Truman, "Health security for all, regardless of residence, station or race—everywhere in the United States." This means not only more medical facilities but more doctors, scientists, dentists, nurses and other specialists.

~ ~ ~

Lending support by her conspicuous presence at luncheons, dinners, and other meetings sponsored by worthwhile organizations occupied a great deal of Eleanor Roosevelt's time. She was all the more pleased to be there when the organization truly did represent her own highest principles—as did the all-woman-staffed New York Infirmary. The bonus in this case was the speech by Bernard Baruch, the financier who had advised both Woodrow Wilson and FDR, particularly with counsel about the development of wartime industries. Like Mrs. Roosevelt, Baruch was soon to become involved in United Nations work, as a representative on the UN's Atomic Energy Commission.

LOUISVILLE, KY., APRIL 26—The other evening, in New York City, I attended a dinner for the New York Infirmary. It was a very distinguished gathering. They were particularly fortunate in getting Bernard M. Baruch to make a speech.

Among other things, he said that his father, whom he described as one of the wisest men he had ever known, had once told him that no man should become a doctor who was looking for any financial return. His reward should be entirely in the good he could do for other human beings. That is a pretty difficult standard to live up to in any age, and I think Mr. Baruch's doctor-father must have been a very fine man.

Mr. Baruch then proceeded to pay the ladies a very wonderful compliment by saying that he thought they would more nearly meet his father's requirements as doctors and, therefore, he believed in the work of the New York Infirmary, which is staffed entirely by women and gives them an opportunity for the best and highest training in the medical arts.

There was a time, many years ago, when this was the only institution in the city of New York where women could get this kind of training. But now they have won their way and they no longer have to face as many difficulties as they did in the past. However, they still have some limitations to overcome, so this institution still fills a great need.

~ ~ ~

"Write to your Representatives in Congress!" "My Day" readers were often reminded—usually with a strong suggestion about what to say. Nonetheless, a legend had grown up around the former First Lady in which many people believed that "Mrs. Roosevelt could and would fix things—by herself." Indeed, Eleanor Roosevelt was a kind of one-person lobby, and she did speak for various interest groups even when she had no formal affiliation with them. Yet on the issue of what was to become of the Office of Price Administration in the postwar economic stabilization program, she recognized that no program would work without public cooperation.

NEW YORK, APRIL 30—It has been a long fight to put the control of our economic system in the hands of the Government, where it can be administered in the interests of the people as a whole. Now Congress, under the influence of powerful lobbies, is rapidly trying to return control to big business. It may be that individual Congressmen do not realize just what they are doing, but they are heading us straight for inflation and accepting the old "boom and bust" ideas instead of sticking to the plan of ironing out the peaks and the valleys and trying to keep us on a fairly even keel.

Chester Bowles, Stabilization Director, and Paul Porter, Price Administrator, are doing their best but, without the support of the people, who are the ones most affected by what happens to OPA, these two men will be defeated by the representatives of the people.

Write to your Representatives in Congress. Writing to me is of very little use!

~ ~ ~

Eleanor Roosevelt threw herself into her United Nations work. Her diplomatic skills were soon given recognition when she was elected chairman of the Human Rights Commission, a task that would absorb the better part of her energy and time for several years. Because Mrs. Roosevelt was especially devoted to the struggle for women's equality, the UN Subcommission on the Status of Women would also regularly draw her attention.

NEW YORK, MAY 1—Yesterday noon, I had the pleasure of meeting at lunch some of my colleagues on the Human Rights Commission of the UN Economic and Social Council. As usually happens, there was some confusion about contacting a few of them. And our French colleague, Prof. René Cassin, was delayed somewhere on an airplane.

Besides myself, only three members of the commission were present. But there were also Henri Laugier, Assistant Secretary General, who is in charge of all of the Council's commissions on social affairs; Dr. Schmidt, who is secretary to all the six commissions now meeting in New York; and Mrs. Joseph Lash, who is secretary for the Human Rights Commission.

This was our first opportunity to talk together, and we found that Mr. Laugier and the gentleman from Jugoslavia preferred to speak in French. The rest of the group felt more at home in English.

After lunch, we drove to Hunter College for the first meeting of the commission at 3 o'clock. The predominant number of members speak English, but everything is translated into French—a little item that I, as chairman, kept forgetting until I suddenly looked at the translator and noticed that his expression was somewhat agonized. I realized then that I had completely forgotten to give him a chance to translate my remarks!

Mr. Laugier made us a serious and inspiring speech, but I think all of us fully realize that our responsibility is great. Being chairman rather frightened me, since I am not very good on parliamentary law! Fortunately, we adopted the rules of procedure which were suggested for the commission, so I only have to keep them before me in case any difference of opinion crops up.

The Economic and Social Council appointed this "nuclear" commission to serve for one year and to make recommendations as to the permanent set-up for the commission. Nine members were invited to serve. They were chosen as individuals, not representing any government, who would be competent to work on the questions which would probably come up in the field of human rights.

It will be up to us to recommend whether this method of choice will be continued or whether the members later will be chosen to represent governments. In view of the fact that the commission will only make recommendations and that the Economic and Social Council, to which the recommendations go, is made up of representatives of governments, it seems to me that the governments will have the final decisions in any case.

The Subcommission on the Status of Women met after our commission ended its meeting, and three of our members had been appointed to serve on this subcommission. I was among the number but, yesterday, having made two engagements for the late afternoon, I could not stay for the subcommission meeting at 5 o'clock. I will, however, be on hand for all the meetings in the future, I hope.

~ ~ ~

The role of Harry Hopkins in the entire Roosevelt presidency was crucial. As head of the Federal Emergency Relief Administration (1933) and of the Works Projects Administration (1935–1938), he oversaw the distribution of $8.5 billion for unemployment relief. Hopkins was Secretary of Commerce from 1938 to 1940, head of the Lend-Lease Administration in 1941 as well as the President's personal envoy to Russia and Britain, and a member of the War Production Board in 1942. He served as Special Assistant to the President from 1942 until 1945. Hopkins was only fifty-six when he died.

New York, May 22—In Washington tomorrow, May 22nd, there will be held a memorial service for Harry Hopkins. Those of his friends who are able to attend will be grateful for an opportunity to think of him and to talk about him to others who still keenly feel his death.

In the last years of my husband's life, Harry Hopkins was probably his closest and most trusted co-worker. He went on missions that required tact and courage, and he met the great men of the world face to face. I cannot remember the time when he looked really strong and, as the years went by, he became more and more delicate. Yet he seemed to be able to rise above his bodily weakness and meet every great emergency. Perhaps it was this quality of indomitable spirit which first drew my husband and Harry Hopkins together.

They met and worked together in New York State while my husband was Governor and Mr. Hopkins had charge of the State unemployment relief program. They got on well then, and when Mr. Hopkins came to Washington to take over the much larger and more serious relief job that faced the nation, my husband felt he was dealing with someone he already knew and on whom he could count. It was not, however, until domestic issues began to be secondary and the war seemed to be growing daily closer to us that the two men really began to work on the whole world picture together.

My husband recognized the weaknesses as well as the strength of the people with whom he worked, and I often heard him take Harry Hopkins to task because, in spite of repeated warnings, he would do the things which he enjoyed doing and then his health would suffer. However, my husband understood the impatience with bodily handicaps which made Mr. Hopkins such a poor patient.

To a man who was handicapped physically in the way my husband was, it was almost essential that he have a few people whom he could trust absolutely and whom he could use as messengers. He had to have the knowledge that his messages would be delivered accurately and that his ideas would be conveyed in the way he wished them conveyed. True, he expected everyone who worked for him to use their own initiative and their own judgment whenever the need arose, but when they were carrying a message, or getting a plan across, any initiative must bear on the ultimate accomplishment, and the personality of the individual must not in any way obscure the job that had to be done.

Harry Hopkins was in himself a very big person. I think it was because of this that he was willing to subordinate himself and to accept the fact that the objects for which he and my husband worked together were more important than any kudos which he might acquire for himself.

In some ways, the comforts and luxuries of this world were matters of complete insignificance to Mr. Hopkins, and yet there was another side to his character. There were times when he felt he wanted to enjoy them all. But always his tongue was in his cheek, and you felt that a little imp sat on his shoulder and said: "Go ahead and have a good time, but you know it has no real value." His was a life spent too fast, and yet it was well spent. Few people have left a greater record of accomplishment to spur their children and future generations of mankind to achievement.

~ ~ ~

Again the German question: to allow rearmaments or not? Whatever controls might be required of the occupying Allied forces in Germany to forestall any rearmament there, Eleanor Roosevelt was for them. She had no faith that Germany could restrain itself from making war again. And Mrs. Roosevelt's antennae were sensitive to the Russian question too: Just what kind and amount of expansion into Eastern Europe were the Soviets planning?

New York, May 23—I am sure that every citizen listened with as much interest as I did to Secretary of State Byrnes' report to the nation about the Paris conference. It seemed to me a forthright, honest story and, in view of all the elements of the situation, it was less discouraging than I had expected.

I was particularly glad to have him say that we still intend to carry out the original agreements and keep Germany from being able to rearm. Some of us have realized that under the surface, ever since those agreements were made, there have been groups of people in both Great Britain and the United States who have not looked upon them with favor.

For one thing, certain people have thought that, when all was said and done, we had beaten Germany twice, and perhaps it would be better to have her as a buffer in central Europe against the spreading out of the Soviet Union and its influence over neighboring states. In addition, there are large business interests in the international field which tie all nationalities together. Thirdly, since Russia only recently granted freedom of religion within her borders, there has been considerable feeling against wiping out the strength of a country which, except during the Hitler regime, was considered a religious nation.

All these interests added together meant that there was a strong undercurrent against carrying out the original agreements. And yet, twice in 25 years, we have been taken into a world war by Germany.

It cannot be said that, in the last year, Russia has taken any pains to allay the fears of those who have been worried about her spreading power. True, she has assured the world repeatedly that her interests lie along the paths of peace, and all of us know that she feels the loss of her sons and the devastation of her land. However, it has been easy for people to say that Russia was relying more and more on the building up of her own power, and less and less on the joint power which won the war and which the founders of the United Nations hoped would win the peace. We must get together with Russia, but it must be a two-way matter.

~ ~ ~

Eleanor Roosevelt was motivated in much of her social and political activity by a sense of noblesse oblige. Like Nelson Rockefeller, cited in this next column for his work on behalf of a relief committee of the United Jewish Appeal in New York, Mrs. Roosevelt came from a long line of well-to-do, well-educated upper-class Americans. Yet explaining her sense of obligation to help those in distress, as surely the European Jewish survivors of the Holocaust were at this time, merely as noblesse oblige does her a disservice. Mrs. Roosevelt's principles were broader, as we can see in this column when she asserts flatly that all Americans, no matter what their class or race or religion, have a moral obligation to give something to the Jewish relief cause—because those who were suffering were fellow human beings before they were Europeans, and before they were Jews.

In the second of these next two columns, Mrs. Roosevelt refers to Fiorello LaGuardia. He was Mayor of New York from 1933 through 1945 and served with the former First Lady as a director of the Office of Civilian Defense in the early years of World War II. In 1946 LaGuardia became Director General of the UN Relief and Rehabilitation Administration.

HYDE PARK, JUNE 11—I wonder how many of my readers know of the Community Committee of New York on behalf of the United Jewish Appeal. The chairman is Nelson A. Rockefeller. The honorary chairmen are Governor Thomas E. Dewey, Mayor William O'Dwyer of New York City, the Honorable Herbert H. Lehman and Bishop William T. Manning. The vice-chairmen are William J. Donovan, John J. McCloy and William S. Paley. And there is a distinguished executive committee made up of men of many races and many faiths.

I bring this to the attention of my readers because I feel strongly that every city, small or large, in this country would help to increase the feeling of brotherhood throughout the world if a similar committee was organized in their midst. The purpose is to help the survivors of the Jewish group in Europe who were the greatest sufferers under Hitler's fascist rise to power.

Of the 7,000,000 Jews who lived in Europe when Hitler first came to power, nearly 6,000,000 were put to death in the most brutal manner possible. The methods used frequently included deliberate starvation and torture. Among those murdered were 2,000,000 Jewish children.

Just the other day, I talked to a man and his wife who had finally managed to come to this country from a concentration camp near Frankfurt. They are educated, scholarly people—he is a poet. They had seen their two children burned to death. How one lives through such torture is only explained by the fact that, within each of us, there is an extraordinary tenacity which clings to life, and if we have any hope held out to us, we will struggle to start again.

We in America, who have been spared such cruelty, have a joint responsibility, I think—whether we are Catholic, Protestant or Jew—to help the 1,400,000 Jewish survivors in Europe to return to some kind of normal living.

This committee in New York is helping these people in 51 countries through a joint distribution committee, which does the work of providing food, clothing, shelter and medical supplies. They are establishing hospitals, helping to rehabilitate schools and community welfare institutions, and giving vocational training. Not the least important work is that of reuniting families—which, in war-torn Europe, is a difficult thing to do—and then assisting in their transportation to and establishment in new homelands.

HYDE PARK, JUNE 15—I see that Mr. LaGuardia is urging us to relax our immigration laws and take in some of the displaced persons from Europe. If Palestine is not going to be opened even to 100,000 Jews, I think we should take the lead in opening our borders to this particular group of persons who have suffered more than any other.

There are many more, however, who in spite of all the efforts made to have them return to their own countries of origin, will have to go to other nations. And here again I think we have a duty to lead in taking our share. It is not fair to ask of others what you are not willing to do yourself.

~ ~ ~

Many great minds have struggled for decades to bring about rapprochement among the competing ethnic, religious, and political factions in the Holy Land. Though Eleanor Roosevelt had no master plan to offer herself, she did propose, many times, that only through negotiations could peace be achieved and that repeated government inquiries on the "Palestinian question" never resolved anything. Uppermost in Mrs. Roosevelt's mind was the need for action to help stranded European Jews seeking entry to Palestine. She apparently had no understanding that even after the establishment of Israel as an essentially Jewish state regional conflicts would continue unabated in the Middle East.

HYDE PARK, JUNE 22—There is an article in "The Nation" by Freda Kirchwey, editor and publisher, which was written in Cairo about the Palestine question and the attitude of British Foreign Secretary Ernest Bevin. This article appears at a very opportune time. Anyone who has been noting what desperate things the Palestinian Jews are doing, in order to hold onto their arms and build up a defense group somewhat akin to underground groups everywhere, must realize the seriousness of the tragedy of the whole situation in Palestine.

I think we should think back over the steps by which we as a nation became involved in this matter. There was a time when we took no responsibility for Palestine. Then Great Britain invited us to take part in a joint commission to study the question.

We knew the conditions in Europe, and so did they. We knew that innumerable Jews in Europe were braving every kind of danger in order to get to Palestine, because it was the only place where they felt they would be at home. We knew the attitude of

King Ibn Saud of Saudi Arabia, and we knew the general Arab position.

There was really no need for a commission of inquiry, but we went along with Great Britain. The obvious reason we went along was that we believed Great Britain would accept the report of such a group and try to implement it. It was only fair to suppose that we both had a clear understanding of what our joint obligations to implement any such report would be.

Now President Truman has appointed a committee to look into this question of implementing the report, but the British Foreign Secretary, Mr. Bevin, has stated that the real reason we are anxious to see 100,000 Jews admitted to Palestine is that we do not want them in New York. He may be right in what he has said, and I am only sorry that we have not made our position so clear that such things could not be said about us.

It might be unwise to bring into New York, which already is larger than any city should be, a great number of any particular group. But certainly throughout this country we could scatter our share of displaced persons without upsetting our economy. We are not yet at the point where an increase in population is a menace. In fact, it would be quite possible to absorb far more than our share of the displaced people in Europe who are seeking homes.

The particular point at issue, however, is that there are 100,000 Jews in Europe who must find homes immediately and they want to go to Palestine. The Arabs threaten dire things. The British talk about the impossibility of increasing the military force. But, surely, our allied Chiefs of Staff could work out some form of military defense for Palestine which would not mean an increase in manpower.

The Arabs are intelligent people and so are we. I cannot believe that they are without mercy any more than we are.

~ ~ ~

Model communities, set up by New Deal legislation and fostered by a combination of private enterprise and government ownership, were among the pet projects of both FDR and his wife. Mrs. Roosevelt was particularly pleased when she could report on the successful evolution of such a community to the stage of full financial independence. Inevitably, from Depression days forward, the Roosevelts and their supporters were met with the wrath of critics who believed government intervention in the financial side of private citizens' lives was unconscionable. Mrs. Roosevelt never tired of pressing her side of the argument.

Perhaps the best known of the Depression era communities created under the provision of FDR's Subsistence Homestead Act was Arthurdale, an extremely poor Appalachian town near Morgantown, West Virginia. When Mrs. Roosevelt visited Arthurdale in 1936, she found the living conditions shocking. It was her report to the President that put in motion the legislative machinery to provide federal government assistance to such financially hopeless Americans. Though Arthurdale developed nicely into a self-sufficient community, with families living for the first time in houses with refrigerators and indoor plumbing, the nature of the project upset critics who believed the government should leave citizens to fend for themselves. In the following column, Mrs. Roosevelt reports on another similarly successful community.

HYDE PARK, JUNE 29—I was very much interested the other day to receive an article sent to me from "Pageant Magazine" on a New Jersey community which has changed its name from Jersey Homesteads to Roosevelt. This is one of the homesteads started in the days of the Depression, and it has had a hard and discouraging career.

A small group of New York City garment workers originally moved out there from the slum areas of the city. Each contributed a small amount of money, and their plan was to run their own factory, live on small garden or farm plots, and have the stores municipally owned. It didn't work, partly because the experience was not there to run this type of community.

Today things are privately owned and run, but I judge from this article that a spirit of cooperation still exists and the community is politically active. They have a high rate of actual voters in elections. The borough council meetings are open to the public, and public issues are discussed there and at specially called town meetings in which the citizens take part.

I was very glad to see this article because so often we are told that these experiments of the Depression years have produced nothing but loss to the taxpayers. The other day, for instance, I received a long letter from the minister at Arthurdale, West Virginia, who runs the community church. It is an encouraging report on the success of the people in the community. Yet I had just read, rather sadly, a diatribe in some paper quoting the cost of the original experiment and stating that the people had not liked the paternalism of Government control, that the Government had now sold the community and only recovered about 5 percent of the original expenditure.

All this may be true, even the part about the people not liking to be helped, and yet I can hardly believe that this was universal when I remember the conditions from which those people came. If at that time some kind of Government help had not come, they and their children today might be costing the taxpayers far more than the loss on that investment in the Arthurdale community.

Children brought up in utter misery, with scant food, children whose parents are too worried to really do anything constructive for them, are the ones we find today in reformatories and later in prisons, or in state hospitals. All of these institutions are supported by the taxpayers, and the greater the number of inmates, the greater the cost.

I am glad that the Arthurdale experiment, like the Jersey home-steads, is now owned by the people; that a private company has taken over the factory buildings; that the school buildings are run by the school system of West Virginia. I cannot help believing that the people who now own those houses and live in those communities have healthier, happier children, and that these children have grown in the past fourteen years to better citizenship than they could have achieved if there had been no Jersey Homesteads and no Arthurdale, or the equivalent in various parts of our nation.

~ ~ ~

Leave it to Eleanor Roosevelt to see the universal in the particular. As she tended her own vegetable garden, appreciating its bounty, she thought of hungry people elsewhere, especially in war-torn lands, and realized the connection between America's surplus and other nation's needs. Mrs. Byrnes was the wife of James F. Byrnes, Secretary of State from 1945 through 1947; Mrs. Nimitz was married to the commander in chief of the U.S. Pacific fleet during the war who was chief of naval operations at the time this was written.

NEW YORK, JULY 23—In the papers last week, there was a nice photograph of Mrs. James F. Byrnes and Mrs. Chester W. Nimitz busily canning. I hope it reminded a great many people that one of the best ways to help the food situation throughout the world is for everyone who can do so to have a garden, and to put up anything they can't eat now, so they can enjoy it next winter.

Of course, if you happen to have a deep freeze, you already know the joys of taking out your vegetables or your fruits and using them all through the winter and spring. Many things are far better put into the freezer than preserved in any other way, particularly now when there is such a shortage of sugar, for one can do so much better in the deep freeze with less sugar.

I have only just finished using up peaches which I put into the deep freeze last summer. I can vouch for the fact that they made very good peach shortcake! The things, however, which give me real joy are those which I have grown myself. I find that peas and beans, beets and carrots, put straight from the garden into the deep freeze, come out just like fresh vegetables. During these two or three weeks while I am away from Hyde Park, everything possible is going into my deep freeze, since I cannot be home to eat part of it now.

~ ~ ~

The annual summertime trek to Campobello Island would have been sad for Mrs. Roosevelt in 1946, the first time in decades that she had visited the Roosevelt summer home without the President. Yet she had the practical wisdom to find pleasure in the delicious details of small things like fresh strawberries.

EN ROUTE TO CAMPOBELLO, JULY 31—After stopping overnight in Portland, Maine, I have driven on up the coast, looking for familiar landmarks as I went. Where was that nut shop or that place where, in the past, I stopped to buy jellies or jams? On the way up to Campobello Island, I used to make acquisitions which my family enjoyed, since it is not very easy on the island to get a variety of food. Gardens are late, but fish is always plentiful there.

I may be in time for the late strawberries, because they ripen slowly. They have a wonderful flavor, somewhat like the ones grown on the Ile d'Orleans, in the St. Lawrence River, near Quebec. These are famous for their delicious flavor. It used to be easy, when we had a boat, to go and come to the mainland, but a storm destroyed our boathouse and our boat last winter.

On August 1, a monument will be unveiled in the little village of Welchpool, Campobello Island, N.B., in memory of my husband, who went there so often in his boyhood and early manhood and loved not only the island itself but the waters all around it. He knew the coast of New Brunswick and of Nova Scotia and was as good a sailorman thereabouts as many of the natives. They asked me particularly to try to be in Campobello on August 1, so I am glad that, with my son Elliott and his family, I will be there. Soon afterward, we will start for home.

~ ~ ~

Turning away the former First Lady from a previously reserved hotel room because she was traveling with a dog (indeed, one with its own national reputation) took more than a little chutzpah on the hotel clerk's part when Mrs. Roosevelt was en route to Campobello. Her spunkiness and sense of humor show through in the column.

HYDE PARK, AUGUST 5—Some of the papers in the Maine area made a good deal of the fact that, on my trip up to Campobello

Island, I could not stay overnight at a hotel in Portland because I had Fala with me. Since it was a hotel rule, the clerk was quite right to stick to it and I had no complaint. I did not know of the rule because I had never stayed in that hotel before, and I would not have telegraphed for rooms there if I had not forgotten the name of the hotel where I usually stay. I remembered this hotel because my son had stayed there when he made a speech in Portland last spring.

The fault was mine, since I had not mentioned that I would have a dog with me. And it made no difference because, when I stopped for supper in Yarmouth, I asked if there were any cabins nearby that would take me in with a dog, and I found a place at once and had a very comfortable night.

~ ~ ~

Again the issue of European Jewish refugees and Palestine. The political situation in Palestine in the immediate postwar period had the same "damned if you do, damned if you don't" quality it has at so many points since. The British ended up with the mandate to supervise Palestine, just as the United States and the Soviets took temporary control in other parts of the world. Given the trauma of the European holocaust, it was inevitable that hundreds of thousands of the remaining Jews would want to emigrate, and most of them would want to settle in Israel. It was equally inevitable that the Arabs, as a people if not as one organized state, would feel threatened by the surge of Jews (historically their adversaries) toward Palestine—their shared homeland. Mrs. Roosevelt had no magic wand to wave to create a solution, but she also had no patience with political jockeying for position or with cruel abuse of helpless emigres. She was losing patience with the British, who were trying to stave off Arab-Jewish conflict but whose rerouting of Jewish refugees struck Mrs. Roosevelt as high-handed and evasive of the real issues.

NEW YORK, AUGUST 19—I think many people must feel as unhappy as I do over the fact that Jewish refugees on ships bound for Palestine are being taken to detention camps in Cyprus. Many of us will agree that resort to force by Jews in Palestine is deplorable, but I don't think it is hard to understand. Palestine does not belong to Britain, which governs it under a mandate. When people are desperate, I suppose that a show of force against them inevitably brings retaliation in kind. The British have certainly had force in evidence in Palestine.

We are faced today with the problem of trying to find homes for many thousands of homeless people in Europe. Some of them do not want to return to their former homes. They will willingly adventure to other countries in the hope of finding better conditions and greater opportunity. A great number of the surviving Jews of Europe—and it is sad to think how few there are—long to go to a new home of their own, and to them Palestine has come to mean that home.

The suggestion that the country be partitioned seems to me no answer to the problem, since the main objection originally to Palestine becoming a home for the Jews was the grave doubt entertained by many as to whether the land would be able to support any more people than were already there. It is understandable that the Arabs are not anxious to have the Jews as neighbors. The Arabs are a nomadic people, leading simple lives, and those who have moved into the orbit of the Jewish people have found the competition difficult and the standard of living higher than that to which they were accustomed. The Jews, however, are not asking for a vast increase in land. They ask to keep what they have, with slight additions for economic needs, and to be allowed to take in refugees.

There are many Jews, even among those in Europe, who do not want to go to Palestine because they see greater opportunity in becoming citizens of other nations. There are many today who are Britons, Americans, French or other nationalities.

Those going to Palestine are mainly in two groups: old people who wish to be surrounded by their own customs and by friendly people for the rest of their lives or young people who have been trained in camps in Europe for specific occupations. The latter are imbued with the desire to develop Palestine and to have it a homeland and a refuge for their people. They have lost so much and seen so much sorrow and suffering that this idea is probably almost like a crusade.

71

We sit safely and smugly in the United States and read of new detention camps in Cyprus. To an ordinary citizen like myself, the motives that Britain might have which would lead to the latest developments in the Near East are very difficult to understand. It looks as though we were forgetting our main objective of peace in this world. It is possible, of course, that what we fear is that the Arabs will go to war with us, but that hardly seems possible.

It seems to be a case of deciding what we think is right for people from refugee camps in Europe who are trying to find a place to build a new life. In Great Britain and in the United States, if we decided what was right, I don't think we would have much difficulty in getting it done.

~　~　~

Hyde Park had become for Mrs. Roosevelt both refuge and shrine. Refuge for her, personally, in that she had privacy in her nearby Val-kill Cottage where walks in the woods and work in the garden or the kitchen helped her clear her always busy mind of other, more worldly concerns. But shrine as well, as the statistics concerning public visitation at the FDR homestead indicate. (Even after forty-five years of history the parking lot at the Presidential Library and Museum at Hyde Park is filled on a summer day with visitors' cars and buses from all across America. If one listens closely while touring the museum, the languages of many countries will be heard as well.)

HYDE PARK, SEPTEMBER 12—I've received a letter from George Palmer, superintendent of the "Home of Franklin D. Roosevelt," giving some figures which I think might be of interest to the public. On a recent Sunday, 9,836 persons passed in front of the grave. During August, 104,311 people visited the grave and 70,031 went through the home. In all, 203,628 people have visited the home, and 304,320 the grave since last April.

Mr. Palmer tells me that they have decided that 2,500 visitors a day are all that can be allowed to go through the house. It will not stand a great crowd at any one time. I can remember that once, when we had a reception years ago, my husband kept urging me to get the guests to pass through the library because he thought too many people were standing on the floor at one time!

~ ~ ~

Henry A. Wallace was one of the more colorful characters on the American political scene in the 1930s and 1940s. After distinguishing himself as a plant geneticist and as an editor of a farmers' journal founded by his father in 1895 in Iowa, Wallace was chosen by FDR as his first Secretary of Agriculture and served in that post from 1933 until 1940. He was always idealistic, hardworking, a serious conservative Christian, and an outspoken political liberal. With FDR's confidence in him growing and Wallace's own ambitions on the rise, he won the nomination for Vice President under FDR and served during the President's third term, 1941–1945. But a certain aloofness and a disdain for the necessary compromises of ordinary political life alienated Wallace from most party leaders and made him less than effective; Harry Truman replaced him on the ticket in 1945.

The consolation prize for Wallace was the Commerce secretariat, where he frequently held forth on a broad range of issues, particularly international affairs. Believing himself the true carrier of the faltering New Deal banner after FDR's death, it must have been hard for him to see Mrs. Roosevelt criticize his ideas in print.

For her part, we see here the thoroughgoing idealism that colored her vision of the postwar world under the presumed beneficence of the newly organized United Nations. Though Mrs. Roosevelt was extremely wary of the possible consequences of allowing the atomic bomb to get into irresponsible hands, she nonetheless really believed the UN—if equipped with some means of forceful control (an idea she never seemed able to define)—would keep the peace. At this point anyway, Mrs. Roosevelt does not yet appear to have recognized the dark implications of Churchill's recently coined term, the iron curtain to describe the political wall between East and West that was rapidly being created by the expansion of Soviet Communist influence in Eastern Europe.

New York, September 20—The "spheres of influence" section of Secretary of Commerce Henry Wallace's speech last week seems to me to have been written without proper explanation. Because Russia has gained a predominant military and political interest in certain countries along her borders, and because Great Britain has always shown the same type of interest in countries along what are known as her "lifelines," and because we in this hemisphere find that we have similar interests with our neighbors, many people feel that we must of necessity accept the fact that there will be spheres of influence in the future. However, I really think this matter requires a little more thinking through.

Within its sphere of interest, each great power is required, by its acceptance of the principles laid down in the Atlantic Charter and in the United Nations Charter, to give freedom of action to the peoples of the various nations in that sphere. And if their interests should clash, the great power, under these agreements, would have to accept whatever differences a smaller nation might choose in religion, politics or economics. Spheres of interest, in other words, can only be held together by mutual agreement, and there is no reason why this concept should prevent our trying to keep the world "One World" and to achieve the basic principles which concern us all.

This can only be done through the United Nations and the organs established under the United Nations. To preserve peace in the future, I count as most important world cooperation through the UN Food and Agriculture Organization, through the UN health and labor organizations, and through UNESCO, which will develop cultural and scientific cooperation among the different nations. The Economic and Social Council, with its various commissions, is designed specifically to prevent friction. When questions reach the Security Council, we must have an organization to enforce its decisions.

Until a decision is made on control of the atomic bomb, our method of joint enforcement is held up. But as soon as possible, a method should be decided upon because, as long as force rules anywhere in the world, we have no choice but to make it a collective force if we do not wish to see the big nations enter into an armament race. And such a race, as Secretary Wallace pointed out in his letter to the President, would lead to war.

President Truman, some months ago, stated that the foreign policy of the United States was his foreign policy, and that Secretary of State Byrnes was negotiating and making the fight for peace treaties as a representative of the President of the United States. These negotiations are bound to develop friction.

The men concerned are representing their governments to the best of their abilities, and are trying to obtain the things which they feel their people, as represented by their home governments, really want. Our representatives are probably more conscious of the thinking of the people at home than are those of other nations. For that reason we have able members of our Senate, representing both political parties, advising the Secretary of State.

NEW YORK, SEPTEMBER 21—An armament race in an atomic world is unthinkable. On this subject, Secretary Wallace gives us a very excellent and true picture. The crux of the matter is that, in time, atomic bombs can be manufactured almost anywhere. The only advantage would be to that nation which used them first, so we would live in a neurotic, fear-ridden world.

Peace—and a peace which will lessen individual armaments throughout the world—must be our aim. Force, if it must be used, must be used only through the one organization which can use it collectively and function for us all.

I think that, on the whole, the debate which has taken place because of Secretary Wallace's speech has not done anyone any real harm. It certainly will not hurt the peace negotiations for the Russians to know that in this country, while we do not want to be a tail to their kite, we do want to cooperate with them in order to give Russia and ourselves greater security—and to attain greater security, coupled with better economic conditions, throughout the world.

~ ~ ~

75

Many wealthy Americans would have been loath to discuss in public any financial arrangements with their domestic servants. Not so Mrs. Roosevelt. She was accustomed to having plenty of help in all parts of her life (secretaries, maids, cooks, chauffeurs, gardeners, caretakers) and just as accustomed to treating them well. As we shall see in later columns, some of the Roosevelts' domestic workers stayed with the family for decades. And so Mrs. Roosevelt was perfectly positioned to bring into the open the economic facts, to do so with honesty, good humor, and a practical political aim as well: to promote the unionization of domestic labor.

HYDE PARK, OCTOBER 28—There is an article in one of the papers today which will bring chuckles to anyone who knows the younger set on Long Island. It is by a butler who tells what's wrong with the employers he's worked for. Although it is amusing and in some ways very true, there is another side to the picture, and I think both sides should be presented fairly.

There is no question but that in the past the employer did not provide "servants" with the type of comfortable living quarters to which they are entitled. But I think it is the exception today when an employer does not give comfortable rooms and furnishings.

I am entirely in accord that a change in the name is desirable. I have always disliked the word "servant." Could one say domestic helper, or is there a better name? The job, if a family and a home are to be well cared for, is a skilled worker's job.

I do not find the story of the woman who served 40 years in one family and then left all she had to her employer's son, rather than to her own relatives, a sad tale. I think she was undoubtedly happy in her work and loved those whom she served. That can be a very rare, close and satisfying relationship. No compensation in wages can possibly measure the tie that exists between employer and employee when years of love and respect have forged the bond.

I think the unionization of domestic employees will be salutary for both the employer and the employee. The employer would have to be more accurate in describing the job and less changeable. The employee would have to be well trained and live up to certain standards, both as to the manner in which the job was done and the time it took to execute it. There would have to be definite achievement and skill in order to obtain certain wages.

The butler who writes this sad and partially true tale does not mention that many a couple in service today is demanding and receiving from $300 to $400 a month in addition to board and lodging, which at present living costs would probably mean an additional $200 a month. There are not many employers, young or old, who can afford that amount of money for help in their household tasks.

Forty or 50 years ago, the monthly rate of pay in households with several employees was $40 to $50 for a cook, $25 to $30 for a housemaid or waitress, and $18 to $20 for a kitchen maid, with room and board for all. These wages rose until about 20 years ago, when a cook received $80 to $100 a month, a butler about $70 or more, and the other employees between $60 and $70 a month. Costs of food and rent were far lower, so that for the salary received by a couple today, one could have a house completely staffed with four or five well-trained domestic employees. It meant less work for everyone, of course, but less pay. I am not sure that in the aggregate, however, those domestic employees of an earlier era really had such a bad time!

~ ~ ~

Unionization and the right to strike could easily be turned to ineffective, illegitimate purposes, in Mrs. Roosevelt's view. Staunch as she was in her defense of labor organizations, she placed the broader national and international needs of working people above the immediate concerns of any specific labor group. John L. Lewis, head of the United Mine Workers, often stirred Mrs. Roosevelt's ire, especially when she suspected he was using his union's support to pave the way for his own political ambitions. And what could be worse, from a New Dealer's viewpoint, than to see a leader of labor, no less, apparently pandering to the Republicans for support?

New York, November 19—For several days now the chief headlines in the papers have been held by John L. Lewis and his threats against the Government. Curiously enough, what he says rarely stresses the one point which I think is important—namely, that the conditions under which the miners today are working may need to be changed. He insists that there must be a strike, but one has the feeling that it is not because every effort to better the miners' condition has failed, but because Mr. Lewis wishes to show his power.

There was a time, a long while ago, when I thought Mr. Lewis one of the best labor leaders in the country. I thought he cared about the men in the mines. I know that the reason he has kept his hold over them is that they thought he cared. They knew that, at the time when they needed help, he was the only person who got them even the slightest consideration. I remember what conditions for the miners were at their worst. I remember what they were in the early '30s, in the black days of the Depression. I have always had respect for the work they do and a desire to see all possible improvements made in their working and living conditions.

The miners still trust Mr. Lewis, and the long-distant past would justify that trust. But a nearer view makes one begin to wonder. For a long time now, it has seemed that John L. Lewis and those immediately around him feel that they rule an empire. The people who make up that empire seem to be there mainly to serve a lust for power which seems practically insatiable. No one could read Mr. Lewis' last letter without being struck by its arrogance.

A strike in the coal mines will mean the stopping of hundreds of industries—industries which are necessary to the rebuilding of the economy in our own country and in the world.

I cannot help wondering which of two things Mr. Lewis is trying to achieve. Number one—is he expecting recognition from the Republican Party if they should win in 1948? Has he entered into an understanding with the owners of the mines whereby, if he breaks the contract with the Government, he hopes to force the return of the mines to the owners and then to make a better contract with the owners? This would make him a great figure in labor. The Republican Party and the industrial leaders might feel that they had someone whom they could safely place in power, because he would be amenable to their interests in the long run, even though he might ask enough for labor to hold his power over them. That power the practical Republican leadership knows is essential.

The only other alternative, of course, is that he does not realize how much resentment a strike in an essential industry is going to cause on top of the other strikes which have only just been settled. It is just possible that what he is doing now may lead to a demand in our country for the nationalization of the coal industry as a basic utility which the people themselves must control.

I would be sympathetic with a plea for better conditions, but I cannot help believing that, at the moment, we have to subordinate ourselves to the paramount interest of getting our economy running full blast. How can the people of devastated countries hope to succeed in this if we don't succeed?

~ ~ ~

If Mrs. Roosevelt had ever been appointed to a professorship on a university faculty, it might well have been in the philosophy department, teaching courses in ethics. She rarely slipped into simplistic thinking as a way to cut through knotty problems but instead held up for others to see the two or more competing sides to many an argument. At bottom, however, Eleanor Roosevelt placed above all else our obligation to show compassion for the weaker individual in any transaction where power was involved in a struggle with a larger, stronger entity. In her view, therefore, tenants deserved protection more than landlords.

NEW YORK, NOVEMBER 30—I am very glad that we are beginning to think and talk about disarmament. This first move made in the United Nations to request all countries to give information on the number of men they have under arms, both at home and abroad, is purely preliminary, but I think it will have a very good effect and will fix attention on the fact that one of the objectives toward which we are working today is a step-by-step disarmament.

We know that this must be general. We know that no single country can disarm without inviting disaster. A weak country is always a temptation to a stronger one. But if all countries, great and small, disarm together and turn their policing powers over to the United Nations, they will find themselves in a far more stable world situation.

~ ~ ~

Probably, at some point in Mrs. Roosevelt's lifelong education and wide reading, she came to know Alexis de Tocqueville's Democracy in America. *Here, in her final column for 1946, Mrs. Roosevelt sounds just like the eighteenth-century French political observer when she singles out the feeling of hopefulness as a central trait in the American character and recognizes the social function of this trait as a kind of gyroscope, keeping the nation usually in balance and away from violent disruptions. She quotes Walter Lippmann, the Pulitzer Prize-winning liberal columnist of* The New York Herald Tribune, *referring to a Roper public opinion poll.*

HYDE PARK, DECEMBER 30—I like very much a sentence in Walter Lippmann's column of December 28, in which he says: "Mr. Roper's figures would, I think, justify the statement that in America the circulation upward in the social order is so free and active that this country is living in a state of slow but permanent revolution."

Nothing more hopeful was ever written. Since the world as a whole lives in hope and always on the hope for the next generation, this is what gives us stability as a nation. A feeling that if you are poor, you and your family are not doomed to be poor forever; that if you are working in a job you do not enjoy, you are not doomed to hold that job forever but may quite probably find one you will like very much better at almost any time; that if you failed to receive or to take advantage of the education you feel essential for success, you still see visions of your children having the opportunities you missed—all of this makes for a restless world, perhaps, but a more stable one. There is a desire for progress in the hearts of all men, and it is the sense of frustration and inability to move forward that brings violent revolution.

In a society such as ours, where changes come about easily, violent revolution is unnecessary. Fortunately for us, our people recognized the need for reform and did not fight it. For that reason, I think, we have more gradual changes and rarely any threat of violence. Even in the days of our deepest depression, the promise Mr. Hoover kept making that around the corner there were "two chickens in every pot and two automobiles in every garage" did not seem so fantastic as to preclude the possibility of believing that it might conceivably happen; and I think that hope stabilized our nation until real help came to the rescue.

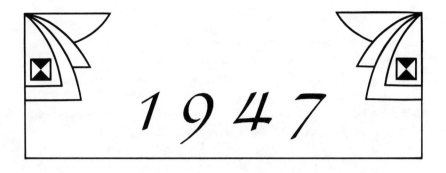

1947

*H*arry Truman put his own stamp on the presidency and the history of American politics in 1947. He started the year by appointing retired Army Chief of Staff General George C. Marshall Secretary of State. Together, Truman and Marshall would quickly evolve a European Recovery Program that came to be called the Marshall Plan, providing economic and political aid in the billions of dollars. The first step toward the overall plan was a recovery aid package of some $400 million for Greece and Turkey aimed specifically at helping those countries resist Communist influence from the Russians, a policy immediately dubbed the Truman Doctrine. The Cold War, as yet unnamed but gaining in recognition as a foreign policy fact of life, was intensifying.

Eleanor Roosevelt was a fierce participant in the political battles of the day, and not only in her capacity at the United Nations. She was among the first to question the wisdom of Truman's notorious Executive Order 9835 (March 1947), which established a Loyalty Program in the government requiring investigation of employees and job applicants and reflecting the growing fear of Communist subversion. By autumn this fear, which Mrs. Roosevelt generally saw as paranoia, led the House Un-American Activities Committee to open an investigation of suspected Communist infiltration of the movie industry. The stage was set for the witch hunts of Senator Joseph McCarthy, the rabid antiCommunist, in the 1950s.

As America itself recovered from the war, housewives were made happy by the lifting of sugar rationing in June, after five years of deprivation. The bitterness in labor-management relations in the immediate postwar years culminated in passage by the Congress over the President's veto of the Taft–Hartley bill, which substantially strengthened employers' hands in their dealings with the unions. Mrs. Roosevelt was a frequent commentator on labor-management disputes, always looking for a way to reconcile the workers' demands with the country's needs. Perhaps reflecting the country's recognition that too much of an apparently good thing might be bad after all (in this case FDR's four-term presidency and the New Deal) the Twenty-second Amendment was proposed, limiting any subsequent president to two terms. Revision of the Presidential Succession Act made the Speaker of the House of Representatives next in line after the Vice President.

Harry Truman took his first major foreign policy crisis—what to do about divided, occupied Korea—to the United Nations, which responded with a resolution calling for a united, free country. (The world would soon see that resolutions were not enough.) In 1947 the President also became the first world leader to address his nation on television. Groping for some form of solution to the worsening tensions in the Middle East, the Truman White House gave its support to a UN proposal for autonomous Jewish and Arab states in Palestine. Eager to clean up and to streamline the executive branch of government, the incumbent Democratic president appointed a former Republican president, Herbert Hoover, to head a commission of inquiry. Another presidential commission, this one working on civil rights, made its report public and set in motion one of the few truly noble reform efforts of the time, a campaign for justice that would continue to occupy much of Mrs. Roosevelt's time and thought.

Symbolically important "firsts" in 1947 included the first supersonic flight, by Air Force test pilot Charles (Chuck) Yeager; another speedster, Jackie Robinson, became the first black major-league baseball player when he signed with the Brooklyn Dodgers. By year's end two great new dramatic characters, both in the same play, had appeared on the American stage. Tennessee Williams' *A Streetcar Named Desire* opened in New Orleans, bringing the brutal Stanley

Kowalski and the fragile Blanche Dubois to life. In times of trouble, Blanche said in her most memorable line, she had "always relied on the kindness of strangers."

But Harry Truman was not to be as lucky: both Republican Senator Robert Taft of Ohio and former Vice President Henry Wallace, now running on a third-party (Progressive) ticket, announced they would oppose him in the 1948 elections. Try as she might, Mrs. Roosevelt could not keep clear of the sometimes acid debate that ensued.

~ ~ ~

Would it be right to characterize Mrs. Roosevelt's feelings about Germany as "Germanophobia"? Late-twentieth-century Americans may find it difficult to comprehend the anxiety anything German could elicit in those who had lived and fought through the two world wars. However, bearing in mind that a reasonable argument can be made assigning primary responsibility for both wars to German aggression—though the Germans were by no means alone in that aggression—it is easier to see how even a highly intelligent observer of the international scene like Eleanor Roosevelt, who would have known the subtleties of how many nations deliberately and inadvertently conspired to bring about these wars, would nonetheless fixate on one all-purpose enemy. In her "My Day" columns we rarely hear Mrs. Roosevelt railing against the Japanese or against the Italian and Spanish Fascists. Whether right or wrong in so unwavering an opinion about Germany, she was at least consistent in articulating its implications, even when she might provoke other people's ire, as with the American soldiers mentioned in this column.

HYDE PARK, JANUARY 3—I have received a letter which voices a strong protest against some of our policies in regard to the Germans.

The nine signers of the letter are worried, first, about the relaxing of many controls in our zone of occupation in Germany, which tends to allow the Germans to run their own country. In answer to this, I would say that the Germans eventually will have to run their own country, and we have to prepare them for the time when they will be left without an army of occupation.

Our safeguard in Germany should be the insistence that there shall be no rebuilding of heavy industry of the kind which would permit Germany again to become a great industrial nation and rebuild a war machine. Small industries needed for export purposes and for the daily life of the people should, of course, be permitted. The one thing to be viewed with alarm is any policy on the part of the United States or Great Britain, no matter what the reason, which would allow Germany again to become a potential war breeder.

The second protest is against granting licenses to GIs to marry German girls and allowing them to bring their wives to this country. I was asked about this question when I was in Germany last year. I said then that I felt that any boy in love with a girl over there should not be allowed to marry until he came home and had sufficient time to be quite sure that his love was not born of loneliness and propinquity in a strange country. Many young soldiers were annoyed with me, but they saw the point. And I still believe that a rule requiring a boy to be home for at least four months before he could bring over the girl he wished to marry would be a safeguard to our present young army in Germany.

These boys are not the boys who fought the war. Many of them have no real feeling against the Germans and do not understand the background of the two World Wars. And as the German girls are quite ready to be friendly, the soldiers are apt to be carried away.

There are exceptions, of course. One boy told me he had been engaged to a girl for years and she had gone to Germany before the war to visit members of her family. Then the war broke out, preventing her return to this country. Now, he had finally found her again in Germany. Naturally, he wanted to marry her, but the wartime rule prevented it. He stuck to his purpose and succeeded. In that case, the boy was right.

The third protest of my correspondents is against the bringing of German scientists and their families to this country. I am trying to find out the reason for this. I thought we were bringing over certain scientists who never were Nazis, but I do not really understand the reasons for doing this.

My correspondents fear that we are building up "a strong nucleus" of Nazi spies in this country and are "strengthening the Nazi cause all over the world." This is a consideration which should not be taken lightly. I think there is no question but that any Germans coming into this country should be very carefully screened. Their background should be examined and tested in every possible way.

~ ~ ~

The automobile accident Mrs. Roosevelt refers to resulted in no serious harm to anyone, although her own car and the one she mistakenly hit while "motoring" through the upstate New York countryside were slightly damaged. She explained in other columns, in a confessional tone, that she had indeed had a lapse of attention while at the wheel and couldn't put the blame on anyone else. Still, awkward though it was to go without a license for a time, Eleanor Roosevelt did have a chauffeur available when she needed him, and there were plenty of sympathetic friends and family to ferry her about. At the time of the accident she was sixty-two.

NEW YORK, JANUARY 16—Today I received the notice of the cancellation of my driving license for reckless driving in connection with the accident I had last summer. I am a little sad about this, since it takes away one of the things that I enjoy, but I recognize fully the justice of punishment for endangering other people. And while I hope that some day the license may be restored to me, I shall certainly not ask for any special consideration. I can only be deeply grateful that no one was permanently injured in the accident.

Perhaps at my age, in any case, it is wise to curtail one's activities. One thing is sure—that if you give up any activity, it is much more difficult to start in again. And since the accident, I have done no long-distance driving, not even from Hyde Park to New York City.

It will be distinctly awkward to have to walk everywhere around the

Hyde Park place, instead of driving. However, at all times and as long as one lives, life administers disciplines, and it is in accepting and obeying them that one learns.

NEW YORK, JANUARY 18—When I turned on my radio the other morning at 7:30, I got the welcome news that in 30 days I may apply for a new driver's license. Apparently, I have to take a test just as though I had never had a license before, and it is so many years since I took one that I have forgotten what is required! I can only hope that, when I do apply, I shall pass the test, but I shall certainly wait until spring so that driving conditions will be favorable!

~ ~ ~

Mrs. Roosevelt used her "My Day" columns and her magazine writing as well as her speeches and her many official conversations with FDR when he was president to report on what she had observed while traveling around the United States and abroad. She knew how hard a task it is to render a complex story in a few clear words. (The subsequent distinguished career in radio and television journalism of Eric Sevareid at CBS proved that Mrs. Roosevelt had a keen ear for recognizing a real pro.)

NEW YORK, JANUARY 20—To finish up a busy day, I attended the American Veterans Committee's foreign correspondents' dinner. These young foreign correspondents spoke on the theme of "The Search for World Order." Eric Sevareid, who was chairman of the sponsoring committee, made a deep impression upon me because of his very evident sincerity. Speaking on "Prospects for Peace," he pointed out that the war had come about not because of any one thing, but because of many things; and achieving the peace therefore was not going to be simple, but complicated.

~ ~ ~

In the monthly opinion poll conducted by the Woman's Home Companion *and announced in the January 1947 issue, Mrs. Roosevelt was named the woman most admired by other American women. Reader-reporters of the magazine mentioned all of 240 women, extending the field of their admiration beyond America to include Madame Chiang Kai-shek of China, Queen Elizabeth of Great Britain, Queen Wilhelmina of the Netherlands, and actress Beatrice Lillie. Mrs. Roosevelt "led by a large majority."*

On January 27 at Lake Success, Long Island, Eleanor Roosevelt was unanimously elected chairman of the United Nations Commission on Human Rights, an eighteen-nation agency of the UN Economic and Social Council. Previously she had been chairman of the so-called Nuclear Commission on Human Rights, a preparatory group that laid the groundwork for the present task of drafting a World Bill of Rights. In this position Mrs. Roosevelt felt it her duty to express moral outrage whenever a particularly egregious case of human rights abuse appeared, especially in her own country.

NEW YORK, JANUARY 31—It seems incredible that a majority of the Georgia House of Representatives actually think that the State of Georgia is so far removed from the rest of the world that they go ahead and approve a "white primary bill" which would bar Negro citizens from voting in the Democratic primaries.

The United Nations Commission on Human Rights has before it the creation of a subcommission on discrimination. Are we going to put ourselves in the position of having the world think of us as a backward nation? A nation that discriminates, and takes away political rights from a large group of its citizens?

We can hide behind a provision in the UN Charter which states that domestic affairs cannot be interfered with unless they menace the peace of the world. But I do not think that will make us very happy, since there is no way of hiding from the thoughts of others.

I believe that a great majority of our citizens will hang their heads in shame if one of our great states actually practices what little Liberia has been trying to do away with. Liberia, I understand, has recently taken steps which seem to promise the full participation in the government of the country by all of her citizens who are able to vote.

I wonder if these citizens of ours, who, in the view of some of our other citizens, are so recklessly abusing their state's rights at the moment, think that this will have no effect on future arguments concerning states' rights. I can well imagine the orators who will cite this particular situation as showing that the citizens of a state should not be allowed to take a stand in opposition to the progressive outlook of the majority of the citizens of the country. This is not a stand which affects just the people of Georgia. It affects the standing of the United States in the world family of nations.

~ ~ ~

A year and eight months after Mrs. Roosevelt left the White House large numbers of people from all walks of life still considered her, or at least her office, as the best place to send a letter asking for information about government activity or services or lodging a protest about one sort of problem or another, governmental or not. The impracticality of continuing to receive such a flood of correspondence meant that it had to stop, and Mrs. Roosevelt announced this in "My Day." Still the fact that she was perceived so automatically as an available investigator and advocate for common people who otherwise would have had no one in particular to write to "in Washington" is testimony to another fact: Eleanor Roosevelt was a real and loyal friend to the masses.

The fear of Communist subversion was spreading like a cancer in the body politic. David Lilienthal had been an important New Dealer as head of the Tennessee Valley Authority (TVA) and was held in high esteem as an administrator not only by Mrs. Roosevelt but by most members of Congress as well. His nomination by President Truman to be head of the newly formed Atomic Energy Commission, however, evoked criticism and a certain amount of character assassination from disgruntled, anxious conservatives. Lilienthal's sponsors had trouble for some time rebutting the vehement attacks on his loyalty by Senator McKellar of Tennessee, always a critic of the TVA. Lilienthal's parents' Czech roots and his Harvard Law School training made him an easy target for those who believed that anyone of Eastern European stock was suspect and anyone from that "uppity" liberal school in New England was doubly so.

NEW YORK, FEBRUARY 19—As the days go by and Sen. Kenneth McKellar, together with a few others, continues to oppose confirmation of David E. Lilienthal as chairman of the Atomic Energy Commission, one begins to wonder just who pulls the strings. Is it, as one newspaper states, that the power companies, because of competition with TVA in the past, are now stirring up all of this feeling against a man eminently well fitted for the job? That would be short-sighted, because TVA has really helped the power companies!

Is it that we are so completely possessed by fear that we do not recognize the ring of truth when a man speaks up for democracy as Mr. Lilienthal did? Is it that Sen. McKellar is really afraid to trust any five men with the development and use of atomic energy? If this is true, we had better remind the Senator that this is not the only country in the world. Atomic energy is going to be developed, and whether it is developed for the good of humanity or the destruction of humanity will depend a great deal on this five-man group.

I would trust a man with Mr. Lilienthal's expressed belief in democracy to head that group. Where his parents were born seems to me to have no relation to the question at hand, which is his fitness to do this job. Where his loyalties lie is crystal-clear to those who can read and understand the English language.

There are not many men with the training and background for a job such as this one and, if we turn down a man who is preeminently well-trained, then we deserve to be handicapped in this race for the development of atomic energy. Instead of leading the world and helping it to use this power for the good of humanity, we will be branded as being so small of vision that we could not control a few men but let them hold us in check.

The world cries out for men, especially those of the United States, to work and produce. We blame workers who go out on strike. How about the members of an important legislative body who go on strike against the group of men who should be developing the world's greatest new source of power?

~ ~ ~

Given FDR's romantic dalliance with Lucy Mercer Rutherford, one might suppose that after the President's death the former First Lady would have been glad to let go quietly of her own title, Mrs. Not so; once married, always married seems to have been her way of looking at it. Ironically, of course, having married a man from within her own family, a man carrying her own last name, ther could never have been any full disconnection from the family name even if she had wanted it.

NEW YORK, FEBRUARY 28—One of my newspaper friends has written to ask me to settle a question which keeps coming up in newspaper offices and also when I am introduced on speaking engagements. Do I want to be called Mrs. Eleanor Roosevelt or Mrs. Franklin D. Roosevelt? Of course, I want to be called the latter.

I have been called that ever since I was married and it would seem very odd to change. I understand perfectly well that a professional or business woman who has made a name for herself may find it difficult and confusing to change her name professionally when she marries, but that does not happen to be my situation. I have never made any name for myself, and as I have always been known as Mrs. Franklin D. Roosevelt, it seems to me simpler and more correct to be called that.

~ ~ ~

Mrs. Roosevelt loved the West Coast and had close friends and family there. Whenever business or political responsibilities would permit, she visited her favorite haunts such as Chinatown in the City by the Bay. The first of these two columns shows that Mrs. Roosevelt used "My Day" sometimes simply to review her social calendar. The second brings her back to more serious purpose: a little politicking for environmental protection.

SAN FRANCISCO, MARCH 13—Yesterday morning, I took a stroll through Chinatown and visited my old friend Suey Chong. He is now receiving goods from China, but he deprecatingly said that silks were still very expensive and therefore the goods made from them were expensive. I am afraid we were not very good customers, but our welcome was nevertheless a warm one. In looking into the shops here, one sees that some goods which were impossible to get during the war, such as rattan furniture, are being produced again, so that an order can be filled in a month or six weeks.

My old friend Miss Flora Rose, who used to be head of the College of Home Economics at Cornell, came over from Berkeley to have lunch with me yesterday. She is just as full of interests as ever, and is now conducting a Red Cross course for the wives of GIs studying at the University of California. They have to live in cramped quarters and she has the greatest admiration for their fortitude and cheerfulness. I am sure that no one ever did so much active work after retirement as does Miss Rose.

LOS ANGELES, MARCH 18—I am confronted daily in the papers out here with some news about a group which calls itself the Los Angeles Smog Committee, under the leadership of William Jeffers. I have no idea what the word "smog" means, but the objectives of this committee seem to be altogether good, so perhaps we should start the same type of organization in every city and town in our country!

They apparently attack any bad situations which creep into the surroundings of any aggregation of people. Today it is the city dumps which have come in for denunciation and vociferous demands that they be done away with immediately because they are "creating a vicious public nuisance." Nearby Long Beach has solved the problem by a method of burning the rubbish which creates no smoke or rat problem. It seems that this committee not only fights against a nuisance which endangers public health, but also suggests methods for improving the situation.

In every locality, I think, one could use a group of public-spirited citizens who would agitate on local questions of this kind—and the first point to be taken up should be housing everywhere!

~ ~ ~

Executive Order 9835, issued by President Truman, set in motion many years of questionable investigations into the alleged disloyalty or (as it came to be called, subversiveness) on the part of individuals and organizations who never before had been guilty of anything more serious than a parking ticket or failing to put their trash out to the curb on the right day of the week. It is to Eleanor Roosevelt's credit that, even at this early stage of the historical phenomenon soon to be called McCarthyism, she recognized and had the courage to state emphatically that repressive legislative and political measures intended to check the spread of Communist subversion actually reflected more insecurity than self-confidence in America's political ego.

NEW YORK, MARCH 27—I was asked about the President's executive order to prevent disloyal employees from working for the Government. I was asked also about the proposals, which are coming up in several parts of the country, for outlawing the Communist Party. I was asked whether I thought it was necessary to take these steps. Therefore I've decided to write today on the feeling I have about all repressive measures.

Such measures always are a sign of lack of confidence in ourselves. If we were sure that our citizens understood the value of democracy and were clear in their minds on the subject, I doubt if we would need such an investigation as the President has ordered. It would be quite easy to eliminate from the Government, by the usual legal processes, anyone who was proved to be disloyal. Naturally, any order of this kind carries a certain amount of danger with it, in that it may be possible to misuse its provisions. If a wave of hysteria hits us, there will be very little protection for anyone who even thinks differently from the run-of-the-mill.

Political conditions in the USSR today still do not recognize the right of individuals to think differently. Only here and in other free democracies can we criticize our Government and have the freedom to think independently. It is, I believe, a very precious freedom, but it requires of us something more than apathetic citizenship. We must really believe in democracy and in our objectives. We cannot live in fear of either Fascism or Communism. We have to be certain that the majority of our people recognize the benefits of democracy and therefore are loyal to it.

Proposals to outlaw the Communist Party seem to me another evidence of a feeling of insecurity. I can imagine nothing stupider than to believe that the mass of people of this country would really find Communism a greater advantage to them than our own democratic system. The danger in outlawing the Communist Party is that we would set a precedent which might work against any change or difference of opinion in the future.

I do not know why we are so prone to fears at the present time. Some people are so afraid of Russia that they are suggesting that perhaps, since we cannot hope always to be the only nation possessing the atom bomb, we should use it fairly soon to wipe out all opposition. That sounds ludicrous, but it has actually been said to me by some people.

Others fear that we cannot manage our economy so as to avoid a major depression. Still others think that it will be impossible ever to make the United Nations strong, because we are all too much afraid of each other to trust in joint action.

All of these attitudes are attitudes of fear. They show lack of confidence in ourselves and in others. For the leading democracy in the world to indulge in them is a very great danger, not to us alone but also to the world.

~   ~   ~

Eleanor Roosevelt could have chosen, as many did after the war, to insulate herself from the continuous stream of horror stories concerning suffering in the concentration camps and in other cruel political contexts in Europe during the Nazi–Fascist era. Instead, she became

95

one of the few who took as their task the exposure of the truth no matter how gothic and unpleasant it might be.

NEW YORK, APRIL 1—I think we cannot be reminded too often of the horrors which human beings have gone through in the past few years. It ought to keep us from doing, through fear, anything here which will lead to the same results again.

The particular story told, which I find hard to get out of my thoughts, was that of a Jewish rabbi who, after years of hard labor in a German concentration camp, was aboard a ship, watching our shores come in sight. The young man standing at the ship's rail beside him was excited at getting home and said: "This gives me a thrill. It must be an even greater thrill for you, Rabbi. Here you will be able to begin life again and be happy."

The rabbi answered: "Deep down within me there are memories which will keep me always from being really happy. Let me tell you something. On one of the days of atonement, as I came back to report after work, the German camp director said, 'Did you pray today, Rabbi?' I did not answer. He hit me across the mouth and said, 'When I ask you a question, answer.' I said, 'Yes, as I worked I prayed.'

"He said, 'Dog, you will see how we treat rabbis who pray to their wretched Jewish God.' He took me out to where a little car stood upon tracks, and put my small son into the car and told me to give it a push. It rolled away from me and, before my eyes, I saw it roll into the gas chamber. Can one remember that and be happy?"

There are not only the Jews who have such memories. There are many, many other people—those who fought in resistance movements when their countries were invaded—who are faced with similar memories.

The other day, I heard of a Belgian organization known as "Les Invalides Prevoyants," whose members are veterans of World War II, with a few from World War I. They are struggling to help the orphaned children of men and women who were shot or died in captivity, or who were tortured in German concentration camps for defying the occupying forces.

Under the law, the state can do nothing for these children. Orphans whose parents died under other circumstances have some rights under the law. But those whose parents, from patriotic motives and of their own free will, chose to defy the German authorities, are left without protection. I hope very much that, when we are helping the orphans of Europe, we will not forget this particular organization in Brussels which must raise money from private sources for the care of these children.

~ ~ ~

That we are all interconnected and have an innate responsibility to share our resources and negotiate rather than fight over our differences were among Mrs. Roosevelt's basic principles. Hence the argument she made in "My Day" columns in favor of expanding the United States' foreign aid package to include Greece, Poland, and Yugoslavia. It was thinking like hers that helped shape the dimensions of the Marshall Plan to rebuild Europe. The widening gap between America and the Soviet Union had rapidly become a theme not only in her columns but everywhere in the nation's political discourse. Former Vice President Henry Wallace, at this point warming up for a run at the White House on the Progressive Party ticket, had taken the growing gap between the democratic West and the Communist Eastern bloc as his topic in several public speeches.

NEW YORK, APRIL 16—When I spoke the other day at an Essex, Conn., forum on the United Nations, one or two of the questions troubled me. For instance, the usual questions on what the Greek–Turkish aid program means to this country came out rather indirectly in a question on whether the Truman policy had hurt the United Nations.

Finally, one gentleman asked whether, if what was now being said was true, it would not be better just to leave the Russians out of all of our calculations, even out of the United Nations—in other words, to organize a world in which two groups would face each other. One, obviously the Russian one, might be weak at present and, therefore, for a time we would be safe. Under this theory, we wouldn't be learning to get on together in one world—instead, we would be preparing for a two-world war.

That, of course, is basically what troubles Henry Wallace. He feels that we are pulling further and further apart, and that, without realizing it, we may be setting the stage for a two-world catastrophe.

~ ~ ~

Though the Roosevelt family homestead at Hyde Park had always been a working farm, which meant serious business, there was still room for fun and for pursuit of the old-fashioned pleasures (like homemade butter) that took inordinate amounts of effort but seemed well worth it.

HYDE PARK, MAY 6—About a month ago, our farmer told us and proved to us that it was highly uneconomical to make butter on a diary farm; that we could sell our whole milk and make more cash; that the cost of the cream and the time consumed in making butter, even though we had an electric churn, was pure waste.

I remembered that, when I was a little girl, my grandmother made butter in a little glass churn on the dining-room table. It was completely sweet, fresh butter, and we thought it the greatest possible luxury. And my mother-in-law always boasted of having her own butter. It seemed somewhat of a wrench to me to give this up, so I loftily said to our farmer, "I will take the churn, and in our cellar we will make enough butter to last both my son's house and mine for several weeks. It can be stored in the deep freeze."

Last Friday, the farmer brought the churn. Our superintendent was on hand. So was I, assisted by Miss Thompson and the cook. We all stood around, prepared for our first lesson.

The farmer first showed us how to wash the churn and the implements. Then, firmly telling me the cost of the cream which he was pouring in, he poured it in, adjusted the cover of the churn, and started it. All of us were spattered with cream. He stopped the churn, looked at the cork in the bottom, adjusted the top, and started the churn again.

Then the five of us watched with pride for fifteen minutes while the electricity did its work. Finally, I inquired how long it took. The farmer said "Anywhere from twenty minutes to four hours. It depends on the temperature." I thought he meant the outdoor temperature and did not realize he meant the temperature of the cream, which in our haste we had forgotten to take.

Time wore on. Miss Thompson decided she had to go back to being a secretary. The two men decided they had to go and eat dinner and attend to a few chores. The cook decided she had to go and prepare lunch. So we left the churning!

Three hours later, I returned. Still no butter. The men tried putting in ice cubes, which spoiled the buttermilk. It came time for the men to do the afternoon chores, and so they said, "Leave it overnight and turn it on in the morning and the butter may come."

The next morning, around 11 o'clock, the cook and I finally finished our lesson and at last the men could go back to their work on the farm. We had learned how to use the electric churn, how to work the butter afterwards, and how to do it up neatly in half-pound packages. For all of that time and all of that labor, we had 13 1/2 pounds of butter!

I am quite sure now that our farmer's economics are correct, but I had fun and I think the cook and I will try it again. It may be a waste of both time and money, but I am still old-fashioned enough to like the idea of having my own butter. I am rather glad, however, that the churn is electric. I think that if I had had to churn by hand for all of that time, I would not be writing about it today!

~ ~ ~

During both the Depression and WW II there were strong incentives for organized labor to cooperate with management and with the government in avoiding strikes or other labor disruptions. Immediately after the war, pent-up frustration over wage controls led to a wave of strikes in many key industries. The public (at least those who were not members of the striking unions) grew frustrated when, for example, telephone service or the supply of basic commodities such as steel, on which so many other industries depend, were interrupted. Also contributing to the diminishing reputation of the unions was the rise to power of the effective but controversial labor leader, John L. Lewis. There were at the same time frequent allegations that Communist sympathizers had infiltrated the leadership ranks of several major unions.

Against this background Congress decided to take action to better control union behavior. Over the President's strong veto, the legislators passed the Taft–Hartley Act and unleashed a storm of criticism from liberals who, like Mrs. Roosevelt, saw the bill as virulently antilabor. The act banned the closed shop (businesses with unions a worker was forced to join simply to keep his job). It also allowed management to sue unions for damages incurred during strikes; it required a sixty-day cooling-off period prior to the initiation of any strike; it required unions to disclose their finances; it prohibited union contributions to political campaigns; and it required union leaders to swear that they were not Communists.

Eleanor Roosevelt, President Truman, and the liberal establishment inveighed against the bill for some time on the grounds that it put far more controls on labor than on management.

NEW YORK, JUNE 10—I suppose it is impossible for any Congressional bill to be put into language which the people can understand. It will be difficult for the average worker to understand the legal language of the Taft–Hartley labor bill passed by Congress last week. In many ways I think labor leaders have themselves to blame for some of their present difficulties—John L. Lewis chief among them, because the people as a whole have come to dread what he can do to our economy. And there are certain union rules which irk the people and which I do not think really help organized labor. These regulations have made the relations between the public and the unions increasingly unsympathetic, and should have been studied and corrected long ago.

The Congress of Industrial Organizations should have got rid of

Communist leaders wherever they existed. The people of this country are more than willing to try to work with the Russians if they recognize on the part of the Russians a willingness to work side by side with other forms of governments and ways of life. However, the constant activity of American Communists, who evidently get their financial support as well as their political direction from Russia, creates suspicion and antagonism here and in some other countries as well.

If the Russian Government still hopes for world revolution brought about by representatives in other countries guided from Russia, it cannot be honest in trying to work cooperatively with other governments as they now exist. I am more than willing to believe that circumstances may modify the way of life and the forms of existing governments in many countries in the years to come, but the changes must come from the free will of the people, not from infiltration of ideas through the influence of outside governments. This is why union leaders known to be Communists should not have been allowed in our labor movement.

Nevertheless, the Taft–Hartley bill is a bad bill, even in its final modified form. I think it will make the work of the National Labor Relations Board practically impossible, and it opens a wide field of labor activities to federal injunctions. I see nothing gained by taking the Conciliation Service out of the Department of Labor. It seems to me that this bill is weighted in favor of the employer. For instance, the bill requires the NLRB to obtain federal injunctions against certain union practices, but there is no provision that the board obtain injunctions against employer practices.

I have not room here to go into this bill in detail, but analyses of it are available and people should study it. I was in complete accord with the labor-reform suggestions made in the President's message, but this bill goes so far beyond that and is so weighted in favor of the employer that I feel that, if it becomes law, it will affect adversely the lives of many people.

~ ~ ~

The foreign ministers of the world's sixteen most powerful nations were meeting in Paris to discuss cooperative efforts to rebuild war-torn Europe. After having fought as allies with the Russians, it was inevitably disappointing and annoying to the Western democracies to find that the Soviets were rapidly developing an antipathy to any further cooperation. In the end, the Soviet Union was the only one of the sixteen to reject participation in the Marshall Plan. We see Mrs. Roosevelt struggling intellectually with what the Cold War eventually taught us to take for granted: that rapprochement between East and West was impossible as long as either side had imperialistic plans for expansion or was driven by fears of domination by outsiders of a different ideological stamp. Soviet foreign minister Molotov was one of Mrs. Roosevelt's staunchest adversaries at the UN.

HYDE PARK, JULY 5—Riding into New York City early yesterday morning on a very slow train, I had ample opportunity to read the whole of Mr. Molotov's statement at the conference of foreign ministers in Paris. I had already read Secretary Marshall's speech replying to the Soviet charges of imperialism.

I must say, after reading Mr. Molotov's statement, that I was very much saddened. The examples which he used as to what the United States, or the committee setup, might demand, were utterly foolish. When you are lending your money, even to a private individual, you like to know the exact conditions which exist, and you wish to have at least a suggestion of the way in which the money will be used. If you approve of the plan, you take the risk.

Lending money is a risk, and it would show very little interest on our part if we did not make some inquiries into the situation and the future plans. This is especially important where it seems probable that money alone will not fully meet the situation and that we might be asked in addition to provide skilled technicians and workers on various levels. That does not mean that we want to control the internal situation in other countries. They are free to refuse a loan. If they take it, it is reasonable that they give a certain amount of information.

Mr. Molotov knows as well as anyone else that we have no desire to control the economic plans of any nation or to take away their sovereignty. We have never tried to infiltrate in Russia and set up a party against the government. The Soviet government might well say that they would not permit that, but they are always rather annoyed when we complain about the political activities in many countries—activities which they must at least have countenanced at some time.

I realize that it must be very hard for them not to think that in this country, as a government and as a majority, people are opposed to the Russian nation. I wish they might remember, however, that the newspapers here represent individual owners and their own particular readers—not the Government or the majority of the people. I wish they might also realize that, while we believe in capitalism and in democracy, we are quite willing to let them believe in collectivism and Communism.

We feel, nevertheless, that all other people in the world should be free to make their own choice. If a very great nation like Russia is so very strict in its control at home when it gains political and military influence, it may be strict in other countries. For that reason we want nations, large and small, to act freely and to make their choice without fearing the influence of well-organized minority groups within their borders.

The Marshall Plan is a bona fide offer to help Europe get back on its feet. Mr. Molotov, in refusing to join the rest of Europe, is creating the very thing he says he fears, which is division instead of cooperation.

~ ~ ~

"It was a caravan, truck & station wagon & my car. The children moved from car to car, Fala stayed with me" Eleanor Roosevelt wrote in a letter in 1947 about that year's trek to Campobello, and in her "My Day" column she declared she got "a lift of the spirit" from the sea air on the Maine coast. Going to Campobello was a family tradition, and any year in which the summertime visit was missed or even curtailed was a year out of balance for Mrs. Roosevelt and her

entire brood. No wonder: The island and nearby communities on the mainland offered extraordinary beauty, wonderfully fresh food, and a blessed escape from everyday business.

Nonetheless, some work went forward while she was at Campobello, including the last stages of a volume of autobiography, her regular columns, and continued thinking about serious political matters. In particular Mrs. Roosevelt felt moved to argue against former Vice President Henry Wallace's plans to run as a third-party (Progressive) candidate for President.

All this is reflected in her next several columns.

HYDE PARK, JULY 16—This morning we are off to Maine—eight adults, four children, three dogs, one a puppy only a few months old, two cars, and a truck loaded with bicycles, bags, typewriters and books. This evening we are going to descend, we hope, on Ogunquit, Maine, to see my daughter-in-law, Faye Emerson Roosevelt, act in "State of the Union." Then we will proceed to Campobello Island, New Brunswick, to spend a month there in strict retirement—devoting half of each day to work on a book and the other half to all the things that our youngsters love to do in a place where life is lived largely upon the water.

One thing which draws me back to this remote island is the sunsets as I look from my porch across the water to the mainland, where two rivers flow in on either side of Eastport, Maine. The sun sets behind the little town.

Eastport and Lubec are the two nearest mainland towns. They are not so very picturesque when you are in the streets, but from across the water they have great charm. I have sometimes thought that Lubec might almost be Mont St. Michel on the coast of France. That is just a little stretch of the imagination, however, and I like both these little towns for what they are. I get a lift of the spirit as soon as I begin to breathe the sea air of the Maine coast.

CAMPOBELLO ISLAND, N.B., JULY 24—I begin this column by saying that I do not believe there should be any third party in 1948, no matter who headed it. I had planned to say nothing on this subject but an article which I saw in one of the Maine papers this morning moves me to make certain remarks.

It stated that the Un-American Activities Committee was going to examine Henry Wallace and anyone suggesting his nomination as leader of a third party because, forsooth, they heard that the people backing a third party were all Communists. This is really too idiotic. Naturally the Communists in this country are going to back a third party—they are a disruptive force and a third party would be something which they would back. But to label all liberals as Communists just because you or I think them foolish to consider a third party is just plain arrogance. When will our sense of humor reassert itself and dominate our foolish fears?

There are in both our major political parties a certain number of liberals. On the whole in the past, I feel that the Democratic Party has had more liberals than the Republican Party. And in general, I think it might be said that the great moneyed interests keep in closer touch with the Republican leaders and their policies than they do with the Democratic leaders and their policies. On the whole I think that it is harder for special interests to ride the Democratic Party and that this party has been the rallying ground for more people who had the general interest at heart. However, it has its conservative group, which we can identify in many votes which have been taken in Congress.

If the liberals of this country want to accomplish anything in the next ten years, they had better work to make one or the other major political party, or both parties, responsive to their ideas. They can do this by making it plain where they stand on certain policies, they can vote for men who stand four-square on these policies, and they can go into the primary campaigns and work wherever they see that good men have a chance of nomination.

The independents, if they have a program and are well enough organized, can elect almost any candidate in any election. The organization of a third party would only mean that the liberals would gain nothing and the conservatives would have every opportunity of carrying their candidates into office.

CAMPOBELLO ISLAND, N.B., JULY 26—Fog which lifts every day for only a short time, but always hangs just over the edge of the island, becomes pretty monotonous—and, until yesterday, that is the kind of weather we have had ever since we arrived here. Someone told me that the people out on Grand Manan Island have been enveloped in fog for 47 days, and I doubt if it has even lifted in the daytime. But a good many of that island's summer visitors are artists and some of the fog effects in this region can be very beautiful. Nevertheless, everyone of us greeted with joy the sunshine and the clearing west wind yesterday.

We packed our lunch baskets and in my son's little power boat we started up the St. Croix River for St. Andrews. Some of our guests had an orgy of shopping at the craft shop there, since wool is again available and the handwoven materials, blankets, and so on, are very well made and very attractive.

Finally, we went to the little island just across the harbor from the town of St. Andrews. We built a fire between two rocks, scrambled our eggs, cooked our bacon, and fed a hungry crowd.

It seemed the right spot to read Longfellow's "Evangeline" to the children, and so I told them the story of Nova Scotia and the Acadian peasants, and then read from a book that had belonged to their grandfather.

"This is the forest primeval. The murmuring pines and the hemlocks bearded with moss and in garments green, indistinct in the twilight, stand like druids of old. . . ."

Few people read Longfellow any more and yet I think he is part of our heritage, both literary and historical. And any child who is not familar with his poems misses something.

I have read a good deal more to the older children up here than to the younger ones. But the other night we found a copy of "Uncle Remus" which belonged to their father, and the little ones were enthralled. However, I found it difficult to read aloud. It really, I imagine, requires a true Southerner to do it justice.

With the older children I have read "The Jungle Book" and we are now deep in a book—which belonged to their Uncle James—called "Connie Morgan in Alaska." It is curious how some books can go on from generation to generation and still hold one's interest. So much that is written deals with contemporary thoughts and situations, but apparently a good story remains enjoyable. We have come across some copies of David Gray's "Gallops" and "Ensign Russell," and all of us, young and old, have enjoyed them.

~   ~   ~

Elliott Roosevelt, fourth of Eleanor and Franklin's children, was in several respects the one who most wanted to be at the center of Roosevelt family life. It was natural then that he should have become the business manager-farmer in the family plan to turn the Hyde Park properties from the style of money-losing, noncommercial farming into something with at least a chance of making a profit for a change. The Roosevelts were not only trying to support themselves (in the style to which they had become accustomed, which had its continuing broad array of expenses for staff and travel) but also to contribute something positive to the local agricultural community.

Though not reflected in her "My Day" columns, the family and primarily Elliott had another project at this time too—a literary one—the editing of FDR's childhood letters. But not without some sibling rivalry: The other children, in particular his older sister Anna, challenged his use of the $10,000 advance from the publisher. It took several family powwows and all of Mrs. Roosevelt's diplomatic skills to get the children back on friendly working terms.

HYDE PARK, AUGUST 19—Last week I acquired from my husband's estate about two-thirds of the land which he owned here in Hyde Park. My son Elliott and I have gone into partnership and we are going to farm the land on a commercial basis. We cannot afford to keep it just as a country place in the way that my husband's mother did. If he had lived, I doubt very much whether he could have continued doing that. We hope now to run the farm on a large enough scale to make it a real business.

My husband and I used to talk of doing this someday and of making our land useful to the other farmers in the vicinity by trying out certain experiments. Whether that is possible I have no idea, but Elliott and I feel strongly that one should not own land unless it produces.

Much of the land is rocks and woods, and that is why my husband planted trees on a good part of it. Where it seems wise, we shall continue the Christmas-tree plantations which he started, and shall sell Christmas trees just as he did. We have good farmland, however, and some that can be made good farmland, and it is a challenge which both Elliott and I will enjoy.

I remember well an old story about J. P. Morgan which may be completely untrue but which I always enjoyed—namely, that he once offered some of his guests either milk or champagne, stating that they both cost him about the same! This land cannot be, for either Elliott or me, a way to spend money. It must be a paying concern. Besides, I think it is more interesting to live where something creative is going on. There is a meaning to every activity which cannot exist where you do something purely for pleasure.

Perhaps the reason I enjoy this idea is that there always seems to be a certain stability about farming. And when the world is in an uncertain condition, as it is today, we cling to the things which seem more stable.

Some of my friends say that the uncertainty of world affairs makes them feel that they do not want to think or build for the future. That seems to me a very unhappy situation. I want to feel that I bend every effort toward making the world a safer place in which to live, and toward giving my children and grandchildren the confidence in themselves which will help them to meet the problems of their day. I want to create surroundings which they can feel are built in a belief that there is to be a future.

~ ~ ~

Mrs. Roosevelt had a resolute confidence in the power of the people under a democratic government to lead their country in the "right" direction. She considered it a sacred privilege to live in a democracy, and for this reason she always took the matter of citizen responsibility seriously. In the context of the emerging Cold War, many people asked her, in letters, in question-and-answer sessions after her speeches, and in press conferences, what they could do to help ensure the prospects for peace. The issue loomed larger as the apparent Soviet threat to world political stability deepened. In the next two columns we see examples of some of the many ways in which Mrs. Roosevelt responded.

HYDE PARK, AUGUST 30—Very few women seem to think, as I do, that at present the most we can do is to convince ourselves and our families and our neighbors that peace has to begin within each individual's heart and has to be lived by each of us every day. Then the quality of citizenship one develops in one's own area, whether it is a village or a city or has wider horizons, will have influence in gradually widening the circle of people who see that peace depends on our daily actions wherever we are.

NEW YORK, SEPTEMBER 6—It interests me that in this country we have not recognized the very simple fact that Communism and Fascism are only dangerous to us if we allow democracy to fail. There may be, as some papers say, "an international conspiracy, headed by Soviet Russia, to break down democratic government wherever it exists—especially our American government—and replace it with a Communist dictatorship." I doubt very much if this is actually so, but it cannot possibly succeed unless you and I do not make democracy work.

Any government which meets the needs of the majority of its people, gives them what they want and the satisfied feeling that they are better off than most of the world, has nothing to fear from Communism or Fascism.

~ ~ ~

Family, lots of it, accounted for much of Eleanor Roosevelt's life story. The combined Franklin Roosevelt and Eleanor Roosevelt clans were extensive in number and diverse in talents and points of view. The President and Mrs. Roosevelt had six children, one of whom, the first of two sons named Franklin, died at less than a year old. The

109

*other children were named Anna, James, Elliott, and John. They all
came to Hyde Park frequently, and Mrs. Roosevelt visited them as
circumstances allowed when she was traveling. There were occasional
ideological battles, but there was mutual sympathy and respect on
most issues—even when son John ran for Congress as a Republican.
The Mrs. J. R. Roosevelt referred to here was either the second wife of
FDR's half-brother James (James Roosevelt Roosevelt) or the wife of
this half-brother's son by his first marriage. Even with a family tree, it
is sometimes difficult to keep all the Roosevelts straight.*

HYDE PARK, SEPTEMBER 9—For twenty-four hours over the weekend, three of my sons and their wives were actually all here together,
also one 15-year-old grandson with a friend. We all dined with
Elliott Saturday night, and for one evening it was almost as though
we had gone back to the days when the boys used to come home and
start arguments with their father.

I never tried to talk much because he was well able to take care of
himself. He led them on, and then, with a twinkle in his eye,
demolished their arguments with facts which, for the most part, they
had never even heard of! Now here we were again, all of us arguing
passionately on ideas, all of us trying to talk at once, even the wives
becoming so interested that they could not help but join in!

I wonder what it is that makes some people able to argue a whole
evening on such subjects as socialized medicine, inheritance taxes,
and what one's obligations are to the future under certain situations
instead of worrying about more tangible things like a new car or a
new fur coat. To me, as the older member of the family, it is
interesting to watch the development, the changes in points of view,
and the better reasoning power in the various younger members. We
separated after 11 o'clock so stimulated by each other's company that
I doubt if any of us went to sleep for hours.

Sunday morning we paid a visit very early to the old house and
grounds, then stopped to see Mrs. J. R. Roosevelt, but she was not
ready to see us so we had to go again after church. My boys are here
so seldom that I always feel they must see their older relatives. It was
a pure coincidence but Sunday was the anniversary of my mother-

in-law's death in 1941, and to the children she has always been a very vivid personality. She adored them and they in turn had a very deep devotion to her.

~ ~ ~

Always a politician but never an officeholder. There were those who said that no one in American political life ever wielded more power without ever having held office than Eleanor Roosevelt. With her access to the media through regular press conferences when she was First Lady, from 1936 onward through her "My Day" column, and all along through much magazine journalism, Mrs. Roosevelt lacked no opportunity for expressing her opinions. Such exposure would have been the envy of even her most resolute opponents. In her one stint as an administrator, in 1941 when she shared with New York City's former Mayor, Fiorello LaGuardia, the job of directing the Office of Civilian Defense, neither the Mayor nor the First Lady had much success in keeping their colorful opinions under wraps while attending to administrative detail. Mrs. Roosevelt eventually resigned, after stirring up enough controversy for even the President to be unhappy.

NEW YORK, SEPTEMBER 13—I have received several letters lately stating how pleased the writers are to hear that I am going to "run for the Senate," and offering me help and support. So far those who would be against me have not written to me in great number. But to all alike I have to reply that I am not going to run for any office! What I have often repeated in the past makes no dent, but one of our prophetic commentators, who never bothers to find out from me whether his statements and prophecies concerning me are correct, is believed without question!

Here I am, therefore, forced again to state—as I did when rumors flew about in 1945 and in 1946—that I not only have no political aspirations, but under no circumstances whatsoever would I run for any political office.

I can hear people say "Why, then, do you accept work with the United Nations?" I accept for the simple reason that it seems to me

111

that there I may make a contribution, both as an individual and as my husband's widow.

I think the arguments within our nation as to how we shall achieve this or that should be settled by younger people. In a short time I shall be 63 years old; and if, in the course of the years, I have gained any wisdom whatsoever, it is the wisdom to know that the Kingdom of God must come on earth through the efforts of human beings and that war in the atomic age will simply mean annihilation, certainly not evolution. With age has come also a capacity for patience; rooted beliefs in certain fundamental things, but an ability to try to understand the motivations of other people; and a kind of interest in human beings which allows for no bitterness toward any person.

~   ~   ~

Mrs. Roosevelt adopted social problems as though they were orphaned children and she herself were Mother Courage. Among the issues she brought to the public's, and thus to Congress', attention was the plight of Native Americans. Shrinking in numbers, their cultures weakened or made extinct by the genocide of earlier generations of settlers' and nationbuilders' westward expansion, the Indians had become America's forgotten people rather than the country's most honored citizens. While one sees in Mrs. Roosevelt's work on behalf of the Indians an obvious sincerity, her persistent optimism that solutions to Indian problems could come through legislative measures missed another more basic point: that, as with the continuing problem of white racism against blacks, much of the Indians' plight was traceable to white racism against the red man.

NEW YORK, SEPTEMBER 30—Many times during the years that I spent in Washington the plight of the Indians, who still live on reservations and are, therefore, wards of the United States, was brought to my attention. The other day a letter came to me from a woman who has just discovered some of the facts concerning the Navajo Indian tribes. She was under the impression that no one knew of the conditions as they exist, and I am sure it must have been discouraging to her when I wrote that not only did I think the Indian Bureau knew all about these conditions but, in all probability, Congress had been told about them a number of times.

The Navajo situation primarily is a population problem. In 1868 the tribe numbered about 9,000 people. Today there are more than 60,000, and they are increasing at the rate of 1,000 a year, which is considerably faster than the birth rate in the nation as a whole.

The Navajo country covers about 25,000 square miles but most of it is semi-desert. Part of the land is timbered and limited almost entirely to use as grazing land, and the soil is severely eroded. The range can carry only about 520,000 sheep, which is roughly ten sheep per person, and the variety raised by the Navajos produces less than $7 per animal per year. About half an acre of irrigated land is the average used by a Navajo farmer and this returns him about $13.50.

Therefore, a little over $80 a year is the overall average income for the Navajo. Only a comparatively few of them are able to earn a little extra income through the sale of minerals, pinon nuts, their arts and crafts and their wood.

Only an act of Congress can appropriate more land for the Navajos, and for years the appropriation bill for the Department of the Interior has stated that no federal funds appropriated in the bill may be used to buy land for Indian use in the states of Arizona and New Mexico.

The most shocking educational conditions exist among these people. There are 20,000 Navajo children of school age, but the total school facilities, including federal and mission schools, will accommodate only 6,000 children. In view of the fact that in 1868 the United States made a solemn treaty with the tribe, promising a school and a teacher for every 30 children of school age, this puts our government in a decidedly unpleasant light. Also, health conditions are deplorable. Roads through the area are poor, and this adds to the difficulties where health and education are concerned.

The Department of Interior has a program designed to solve some of the problems of these people who once owned this white man's land, and it would seem advisable for Congress to respect the treaty even if it was made with a conquered people who no longer can menace our power.

It is interesting to note that 3,400 Navajos were in World War II and 15,000 were engaged in war work. Their war bond purchases and their contributions to the Red Cross were remarkable, considering their small incomes.

~ ~ ~

The House Un-American Activities Committee: HUAC took on a dreadful meaning for over ten years, from the late 1940s to late 1950s, no matter what one's political stripe. Conservatives who had become truly fearful of Communist infiltration in all walks of American life knew that the presence of Communists threatened the very fabric of democracy. Liberals, even those who like Mrs. Roosevelt despised the Communist style of politics, thought that HUAC, if it was supposed to have been a cure for the dreaded infection, had become worse than the disease itself. Many a film-making career was ruined by HUAC— big people and small, as Woody Allen was later to show in his film about the scandal, The Front. *As actors and directors and others were blacklisted because of their alleged Communist tendencies, anxiety and anger spread ever more deeply throughout the industry.*

NEW YORK, OCTOBER 29—I have waited a while before saying anything about the Un-American Activities Committee's current investigation of the Hollywood film industry. I would not be very much surprised if some writers or actors or stagehands, or what not, were found to have Communist leanings, but I was surprised to find that, at the start of the inquiry, some of the big producers were so chicken-hearted about speaking up for the freedom of their industry.

One thing is sure—none of the arts flourishes on censorship and repression. And by this time it should be evident that the American public is capable of doing its own censoring. Certainly, the Thomas Committee is growing more ludicrous daily. The picture of six officers ejecting a writer from the witness stand because he refused to say whether he was a Communist or not is pretty funny, and I think before long we are all going to see how hysterical and foolish we have become.

The film industry is a great industry with infinite possibilities for good and bad. Its primary purpose is to entertain people. On the side, it can do many other things. It can popularize certain ideals, it can make education palatable. But in the long run, the judge who decides whether what it does is good or bad is the man or woman who attends the movies. In a democratic country I do not think the public will tolerate a removal of its right to decide what it thinks of the ideas and performances of those who make the movie industry work.

I have never liked the idea of an Un-American Activities Committee. I have always thought that a strong democracy should stand by its fundamental beliefs and that a citizen of the United States should be considered innocent until he is proved guilty.

If he is employed in a government position where he has access to secret and important papers, then for the sake of security he must undergo some special tests. However, I doubt whether the loyalty test really adds much to our safety, since no Communist would hesitate to sign it and he would be in good standing until he was proved guilty. So it seems to me that we might as well do away with a test which is almost an insult to any loyal American citizen.

What is going on in the Un-American Activities Committee worries me primarily because little people have become frightened and we find ourselves living in the atmosphere of a police state, where people close doors before they state what they think or look over their shoulders apprehensively before they express an opinion.

I have been one of those who have carried the fight for complete freedom of information in the United Nations. And while accepting the fact that some of our press, our radio commentators, our prominent citizens and our movies may at times be blamed legitimately for things they have said and done, still I feel that the fundamental right of freedom of thought and expression is essential. If you curtail what the other fellow says and does, you curtail what you yourself may say and do.

115

In our country we must trust the people to hear and see both the good and the bad and to choose the good. The Un-American Activities Committee seems to me to be better for a police state than for the USA.

~ ~ ~

One of Eleanor Roosevelt's better literary products is her eulogy of a loyal New Dealer, John Winant. Educated at Princeton and Dartmouth, Winant was a public servant on the state, national, and international levels. He served as Governor of New Hampshire, and held several administrative posts in the world of labor-management relations including, in 1939, Director of the International Labor Office in Geneva. Under FDR's leadership, Winant was Chairman of the Social Security Board from 1935 through 1937, Ambassador to Great Britain in 1941, and United States Representative to the European Advisory Commission in 1943. His was just the kind of diverse, flexible career that Eleanor Roosevelt most admired.

NEW YORK, NOVEMBER 5—Just before one o'clock this morning, I turned on my radio to hear the last news of the night. We went from the strains of band music straight to the announcement of John G. Winant's tragic death.

My husband and I both admired him and, what was more important, we trusted him completely. He was an unselfish public servant who gave himself completely to his work during the war, and is as truly a war casualty as any of our other solidiers. In peacetime as well he was a valuable public servant, with a broad vision and a deep sympathy for all men.

He helped us win the war, and I am sure that, if he had kept his health, he would have filled some vital niche in the battle of winning the peace. He had imagination enough so that he might have helped us to find the thing we need above all others today—the key to building confidence between the eastern European states and ourselves.

I knew he was ill last summer when we were together at the Hobart–Smith College commencement. The pain and the desperate weariness could not be hidden then, and since then he has worked unceasingly. He had been to Switzerland and Great Britain this past summer, and has written feverishly, finishing his memoirs. His friends watched with deep misgivings, begging him to rest yet knowing quite well that something within him would not let him rest.

For his family, this way of going must have been a sad shock. But they have a heritage from him which they can cherish all the days of their lives, for no one who knew the motives from which he acted could ever believe that courage and unselfishness were not the mainsprings of whatever he did.

In the International Labor Organization and in the Social Security Administration, Mr. Winant has left two great achievements to which he contributed much. He was director of the former for many years, and he organized the latter. The ILO might easily have been lost during the war years if it had not been for his foresight and action in moving its headquarters from Switzerland to Canada. The setting-up years of any experiment such as the Social Security Administration are crucial years. It was he who built the good foundation.

My husband counted on him heavily. And when people tried to belittle him, as is always the case with any man in public office, my husband would smile and hardly bother to refute the statements, for he knew so well that big men cannot be touched by little people.

The statesmen and the people of Great Britain will mourn him, for they know better perhaps than our own people what his service as Ambassador to Great Britain meant to us all during the war.

The people of his own state of New Hampshire were fortunate to have him as governor during the years of depression, for they owe many of their best developments to that period.

The record is a good one. One can say: "Well done, thou good and faithful servant." But the heart weeps for the loss of a friend and for the loss of the possibilities for service which still lay before him.

~ ~ ~

The UN called itself back into session toward the end of the year in Geneva, and Mrs. Roosevelt felt the contradictory tug of loyalty to home and hearth working against her sense of duty to an organization she believed in deeply. During the late fall Mrs. Roosevelt was also dealing, as best she could, with the apparent breakup of her daughter Anna's marriage. But neither sympathy nor persuasion did much good: The couple separated in early December while Mrs. Roosevelt was at work in Geneva.

NEW YORK, NOVEMBER 29—There is always a little excitement about going off to a new job, but as I grow older I find that I regret the things I leave behind. The lovely pink light in the sunrise sky as I awake on my porch at Hyde Park, the morning walks in the woods with a little black dog cavorting happily beside me or dashing off after the squirrels, the beautiful bluebird I saw unexpectedly take wing across my brook the other day, the family and friends I like to have around me, the Christmas preparation which I enjoy—all these are hard to leave. Only the sense of something tangible accomplished, that may be of value in the future, will seem to me to make this trip worthwhile.

~ ~ ~

Spirits ran high at the UN meeting in Switzerland, at least in the Commission on Human Rights that Mrs. Roosevelt chaired. Somewhat to its own surprise the commission finished preparing a draft declaration of human rights that would occupy much debating time in the UN for several sessions to come. While Mrs. Roosevelt could not have foreseen the intramural political struggle that lay ahead of the declaration, she did sense that the groundwork for an unprecedented agreement among nations had indeed already been laid.

GENEVA, DECEMBER 18—As a result of the work the Human Rights Commission has done here, I feel that the governments in the United Nations will have some very good working papers to consider and comment on—a draft declaration of rights, a draft convention or covenant on rights, and a report on methods of implementation. I hope that these documents will receive close attention in every government.

GENEVA, DECEMBER 19—Despite the many difficulties, the Human Rights Commission actually managed to finish its work here on schedule. Without any question, I've been almost a slavedriver as the chairman, but one of the members came to me and said he felt that, on the whole, we'd accomplished more because we had set a date to finish our work and had stuck to it.

In the last few days I've received several telegrams, from people in widely different parts of the world, telling me they were greatly heartened by the fact that both a declaration and a convention on rights are to be presented to the governments, and that work has also been done on implementation clauses, which, of course, will eventually be included in the convention after the various governments express their views.

~ ~ ~

She could be royally gracious and pugnaciously blunt; it just depended how one rubbed her. Henry Wallace rubbed Mrs. Roosevelt very much the wrong way. No doubt behind the almost vitriolic putdown of Wallace's plan to run as a third-party candidate for president in 1948 was Mrs. Roosevelt's residual loyalty to FDR—whose programs she believed Wallace had criticized too often, had essentially abandoned by becoming too radical. And he, after all, had been FDR's own vice president! The criticism Mrs. Roosevelt levels here at Wallace does not reflect very well on her husband's political savvy in having chosen Wallace as his running mate in the first place. Whatever her motivation, in this New Year's Eve column she goes out, like the year, with a bang.

HYDE PARK, DECEMBER 31—So Henry Wallace is really going to head a third party and run for President in 1948! What strange things the desire to be President makes men do!

He has probably forgotten, but I remember his coming to see me in the summer of 1945 in Washington. At that time, I felt very strongly that it would be good for the country if Henry Wallace, whom we all believed in and admired, would leave active politics and become the leader of the independents of the country. Their vote had increased greatly in the years between 1929 and 1945, but they needed leadership and organization.

They were neither Republicans nor Democrats. They were primarily interested in getting the kind of leadership which would keep them free of economic depressions. And they wanted to continue what had been a peaceful but steady revolutionary movement which had given us, over the years, a greater number of people in the middle-income brackets and fewer people in the millionaire group or in the substandard-income groups.

This had been accomplished in smaller countries like Norway, Sweden and Denmark, but it was a little more complicated in a country the size of ours and had to come more gradually. It could be done under our capitalistic system with proper regulation and was being done, but the independent vote of the country was very largely responsible for the way our economy and social thinking was developing.

I felt that out of politics Henry Wallace could do a tremendously valuable piece of work to keep both of our political parties on their toes; to make both of them less prone to act for purely political reasons; to make both of them realize that to win any election this independent liberal vote was essential and must be courted by deeds, not words.

The women of the country belong largely in this group. They are not hidebound and they are very practical. They know that well-being spread over a great number of people is a safeguard and the best defense of one of our most important freedoms—freedom from want. The young people of the country needed leadership to be in this group; and to feel that they had with them an older man of complete integrity would have been a tremendous inspiration.

At that time, Henry Wallace told me he believed it was his duty to stay and work in the Democratic Party. I knew then, as I know now, that he was doing what he thought was right. But he never has been a good politician, he never has been able to gauge public opinion, and he never has picked his advisers wisely.

All of these things might have been less important if he had been a disinterested, nonpolitical leader of liberal thought, but as a leader of a third party he will accomplish nothing. He will merely destroy the very things he wishes to achieve. I am sorry that he has listened to people as inept politically as he is himself.

1948

It was a year of escalating conflicts on all fronts. The aggravated political tensions, at home and in foreign policy, were dizzying even to observers as cool-headed and astute as Eleanor Roosevelt.

In January the Supreme Court decided that discrimination on the basis of race, concerning admission of a law school applicant, was unconstitutional, thereby establishing a precedent for subsequent school desegregation rulings. The next month the President introduced civil rights legislation and called for an end to all school segregation. In March the high court voted that religious training in the public schools was unconstitutional. Mrs. Roosevelt was outspoken on civil rights issues. She supported Truman's initiatives, gave the high court praise, and through her column brought particularly offensive examples of racial discrimination to the public's attention.

Civil rights was the hottest issue when the national party conventions rolled around in July. The Democrats nominated Truman, with Kentucky's Alben Barkley as his running mate, then adopted a platform emphasizing civil rights. Outraged Southern conservatives—the Dixiecrats—walked out, regrouping just days later to form the States Rights Party with Strom Thurmond of South Carolina at the helm and a platform that urged preservation of racial segregation. Other dissident liberal Democrats organized the Progressive Party, with former Vice President Henry A. Wallace as leader. The GOP chose two governors as nominees: Thomas E. Dewey of New York for president and Earl Warren of California for vice president.

Truman called a special session of the Congress in the summer to deal with, among other things, civil rights legislation and the repeal of the Taft–Hartley Act, but he came up short, with none of the bills he desired. Only an all-out 10,000-mile whistle-stop campaign across the country by the President saved him in the November election, where he narrowly beat Dewey. (The race was so tight that some major newspapers had printed DEWEY DEFEATS TRUMAN headlines—which the President, of course, showed off with glee the moment his own victory was clear.) The Dixiecrats garnered thirty-nine electoral votes, but the Progressives didn't win any. Each of the two minor parties nevertheless collected about a million popular votes. Eleanor Roosevelt backed Harry Truman and several times criticized Henry Wallace in her "My Day" columns, but unfortunately she could not give her undivided attention to the campaign; her status as a UN delegate demanded too much of her time.

Strikes continued to disrupt the economy or to advance the cause of labor, depending on one's viewpoint. President Truman was caught in the middle. In May, when a national railroad workers' strike crippled transportation, Truman called out the Army to run the railroads. The White House had been unsuccessful earlier in the year in trying to avert a coalminers' strike by 200,000 workers that lasted almost a month. Although the compromises that settled the dispute were partially negotiated by UMW President John L. Lewis, he was nonetheless fined $20,000 under Taft–Hartley and his union was assessed $1.25 million for contempt of court. When Eleanor Roosevelt addressed the labor-management dispute in her column, she didn't mince words: She labeled John L. Lewis a suspiciously self-serving union leader. On the other hand, she showed sympathy for the workers, as long as their strikes didn't threaten the overall economy. When work stoppages *did* pose such a danger, she called for a quick resolution of the issues—for the good of the nation.

Tensions were rising on the foreign-policy front as well. The Soviets barred a UN commission, charged with overseeing elections in Korea, from entering North Korea. In June the Soviets blocked access to Western-held sectors of Berlin for two days; Truman ordered American military planes based in Europe to fly in food and fuel. By fall two independent competing republics had been declared in Korea, setting the stage for inevitable conflict between Soviet and American policies there. But certain happier notes in foreign affairs also emerged in 1948. The Organization of American States began its existence with meetings in Bogotá. The United States gave more than $5 million in aid to Europe through the Marshall Plan. Israel declared its independence in May; the U.S.A. was first to recognize her, and Eleanor Roosevelt was among the first to applaud this development. The United States won the team competition at the London Olympics, the first since 1936. But a wise old man of American politics, Bernard Baruch, coined a phrase in 1948—*cold war*—that best summed up the fundamentally dark undercurrent of international developments.

The Communist scare in America continued to intensify, with Representative Richard M. Nixon engineering through the House a bill that would have required all Communists to register with the government. (The Senate never passed it.) Repeatedly Mrs. Roosevelt called for cool reason in an increasingly hot emotional climate. The Whittaker Chambers–Alger Hiss case, concerning alleged Communist activities, occupied the public's attention for weeks because of its witch-hunt drama.

Rounding out the year, T. S. Eliot (claimed by both America and England as a national poet) was awarded the Nobel Prize for Literature; Columbia Records introduced long-playing records (LPs); and another Columbia, the university in New York, got a new president, Dwight D. Eisenhower, for whom even bigger things were in store.

~ ~ ~

Astrology is probably either an inexact science or an arcane art, but it is intriguing to see how certain people seem indeed to embody the characteristics of particular astrological signs. Born in October, Mrs. Roosevelt was a Libran, one of those for whom the symbol is the scales, the balance. Reading dozens of her "My Day" columns one cannot help but notice how often, certainly in the better ones, the issue of achieving a balanced point of view, or of trying to reconcile and harmonize opposites, comes through. The Libran personality, so astrologers say, also combines in highly creative tension the dual tendencies of idealism and practicality.

HYDE PARK, JANUARY 7—In a recent magazine article, "A Thought for 1948," Henry Seidel Canby chose a quotation from Thoreau which any one of us might think of many times a day: "Our life is frittered away by details. . . . The nation is ruined . . . by want of calculation and a worthy aim. . . . It lives too fast." Thoreau, of course, retired to the woods. When he wanted to write a book, he simply lived a hermitlike life, cultivating beans and corn and going into the village as rarely as possible.

This is a simple expedient if you have no responsibilities or if you feel that the particular work you want to do is more important than any of the other things which crowd your days. Very few of us can have that feeling of dedication to one particular part of life, but we can, I think, both personally and nationally, rid ourselves of a great deal of unnecessary detail and, as Dr. Canby suggests, "Live deep instead of fast."

It is not always as simple as he suggests, however, and it is not always a question of just finding out what is the most important thing you want to do and then cutting out everything else. There are people, of course, whose work is so important that it is right for them to subordinate their families, their friends and all other interests in order to achieve what they feel called upon to do. For most of us this would be extremely difficult, since we wonder whether anything we do is more valuable than something done by some member of our family or by some friend, and we feel called upon to contribute to the work of others as well as to accomplish what we can ourselves.

Through good organization and with careful thought, I think the proper balance can be achieved by a removal of as much of the detail as possible that fritters away time. To live deeply requires a capacity for feeling—and that, too, is something which must be developed. For the most part people's emotions, when untrained and uncontrolled, are apt only to stir the surface and not to reflect themselves in thought and in action.

Nature is a good teacher and, though we cannot all be Thoreaus, we can accept her lessons when we have the opportunity and can gain some of the peace and contentment that comes with the development of an ability "to live deep instead of fast."

~ ~ ~

Many "My Day" columns grew out of press releases sent to Mrs. Roosevelt by public relations offices of worthy organizations such as the American Heart Association. These groups knew of Mrs. Roosevelt's passionate concern for the physical and mental well-being of the American population—indeed, of the whole world's population—and knew she was a good bet to give their respective causes some exposure. Mrs. Roosevelt often used the press release (the one here has become the heart of her column) as a jumping-off point for broader reflections on the subject at hand—in this case the health of Americans.

HYDE PARK, JANUARY 23—The week of February 8 has been designated National Heart Week, and I think the public's attention should be drawn to the following statement made by the American Heart Association: "Heart disease causes greater mortality than the combined total of deaths resulting from the next five leading causes: cancer, accidents, nephritis, pneumonia and tuberculosis." The American Heart Association is composed of outstanding heart specialists and many laymen who have awakened to the fact that it is time to organize a nationwide program to fight this disease which takes such a heavy toll.

There are three main objectives in this program: (1) Research, for which money must be provided. (2) Education of the public, for which money is also needed but which can be carried on by laymen as well as by doctors—and even by volunteers, once they realize they have a part to play in telling people what can and should be done to prevent the great toll of deaths every year. (3) Service, which means bringing the benefits of the best medical knowledge within the reach of every citizen in every community.

This is not something that doctors can do alone. You and I must be aware of the need and, through voluntary agencies, must do as good a job on diseases of the heart as has been done by those agencies which have almost stamped out tuberculosis and those which are working year in and year out on infantile paralysis.

In 1945, so many people were aware of the dangers of tuberculosis and infantile paralysis that they gave four hundred times as much toward preventing and curing those diseases as they gave for the prevention of heart disease. And the general public gave one hundred times as much to educate people in the prevention of cancer and in the research and care that is needed. But we let the ravages of heart disease among children and adults go on from year to year, with much less awareness of the price we are paying.

There are many things besides giving money which can be done to combat all disease. One of them is to keep people, young and old, in better health all of the time.

This is partly a question of food—and one of the things on which our food depends is soil conservation. We must take care not to destroy the essential things in the soil that are needed to produce the proteins which people must have to be strong. A campaign should sweep this country, drawing together the farmer and the man who works in the city, because what is done on the farm affects every city dweller.

Food affects mental as well as physical health. The statistics, which horrified us during the war, on the general health of our young men should be studied with extreme care, since these statistics affect our nation in peace as well as in war. They affect the health of every child and every adult.

Every farmer who farms well can feel that he has done his share to contribute to the prevention of conditions which make all people more prone to the diseases which we have to fight in an organized way.

~ ~ ~

Albert Einstein and other scientists and foreign-policy planners who had worked inside or on the fringes of the Manhattan Project that created the atomic bomb in 1945 later became advocates for the peaceful use of atomic energy and for the establishment of one world government. Einstein in particular had had a nightmare vision of what the next world war would inevitably entail, with nuclear weapons wreaking havoc across all world civilizations. To him, nationalism was the central problem, with its fierce pride and territorial protectiveness the tendencies that make war once in every generation a near-certainty. Only through the abolition of nationhood as we know it and the substitution of a single world government did civilization stand a chance to survive went the argument. Many writers joined the campaign as well, among them New Yorker columnist and children's book author E. B. White. Idealistic though Eleanor Roosevelt was on many points, she here strikes the cautionary note.

HYDE PARK, JANUARY 29—A bulletin of the atomic scientists is accompanied by a letter in which Prof. Albert Einstein states that only a world government can keep the world safe from destruction.

The scientists who made the atomic discoveries, which have such great potentialities both for destruction and for improvement in the conditions under which people live, naturally feel a great sense of responsibility and desire to see their discoveries used for the good of humanity. Apparently, by the proper use of atomic energy, we could revolutionize many things related to the basic needs of people— power, production and soil conservation. The scientists therefore feel that it is very wasteful for us to concern ourselves with the production of bombs when there is so much to be done on the constructive side.

I can quite understand why men like Prof. Einstein feel that a world government would answer the problem, but any of us who have worked in the United Nations realize that we will have to learn to crawl before we learn to walk. If the great nations find it so hard to agree on the minor points at issue today, how do any of these hopeful people think that a world government could be made to work? People have to want to get on together and to do away with force, but so far there are many throughout the world who have not advanced to the point of really wanting to do this.

~ ~ ~

Her eulogy of Mohandas K. Gandhi was brief although Mrs. Roosevelt admired him and knew the story of his remarkable life and career very well. Her biographer Joseph Lash, in fact, turns to Gandhi's development into a humanitarian pacifist leader as a model for comparison to Eleanor Roosevelt's life: "Gandhi on his return from South Africa, a relatively young man of forty-five but the hero of Indian nonviolent-resistance to the British there, told Indian National Congress leaders he had to take time away from the centers of power to reacquaint himself with the India of the countryside and the mills. For almost two years he travelled barefoot, third class on trains, and along dusty roads with the poor. Even in South Africa he had given up everything he owned and treated all people as part of his family. . . .

"Such a Wanderjahr of identification with people from different walks of life represented in Eleanor's eyes indispensable apprenticeship in politics, especially for cultivated, upper-class Americans who aspired to democratic leadership."

HYDE PARK, FEBRUARY 2—It was with horror that I heard the news on Friday that Gandhi had been shot. Somehow, for this man of peace, who never hurt anyone, to come to a violent death at the hand of one of his countrymen seems almost impossible to believe. One realizes that the assassin was probably crazed. It is a hard blow to India, especially at the present time when she is beset by difficulties and trying to build an independent nation after so many years of subjection—years in which Gandhi played a great part to bring about her freedom in peaceful fashion.

There is no doubt that Gandhi had great spiritual qualities, and one can only hope that, even though he is no longer with his people, his influence will grow and help them through the years. This same influence had much of value to give to the rest of the world, and one hopes that the very violence of his death will turn people away from violence—which certainly brings none of us any good at the present time.

~ ~ ~

Sometimes a "My Day" column was a compendium of brief thoughts on several topics. In such columns Mrs. Roosevelt faced what for her was always a literary problem: how to make artful transitions. In the next column we see a transition that is not her best but at least does the trick. She wanted to tip her hat to the ILGWU for its poignant art show in New York and then go on to talk about starving children in Europe. Perhaps logic was a bit strained, but the heart makes other kinds of connections. Chester Bowles, elected governor of Connecticut in 1948, became American ambassador to India 1951–1953.

HYDE PARK, FEBRUARY 3—Few people would associate a labor union with an art exhibition, but in 1944 the dressmakers' union local No. 22 raised $4,157.50 for the New York War Fund by their benefit art exhibition, and this year they are going to have a similar art show for the benefit of the Damon Runyon Cancer Fund.

The International Ladies Garment Workers Union has an enviable record for the welfare and artistic projects which they have undertaken and carried through. We certainly hope that the cause which is to benefit from this exhibition will help to attract those who might otherwise think that only in museums and art galleries can interesting paintings be found. These exhibitors are workers and yet they produce creditable works of art.

Art in any form is a valuable medium which does bring home to people many things which we might not otherwise understand. I thought of this as I looked at the cover of a Sunday newspaper's magazine section. It was a photograph of a Hungarian peasant woman's drawn face and, beside her, the sad, upturned face of a child. The eyes do not look as though they ever smiled.

This picture was a fitting prelude to an article by Chester Bowles, chairman of the International Advisory Committee for the United Nations Appeal for Children.

131

The article is a report on Europe's children and was written at this time because the United Nations Appeal this month is making a worldwide drive for funds.

Many nations that will have to be recipients are nevertheless offering to give whatever they have which is surplus. For instance, Poland and Yugoslavia, which lack many things that they must look to the Children's Emergency Fund to supply, have offered some sugar and some cotton—a token that all nations wish to do whatever they possibly can for the welfare of their children.

This article by Chester Bowles, who has just completed a tour of Europe, would indicate that he has been shocked by the realization that the needs of children in devastated countries are not clearly understood in our own country. But he knows, as most of us know, that if any of the people in the United States could for one minute find themselves living in a devastated town, there would be no question about the flow of the necessary things to feed and clothe the neighbor's child.

I personally wish that our country could give to the United Nations Appeal for Children in the same way that we gave to UNRRA. Of course, private individuals and organizations can contribute, but this will not take the place of contributions which governments can make.

And I feel that children should be helped without any discrimination because of their race or religion or the political beliefs of their parents. These are the children who will live with our children in the world of the future—if they do not starve to death in the meantime. If they even come near starving, it will warp their minds and their hearts and they will not be good neighbors to our children in the years to come.

~ ~ ~

As Eleanor Roosevelt watched the Red scare of the late 1940s heat up into a genuine witch hunt for Communists in all walks of life she strained for a way to educate the public and certain legislators about the difference between theoretical Communism as an ideology and practical Communism as a political strategy that included the idea of violent overthrow of the status quo to achieve its aims. In this case Mrs. Roosevelt was a dreamer in her belief that education could quell the anxieties and hatreds felt by the Communist-hunters.

HYDE PARK, FEBRUARY 24—I think the thing that needs to be settled today is whether a statement that you believe in certain economic and political theories known as Communism implies that you also believe in the overthrow of your government by force. Once that point is established, then this whole situation which bothers so many would be cleared up, I think. A belief in the principles of Communism, provided you did not intend to work to bring this form of government into being through violence, would not be any more dangerous than a belief in Socialism, which has been preached in this country for many years without marked advance.

You hear people say they want to outlaw the Communist Party, forbid its existence in our country, deport citizens who are Communists. It seems to me that this attitude is valid only if it is proved that being a Communist means that you believe in the use of force against the existing government.

~   ~   ~

The heavy weight of being a citizen in a democratic society was the subject of an address Eleanor Roosevelt gave at Pennsylvania's Bryn Mawr College; the hope she placed on the next generation of leaders was enormous. A few days afterward, the respect Eleanor Roosevelt had won for herself as a tireless worker for the causes of democracy and humanitarianism was acknowledged when the National Council of Jewish Women presented her an award. By this time in her career, no one could mistake Eleanor Roosevelt for anything but the most compassionate and loyal supporter of the Jewish cause. The irony is, suggests biographer Joseph Lash, that when she was a younger woman (for instance, during World War I) some of her private correspondence had had a strong anti-Semitic strain. Lash sees the great progress Mrs.

Roosevelt made toward complete open-mindedness as testimony to her lifelong capacity for growth and learning.

NEW YORK, MARCH 13—The wheels of the train to Philadelphia kept saying to me: "What are you going to say tonight? What are you going to say tonight?" I felt I should have something really significant to say, but I could not talk as usual just about the United Nations and its objectives. Many of those in the audience would be young people looking for something by which to live. And as the train wheels went around, my thoughts went churning around: "What are you going to say? What are you going to say?"

In the end, I arrived at Bryn Mawr more or less unprepared, with only a few vague ideas floating around in my mind, but then, as I faced the audience, the thing I wanted to say was entirely clear. Democracy stands at the crossroads. We are citizens of this great democracy and it's up to us to find out what we can do to make democracy lead instead of standing still. The United States must really decide on her policies, domestic and foreign, and go through with them and, above all, make every one, from the highest to the lowest, act with integrity.

We have not always kept our word and this has done us harm, but our failures have been largely caused by confusion, not by evil intent. Other nations may have been somewhat clearer on their own interests, but they have been no clearer than we have been on thinking of the joint interests of the world and seeing that the policies decided on were lived up to.

One cannot wipe out the past, but one can make changes in the future. God grant that, in our schools and colleges today, there are young people who will be strong spiritually and morally as well as physically, who will not be afraid to pick up the pieces of this shattered world and try to bring it into some kind of unity.

HYDE PARK, MARCH 19—I want to tell you how deeply moved I was by the dinner given for me in New York on Monday night, when the National Council of Jewish Women presented their "Woman of the Year Award." The fact that Supreme Court Justice William O.

Douglas came from Washington to speak, and that each speaker tied his own thoughts in with some of my interests, made it a very memorable but very solemn evening for me. It impressed upon me the great responsibility which all of us carry who are given an opportunity to touch, even in a small way, the great tide of public work which is going on today.

~ ~ ~

Off to Europe again for the next round of United Nations meetings, Mrs. Roosevelt made a social call at Windsor Castle to see King George VI and Queen Elizabeth, who had been her own guests at both the White House and at Hyde Park.

LONDON, APRIL 7—I spent the weekend at Windsor Castle with Their Majesties the King and Queen. They were, as always, charming and thoughtful, and it was deeply touching to see their loyalty to my husband's memory. Queen Mother Mary, who was there, is a perfectly remarkable person and shows great interest in everything that goes on in the world. She took my breath away on Monday morning by being up and dressed to say goodbye to me.

Princess Elizabeth and her husband, the Duke of Edinburgh, and Princess Margaret Rose were also there. And on Sunday night, the Duchess of Kent came over. Her second son was my husband's godchild. She told me she was going to bring him to the unveiling of the statue in Grosvenor Square and, though he is only five years old, she hopes he will remember it all his life.

On Saturday evening after dinner, we were taken on a tour of the castle. One could not possibly remember all the art treasures there, but it was a feast for the eyes. When one realizes that William the Conqueror built this castle as a fortress for the defense of London and that, from that time on, it has gradually grown and has been lived in by all the people whose portraits hang on the walls, one finds it hard to believe.

It is in seeing things like this that one gains an understanding of what traditions really mean—traditions and customs that go back

135

hundreds of years. For instance, while at dinner we heard the sound of bagpipes, and then the doors opened and a piper, resplendent in his kilts, marched around the table playing various selections. Mr. Churchill whispered in my ear, "This is a Windsor custom. I have been here when a number of them have come marching around."

On Sunday morning, we attended the service in St. George's Chapel. I particularly enjoyed the singing of the little boys who attend the choir school. They look like angels, though I'm quite sure they have all of the normal boyish defects!

Much of the food served at Windsor Castle has to be grown on the place or entertaining would be impossible even for the King and Queen. And I was told that the traditional uniform worn at the castle was worn during my visit only in my honor. When one talks to people who have houses to run, one begins to realize the daily difficulties of living which the British, rich and poor alike, have to bear. Fats are extremely short, and every one to whom I brought a small bit of soap has been overjoyed.

~ ~ ~

The British government had unveiled an impressive sculpture of President Roosevelt in London's Grosvenor Square, situated in one of the city's most charming neighborhoods. Mrs. Roosevelt and other members of her family were in attendance at the unveiling, and she was deeply moved by the continuing British enthusiasm for her husband. Writing to her daughter, Anna, she said, "What friends Father made everywhere for the United States. It ought to bring tangible results to us in the future if we are wise."

Zurich, Switzerland, April 17—Even two or three days after the unveiling of my husband's statue in Grosvenor Square, crowds still filled the square and moved slowly around the statue. The Lord Mayor told me that people were coming to the city just for a day, even from Scotland and Wales, and were spending part of their day in a pilgrimage to Grosvenor Square.

~ ~ ~

What would Mrs. Roosevelt think forty years later about the scandalous rise in homelessness among the urban poor, about the scourge of drug and alcohol addiction that puts so many people more or less permanently on the street? In this column she says "I don't think I like the way we live these days," and one can only suspect that were she to see New York in the last stages of the century rather than in the middle, her sense of outrage might be even deeper.

NEW YORK, MAY 15—A curious thing happened to me the other night. I came out of my apartment house and walked toward Eighth Street to attend a lecture given by Eugene O'Neill, Jr., at the New School for Social Research. Suddenly, I saw on the sidewalk the figure of a man. He lay there drunk or ill or asleep—very thin and very poor-looking. People glanced at him and hurried by. Some of us made sure that he was breathing. But here in a big city, what did one do with a stranger who lay senseless and helpless on the sidewalk?

What we did was to report him to the first policemen we met—which I suppose was the proper thing to do—but it left me feeling very odd. The story of the Good Samaritan kept running through my head, and I wondered whether it was possible in a big city to feel the same responsibility for your fellow man as you would feel on a country road.

I don't suppose the man was worthy, and I doubt if you can take a man you see lying on the street and have him carried into an apartment house. But leaving him there seemed heartless and senseless and inhuman, and I don't think I like the way we live in these days.

I had no further responsibility after we found the policeman, but the incident haunted me all through Mr. O'Neill's lecture about my husband as a man of ideas and a man of letters. And the next day, at Lake Success, as we argued about human rights at a committee meeting, I wondered how many human rights that poor man had. At

137

heart I imagine I am really a country bumpkin—I like to know my neighbors and to have some sense of responsibility for them.

~ ~ ~

In early June 1948 Eleanor Roosevelt could not have known that the Senate would eventually refuse to pass its own version of the Mundt–Nixon bill that had recently made it through the House of Representatives. And so the bill, requiring anyone claiming to be a Communist of whatever kind and for whatever reason, even if purely philosophical, to step forward and register with the government, turned out to be moot legislatively but still had intense political repercussions. Given the rash of attacks being made more and more frequently on the mere idea of belonging to the American Communist Party or of having even an openness to the theoretical possibility that Communism might have something to offer in political terms, no one in these days wanted to declare himself a Communist in the U.S. unless absolutely necessary. Mrs. Roosevelt knew that many individuals' civil rights would be threatened should the Mundt bill pass the Senate.

HYDE PARK, JUNE 1—It is a curious thing that, among those aligned against the Mundt Bill, one finds people belonging to the extreme left and to the extreme right, and also those in the middle—the moderate liberals, like myself, who dislike seeing us fight Communism by extreme measures. I feel that, in using repressive measures, we are not only underlining our fears that democracy cannot stand up against the superficial attraction of Communism, but we are resorting to the very measures which dictatorships—both Fascist and Communist—use to stay in power.

Our Attorney General has just come to the conclusion, according to the papers, that Communism all over the world stands for the overthrow of existing governments by force and that therefore no one who declares himself a Communist can be a good citizen of a democracy. I have known a number of theoretical Communists who certainly were not going around with guns.

The only ones that I think have any real justification in being Communists, and who might possibly be tempted to overthrow any government by force, are those for whom democracy has not provided the basic needs of decent living. That is the point on which I wish we would focus our fight against Communism—not on repressive measures which drive Communists underground, but on the development of democracy so that no human being can find any great attraction in the rather drab program of Communism.

~ ~ ~

The Red scare of the 1940s and 1950s had at its heart, among other dislikable qualities, the tendency to brand entire ethnic groups as suspect. The "DPs" Mrs. Roosevelt refers to in this column are displaced persons, people who were uprooted from their homes and, often, their homelands during the war and who now, under the new political circumstances in postwar Europe, either could not go home or would not want to for fear of persecution. Many of them were Eastern European Jews; some were lower-class Catholics from the Latin countries. Certain congressmen in the United States made a habit of labeling all DPs "bums and loafers," and on the basis of this prejudice worked out a legislative position on such issues as immigration law so that passage to America and a chance at a new life would be permanently blocked for these hapless victims of the war.

NEW YORK, JUNE 12—I am sorry to see that in the debate in the House on the bill to admit 200,000 Displaced Persons into the United States, Representative E. E. Cox (Democrat, Georgia) opposed the bill on the grounds that the inhabitants of DP camps are "the scum of all Europe—an aggregation of loafers. As a whole these camps are the hotbeds of revolutionists and if these people come here they will join those who are gnawing away at the foundation of our constitutional government."

He was joined by Representative Edward Gossett (Democrat, Texas).

All one can say about these gentlemen is that they never visited these DP camps or they visited them with an amount of prejudice and ignorance that prevented them from seeing the most self-evident truths.

The people in the camps are certainly not revolutionists. They would naturally not be in favor of a regime that condemns any human being to spending an indeterminate number of years in camps scattered throughout Europe. Most of these people have skills and are anxious to work, and some of them have professions and were men of note in those professions before they were forced to leave their homes.

The record of similar people who have been allowed to come into our country has been remarkably good. They make successful American citizens and it is un-Christian and uncharitable to brand people as "bums and loafers" when they are the victims of circumstances beyond their control.

~ ~ ~

Alliances between nations bear some rough resemblance to relationships between friends, so when an alliance that has recently been tested by the cruel challenges of war unravels, it is inevitably disturbing— particularly to the party who wants it to continue peacefully. Mrs. Roosevelt was among the earliest to face the fact that the Russians could no longer be trusted as allies. The Soviet actions that temporarily blocked some access to the Western sectors of Berlin were probably the last straw. After that, Mrs. Roosevelt knew when she was debating with her Russian colleagues in the UN that she could no longer consider them trustworthy friends.

NEW YORK, JUNE 17— Last night I read in the evening papers that the Russians have taken again to their irritating tactics in Berlin and have prevented 140 coal-carrying railway cars from entering Berlin from the Western zone in the last few days and have shut off the auto bridges over the Elbe. This was reported by Allied authorities, and by that is meant the Western Allies. British authorities stated that only trains bound for the Western sectors of Berlin were halted. Those destined for the Russian sector went through unmolested.

An excuse was given, of course, but these tactics explain why we no longer seem to consider that the Russians are our Allies. This is a shock and makes one look backward and wonder where this point of division began. Somewhere the Soviet Union, Great Britain and the United States got off the track. Instead of agreeing together, as under the United Nations Charter the great nations were supposed to do, they started to disagree and the disagreement has grown greater and greater until now it is almost difficult to find any point at which we can agree.

~ ~ ~

Family before country, and country before political party: Eleanor Roosevelt would no doubt have agreed with this set of priorities— though she, FDR, and her children (especially the boys who served in the war) were all ready to die for the nation if it came to it. But did Mrs. Roosevelt always "vote Democratic"? Here we see her praising one of Congress' most distinguished women members, the Republican representative from Maine.

HYDE PARK, JUNE 24—You cannot find much news in the papers these days except that about the Republican Convention, nor can you listen to the radio or turn on the television and get anything but the convention.

There is one Republican victory that I am really happy about, and that is the nomination for the Senate which has been won by Representative Margaret C. Smith of Maine, who ran against several very fine gentlemen. It is a well-deserved victory. She has done her job as Representative in Congress conscientiously and has shown ability and integrity. Though we are of opposite political parties, I want to speak this word of appreciation and congratulation.

~ ~ ~

Happy days in the country at Hyde Park seemed to Mrs. Roosevelt well-earned respites from the constant swirl of UN meetings at Lake Success, Long Island, and the social appointments and speaking engagements that ordinarily kept her moving at a rapid clip when she was in the city. And Eleanor Roosevelt was probably never happier than when her house was full of children. From the kids' viewpoint the fun of summering at Mrs. Roosevelt's Val-Kill Cottage at Hyde Park is easy to understand. There were fields and woods to roam in, a safe swimming pool to splash in, and a bottomless well of good food and good will to indulge in.

The granddaughter to be married in Phoenix is Anna Roosevelt's first child, Anna Eleanor Dall whose nickname was "Sistie."

PHOENIX, ARIZ., JULY 8—This is working out as a very successful summer. But to most people it might seem as if we were running a children's camp at Hyde Park, for we have had an average of nine children steadily since early June! When one or two leave, others arrive. However, they all fall into the routine very quickly, and it seems to be enjoyable for them. At least I have heard no complaints.

One of Elliott's sons likes working on the farm. He has a friend with him who seems quite willing to go along with whatever he does, whether it is helping with the cows or mowing the lawn, and he must be enjoying it for he has asked his mother to please let him stay for a longer visit.

Those who ride take care of their own horses. The littlest ones play in the sandbox and swing in the swings by the brook and swim in the pool. All the youngsters spend hours of every warm day in the pool. The two children who are not quite three years old have to wear life belts, but they go through all of the motions of swimming and evidently learn from just watching the others.

I am looking forward to having Franklin Jr.'s younger boy, Christopher, with us for ten days this month and possibly we may be able to get a longer visit from young John Boettiger, who is nine. Elliott's four children, with their friends, and my cousin, Mrs. W. Forbes Morgan, with her two children are our steady, permanent summer residents.

We picnic by the pool for luncheon every day, and that seems to be a perfect idea because the children do not have to take off their bathing suits, which always creates sadness and controversy.

We went off Sunday, the Fourth of July, for our annual picnic in a particular spot where there is a wonderful, rushing stream that has quite a deep waterfall and dark green hemlocks on either side growing out of the rocks. It is a beautiful place, and the children had a wonderful time following the stream along the rocks. They returned, dripping water from head to toe, having all fallen into a pool.

I read poetry after lunch to the six- and seven-year-olds and have found that Robert Louis Stevenson's "Poems of Childhood" are as much enjoyed by this generation as they had been by my own children a generation ago.

I was sorry to leave them all on Tuesday, but Miss Thompson and I left for Phoenix bright and early. This trip is partly business and partly pleasure. I have not been anywhere in the United States away from the East in a long time, and I think if one wants to gauge the popular feeling of the people throughout the country one has to get away from the Eastern Seaboard, if only for a day.

I am, of course, excited about my grandchild's wedding, the first in the family. I suppose this should make me feel very old, but, strangely enough, it does not seem to affect me that way at all!

~ ~ ~

Those who got hooked on the marvelous BBC television series "Upstairs, Downstairs" know how fascinating can be the story of any great public family's life when told through the eyes of a keenly observant domestic worker. Henrietta Nesbitt, the Roosevelt's housekeeper at the White House, had seen the family at its best and worst. Despite the President's own somewhat persnikety and often annoying demands on the two White House kitchens, Mrs. Nesbitt could still tell a sympathetic story. In Eleanor Roosevelt's autobiography, On My Own, *Mrs. Nesbitt is also given warm thanks.*

HYDE PARK, AUGUST 13—It has been a little hard this summer to read the many books that have come my way, but I finally did get a chance to enjoy "The White House Diary" by Henrietta Nesbitt.

When I read the message from Mrs. Nesbitt on the flyleaf, I was a little overcome and embarrassed, because Mrs. Nesbitt is truly kind to all of us. It is true she didn't always like all of our friends and some of the visitors seem to have been a real trial, but so far as my husband and myself and the children are concerned she was certainly a very charitable and generous friend.

Some of the recipes she gives still make my mouth water, and I wish she were still doing some baking and I could ask her to send us some of the things we all liked so much.

Of course, there are a few slight inaccuracies in the book, but it is interesting and readable. Mrs. Nesbitt's viewpoint was all her own, and she perhaps had the opportunity of knowing people better in certain ways than anyone else in the house. Luckily, she seems to have been able to keep some sense of humor through these trying years in the White House, and I will always remember gratefully how she and Mr. Nesbitt came together and tackled a very big job because I asked them to do it. She says very generously that it was a life-saver for her, but it was also a life-saver for me.

I always got on well with Mrs. Nesbitt. My husband became difficult about his food in the last few years, and with rationing troubles it became more difficult to give him the things he really wanted.

The greatest sacrifice which Mrs. Nesbitt made for him was working with his mother's cook, whom he kept after Mrs. Roosevelt's death in 1941 to cook two meals a day for him in the White House and to go to Hyde Park when he went there. Some of my time was spent mediating between Mrs. Nesbitt and Mary, the cook, who had her own kitchen on the top floor of the White House. When I was away, Miss Thompson took over the job of mediating.

One of my daughters-in-law used to worry a great deal about our White House food, which she did not consider very good, and as I had never been able to pretend that I knew anything about food, I had to be very humble about her criticisms and try to remedy the defects. Not being conscious of them myself, I'm afraid I was not very successful. Thus I was very grateful when our daughter joined our household after her husband went overseas, because she could interpret what had then become Franklin's whims far better than I could.

All in all, I think Mrs. Nesbitt deserves the gratitude of every member of our family for her patience and efficiency during the busy years in the White House, and I only wish our paths crossed more often today.

~   ~   ~

Henry Wallace cast himself, as the Progressive Party presidential candidate, in the role of the only true descendant of FDR's New Deal. Everyone else, Wallace asserted, had taken a wrong turn. He promised his followers "a century of the common man" and swore he would rally a "Gideon's Army" in the name of domestic equality and international peace. His positions on several issues were far to the left of the Democratic Party and he was the quintessential dissident politician.

At other times in American history such a political posture might not have elicited much response, but in the late 1940s, in the atmosphere of anxiety over so-called Communist subversion of the American way, Wallace became an inevitable target for those who believed the American way had no room in it for any other way, even theoretically speaking. It is much to Eleanor Roosevelt's credit that she, who was never a fan of Mr. Wallace and disapproved of most of his positions at this time, stood up to defend his right to speak unmolested and unharassed anywhere on the campaign trail.

HYDE PARK, SEPTEMBER 2—It is very unfortunate that Henry Wallace has not been allowed to speak unmolested at several stops on his trip through the South. Anyone who is a candidate for the Presidency of the United States certainly should have the right to be heard. If one disapproves of his stand personally, one does not have to go to listen to him. If one wants to listen to him, then he should be treated with respect whether one intends to vote for him or not.

145

It is reported in the press that as eggs and tomatoes flew in Mr. Wallace's direction as he attempted to make speeches in North Carolina, there were cries of "Communist" and "nigger-lover." These things do not hurt Mr. Wallace. They hurt the section of the country in which they occur. I hope that he loves his neighbor no matter what the color of his skin, because that is what Our Lord said we should do, but the epitaph "nigger-lover" fits no better than the epitaph "Communist."

I did not like Mr. Wallace's statement about his Communist supporters the other day. I thought it was too naive and it begged the question. But I still believe that Mr. Wallace himself is not a Communist, nor does he intend to overthrow the Government of the United States by force. In fact, I think if anyone tried to do such a thing, Mr. Wallace would line up in opposition.

Whether this trip into the South is wise or unwise I do not know. But as long as he has undertaken to go and stand before the voters of the country and tell them what his views are, I think the least that the voters can do is to listen to him or to stay away from the meetings.

~ ~ ~

Mrs. Roosevelt had a knack for spotting the political leaders of the future as they developed their talents and outlooks in the early stages of their careers. In this one "My Day" column she singles out, for the voters' attention, a future ambassador to India (Chester Bowles), a future vice president and presidential candidate (Hubert Humphrey), and another future two-time candidate for president (Adlai Stevenson).

NEW YORK, SEPTEMBER 11—In addition to the Presidential side of the coming elections, I have a special interest in some of the candidates running for Congress and state offices. Among them is Chester Bowles, who is running for governor of Connecticut.

Mr. Bowles can speak with authority on price control and the way to prevent inflation. When we had OPA we did not have all we wanted, perhaps, but at least all of us were treated on the same basis, rich and poor alike. We received an equal ration, and prices in wartime did not equal those we have had since the theory of returning to the old methods of no control at all was accepted and given a fair trial both by Democrats and Republicans.

The State of Connecticut has an opportunity to vote for a governor who is a real liberal and who is capable of thinking through the problems that face us today. I hope Mr. Bowles is successful in his quest for the office he seeks.

In Minneapolis, Minn., there is a young man who has proved himself a good mayor and now is looking toward Washington. He is Hubert Humphrey, and he is running for the Senate seat now occupied by Joseph H. Ball. He showed courage at the National Democratic Convention, and leadership and organizing ability as well. He might infuse new life into a Congress that certainly needs it, and he would certainly stand for more liberal domestic policies than his opponent.

There are many other Democrats, such as Paul Douglas and Adlai Stevenson who are running for office in the State of Illinois—one for governor and one for senator. Both of them are liberals.

Mr. Stevenson had a very long and unique experience in preparing for the first United Nations General Assembly meeting in London. He learned what negotiation with other nations meant, and it certainly will help him in the national scene, where patience and the art of negotiation must be practiced much as it is practiced in the international field.

In California, Chet Holifield is a young liberal who deserves our support. And, of course, I have a special interest in Helen Gahagan Douglas, who has made a great success as a congresswoman and who has done it through her constant interest in such things as affect the daily lives of the people.

These are just a few candidates picked at random who should inspire those who care enough about our government to get out and work in the coming elections. There are many more, and everyone who looks around his own locality probably will find them and feel the urge to work for them. If we want to have a hand in shaping the future, it is only through work at home that we can hope to have any influence at all.

~ ~ ~

Eleanor Roosevelt embarked for France on the SS America *in the
middle of September. The UN General Assembly had chosen to
meet in Paris to avoid the distractions of the last weeks of the
American presidential campaign. The days just before any major trip
are usually a whirlwind for most travelers; for Mrs. Roosevelt they
were a double whirlwind. But she managed to find free time for a
night at the theater to see one of the hottest plays on Broadway in
years. Alas, she didn't like it, finding its main character, Stanley
Kowalski, too crude and vulgar to amount to good entertainment.
We see here what Mrs. Roosevelt's aesthetic principles were: the
theater, or art generally, ought to be uplifting, and though realism
was fine, rubbing our noses in the seamy side of life was hard for her
to justify. Rarely did anyone then or since dismiss the vibrant Marlon
Brando, who played Stanley, as Eleanor Roosevelt does here.*

EN ROUTE TO PARIS, SEPTEMBER 21—A few days before leaving for
Paris, while I was in New York City, I went to see the Pulitzer
Prize-winning play, "A Streetcar Named Desire," by Tennessee
Williams. I had to compare it with "Tobacco Road," since both seem
to have the same qualities that made them box-office attractions.

In "Tobacco Road," however, I could see that if one had never
been around this country, the play might be enlightening regarding
conditions that do exist in our own country. Perhaps there are
fortunate people who have never visited a state insane asylum and so
have no idea of the number and variety of people and circumstances
that make up the tremendous population not only in state asylums
but in private sanitariums all over this country.

There may be fortunate people who have never seen certain kinds
of sordid poverty. Perhaps they need to recognize types and the
results of such surroundings.

I am not sure, however, that a theater and an evening's so-called
entertainment is the proper place for this type of study.

"Streetcar" is a play that is well acted, but the people in it never seemed to become quite real. If they had, I think it would have become unbearable to suffer with them.

As it was, one looked at people who seemed somewhat far removed, and one felt one was examining something in a laboratory. I can understand that actors and actresses would consider this play a great opportunity for showing their abilities. There certainly is a sense of tension and of something crude and almost animal-like that seems to envelop the audience.

I did not feel, however, that I had gained anything when the evening was over. On the contrary, I felt a little soiled in my mind and quite ill, as though I would like to be rid of a mental and emotional experience and was not able to do it.

There is a certain kind of healthy vulgarity that one can endure, perhaps with some embarrassment but still with amusement. There are certain other types of artistic and emotional expression, however, that show degeneracy of the spirit with the individual and with the nation.

~ ~ ~

Probably never in the history of American oratory has someone whose style of speaking was so consistently criticized as shrill and off-putting been invited to address so many audiences on such a wide range of subjects as was Eleanor Roosevelt. Early in her public career she had even taken speaking lessons to help her bring the tone of her high-pitched voice down a bit. When she was invited to address a gathering of diplomats and the faculty of the Sorbonne by Dr. René Cassin, the noted French jurist who had been helping the UN Commission on Human Rights, Mrs. Roosevelt knew she was facing one of the most challenging tasks of her life. Not only would she have to speak in French, in which she was competent but not fluent, but also she would have to discuss the tense international situation.

It looked increasingly as though Stalin really would risk provoking a war to get his way with the Eastern European nations into which Soviet influence and control had spread. The Soviet blockade of Berlin was still fresh news. Mrs. Roosevelt consulted with Secretary of State

*Marshall and then prepared her speech. Joseph Lash says that though
her letters to friends show that she came to the speech "with a sense of
complete futility and hopelessness," outwardly "she was unruffled, her
gravity mixed with smiles." Durward Sandifer, Mrs. Roosevelt's
personal political adviser, commented in a letter to his wife, "Once she
got a big laugh when she interpolated that having raised a large
family she thought she was a master of patience, but she never really
knew what patience was until she came into contact with the Russians
in the Human Rights Commission."*

PARIS, OCTOBER 1—I must own up to the fact that speaking at the
Sorbonne seemed to me altogether too great an honor for a woman
who never even had earned a degree after four years' work in college.

I was nervous and apprehensive, but there is something in the
atmosphere of an old building like that and its beautiful hall that has
an invigorating effect on speakers. Of course, the French language
lends itself to oratory, and long before I spoke I was lost in the
admiration of the way this language provides the words to say things
that one would find it difficult to say in almost any other language.

~ ~ ~

*When confronted with the political and moral reality of apartheid
represented by the white government of South Africa, Eleanor Roosevelt's
hackles rose, and her instinct was to strike at least a rhetorical blow
for the equality of the races.*

PARIS, OCTOBER 9—One amendment, presented by the delegate for
the Union of South Africa, created a great effect upon a number of
the members of the committee. I immediately asked to speak, but
now I think it was fortunate—since there are many other amend-
ments yet to be presented—that the opportunity was not given to me
yesterday. I now realize I would have spoken with too much emotion
and perhaps not as objectively as the conditions called for.

As far as one can judge, the present government of the Union of
South Africa must live under a cloud of fear. I realize I do not know

the exact numbers of the white population, and perhaps if I did it might explain to me their basic philosophy as regards all peoples of color and even extends itself to the position of women.

The fundamental human rights and freedoms that the Union of South Africa is willing to accord all peoples do not include, I gather, any social rights and I doubt whether they include equal economic rights.

It was a strange speech, and when you looked around the table where 58 nations are represented you wondered how any nation could live in the world of today and hold such a philosophy.

It was rumored the other day that the Union of South Africa wishes to withdraw from the United Nations because of their difference in point of view. But I think if they make such a decision in the world of today, in which so much of their own population cannot even be drawn into the circle of social acquaintances, they will be standing still while the rest of the world moves forward in a spirit of fraternity and equality.

~   ~   ~

No publisher ever persuaded Eleanor Roosevelt to write her own version of what John F. Kennedy produced in his Profiles in Courage. *If she had written such a compendium of brief biographies of historical characters she most admired, many unsung women would no doubt have been given substantial attention. Mrs. Roosevelt often used her "My Day" column to spotlight relatively (or even completely) unknown women who had made important contributions to human affairs.*

PARIS, NOVEMBER 2—Last night I again met a woman who was an active organizer in the Resistance movement, and among her duties was the carrying of messages to the Channel to be taken to England. She always wore a German Red Cross uniform and got by for a time with only two German words, "ya" and "nein," by always pretending to be in a hurry. Her good luck didn't hold out too long, however, and she ultimately was imprisoned and tortured. Her nose was broken three times. Her back was scarred. Her hands were burned. Her face is covered with cigarette burns, which are hardly visible now unless you look closely, but she never gave up a secret.

One cannot hear these stories of heroism of the French women and not have a profound respect for the courage and patriotism that made them carry out dangerous missions day in and day out.

I also remember a little Dutch woman who wrote to me that she never opened the door during the war without wondering what might lie beyond it. And that is true of every occupied country. Yet the women lived their lives apparently attending to very humdrum jobs while weaving dangerous and difficult tasks into the pattern so successfully that they got by for weeks and months and even years.

~   ~   ~

The UN Human Rights Commission examined every facet of the human rights phenomenon. The aim was to produce the broadest acceptable declaration of human rights. Sometimes, however, issues were raised, that seemed beyond the Commission's scope. Whether the right to linguistic freedom, the right to education in the language of one's choice, should have been included has been debated many times. The movement for bilingual education (and bilingual printing of official government documents) in the United States, where Spanish is the predominant second language, and in Canada, where French dominates a whole province, is still very much alive. Eleanor Roosevelt took a somewhat jingoistic position on this one by advocating, at least implicitly, that when a foreigner comes to America, he or she ought to learn to speak "American," and that of course means English.

PARIS, NOVEMBER 30—We spent last Saturday morning discussing three new articles, proposed by Russia, Yugoslavia and Denmark. All three of them had to do with rights of minority groups. Denmark was concerned only about the rights of groups to have the language they preferred used in schools and the right to set up schools of their own if they wished. So far as I was concerned the point brought most clearly before us was the fact that this was not a subject on which a general article could be written for a universal declaration. All of the Americas' delegates declared that this problem did not exist with them because people who come to our shores do so because they want to become citizens of our countries. They leave behind certain economic, religious and social conditions that they wish to shed and prefer to be assimilated into the new country that they are adopting as their own. They are accepted by us with that understanding, and from our point of view we would like to see the committee recognize the fact that the European problem should be handled differently.

~ ~ ~

Occasionally Eleanor Roosevelt the tourist took over the "My Day" column from Eleanor Roosevelt the social commentator. When she spoke in her tourist voice, like most of us when we travel, she tossed off colorful observations and even some cultural judgments that may have had little basis in well-researched fact but nonetheless seemed true at the time. Mrs. Roosevelt's saving grace was a sense of humor and a sense of compassion about the quirks, inconveniences, and pretensions of every culture, no matter how modern or unsophisticated.

PARIS, DECEMBER 3—Anyone who is trying to travel anywhere by any conveyance during these days in Europe is completely upset by the weather. Even those of us who simply have to go from our hotel to our offices and committee meetings in the Palais de Chaillot find ourselves traveling around in a kind of dense fog that makes one wonder whether at night it will be possible to get home.

Planes are not flying; trains have accidents; automobiles go over embankments. Altogether, if one could be a person of leisure and stay at home it would be a pleasure. There might be one drawback to that, however. The houses over here are so cold that, in spite of having learned to wear warm clothes, no one enjoys sitting around indoors.

I was talking to someone the other day who had been over here working with the Quakers during the winter right after the war ended. She told me she had a little attic room with no heat and no hot

153

water. She worked out a way of getting a bath by going on different days to friends in different parts of town who had hot water for a few hours on certain days and permitted their friends to share it with them. She couldn't bear getting into her clothes in the morning after she left them lying on a chair during the night, so she evolved a method of taking them to bed with her and thus keeping them warm.

There are many apartments here that have no central heating, and the difficulty of getting coal and even wood for fireplaces makes is sometimes impossible even to have an open fire.

There is always a silver lining in every cloud, though, and those of us who are going back to the United States will appreciate more than we have in the past the comfort of a warm room. In the apartment in New York City where Miss Thompson and I spend an occasional night, we sometimes complain that we have too much heat. But I think both of us now feel we will be as quiet about that as we are about some of our other difficulties, which arise occasionally from the fact that we do not understand the way people live in Europe.

For instance, I dashed away from a meeting one day, hoping before lunch to visit a little shop where I was told they had attractive lingerie. But the door of the shop was firmly locked and a notice, in French, said: "Closed from 12 to 2 for lunch."

When I was talking to a Frenchman yesterday regarding the difference in the average woman's life here and the average woman's life in the U.S., he said, "Well, of course, our women regard a meal as something really important and a work of art, and they rarely take less than four hours to prepare it."

Then he added that when he was in the United States he saw how many American women, with the help of canned foods and mechanical devices, put a meal on the table in a very short time. But, he maintained, that is not the kind of a meal that French women would prepare or think sufficient, a remark that is completely truthful and which denotes real difference in the tempo of living in the U.S. and Europe.

The people take longer to enjoy life as they live it here, and I am not sure they may not get more out of if than we do at home. We

Eleanor Roosevelt's heart, soul and mind went into her Val-Kill Cottage at Hyde Park, New York, seen here from the front side. Built in 1926 as the shop for Val-Kill Industries, a furniture-making business Mrs. Roosevelt ran with two friends to help local young farmers expand their incomes, the house was remodeled in 1936 when the factory closed. It became an 18-room "country retreat" for entertaining countless guests and family. Following FDR's death, Val-Kill became Eleanor Roosevelt's permanent home. *(Photography by Michael Malone © Wappingers Falls, NY)*

In honor of the late President, the Navy commissioned an aircraft carrier the "U.S.S. Franklin D. Roosevelt" on October 27, 1945. The new President, Harry Truman, congratulated Mrs. Roosevelt, who spoke at the Brooklyn Navy Yard ceremonies on her family's behalf. *(UPI/Bettmann)*

When FDR died, expressions of loss and grief poured into Hyde Park—for Mrs. Roosevelt and her family, and for the United States—from all over the world. Seen here in April 1946 at the FDR Library, the former First Lady examines some of the several hundred foreign-language newspapers that had carried the story the year before. The exhibit was organized for the dedication of FDR's home as a National Historic Site. (UPI/Bettmann)

By the fall of 1946, Mrs. Roosevelt was deeply involved in her United Nations work. Her style of diplomacy placed a heavy emphasis on intimate, face-to-face communication, not only with allies but with difficult colleagues. The Soviet representatives, Vyacheslav Molotov (right) and Andrei Gromyko (center) wielded great power; but they met their match in Eleanor Roosevelt. *(UPI/ Bettmann)*

The initial delegation of the United States to the United Nations was as bipartisan as any that America would ever send there. In this 1946 photo, Mrs. Roosevelt huddles with John Foster Dulles (left), a conservative who, under Republican President Eisenhower, became a primary architect of U.S. foreign policy in the cold war; and with Adlai Stevenson (center), a liberal who twice ran unsuccessfully for President as a Democrat.

The Voice of America radio broadcasts took on increasingly strategic importance for foreign policy as the cold war heated up. Mrs. Roosevelt frequently gave short speeches for VOA, usually about the need for international cooperation in the war recovery program, on human rights, or about the perils of the arms race. Speaking in New York on April 12, 1947, Mrs. Roosevelt addresses the Russian people over a microphone that reads "Voice of the United States of America." *(UPI/Bettmann)*

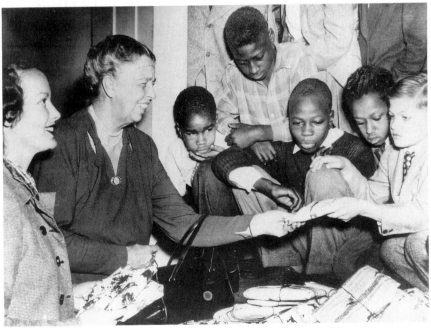

The Wiltwyck School for underprivileged boys, in the Catskill Mountains near Hyde Park, was one of Mrs. Roosevelt's favorite charitable projects. She held annual picnics at Val-Kill and a Christmas party at the school. Attending this party with her, in 1947, was Faye Emerson Roosevelt, son Elliott's third wife. *(UPI/Bettmann)*

A young, famous and hugely successful Frank Sinatra was Mrs. Roosevelt's dinner companion in Los Angeles on June 5, 1947 at a ceremony commemorating Jackson Day. FDR had already begun to pass into the realm of legend, as the miniature sculpture in the singer's hands suggests.

The film might well have been made even if Franklin Roosevelt had lived to see the end of WWII, but his death surely gave impetus for the creation of "The Roosevelt Story," a documentary about the man, his family and their accomplishments, which premiered in New York in August 1947. Mrs. Roosevelt attended with her son Elliott. *(UPI/Bettmann)*

Visiting London on United Nations business, Mrs. Roosevelt called on Winston Churchill. When this photo was taken in April 1948, Churchill was in between stints as Prime Minister. Mrs. Roosevelt's acquaintance with him had grown over the years from the many meetings and formal banquets he had attended as a guest of FDR at the White House and in numerous foreign capitals. *(Wide World)*

It was one of the greatest triumphs of her life even after a host of painful compromises: the United Nations "Universal Declaration of Human Rights." As Chairman of the UN Commission that drafted the document, all of Mrs. Roosevelt's diverse diplomatic skills were fully utilized, including her patience and good nature. At the UN temporary headquarters on Long Island, near New York, in November 1949, she studies a newspaper between committee meetings and savors her success. (Left: *Leo Rosenthal*) (Below: *United Nations*)

There was a seemingly endless string of testimonial dinners in Mrs. Roosevelt's behalf, though she often perceived such events as intended more to honor her deceased husband. In April 1949 she was feted in New York by the Bureau of Intercultural Education whose work she had long and vigorously supported. Enjoying her company is Bernard Baruch, the financier, statesman and New Deal advisor.

Biographer Joseph Lash portrays Mrs. Roosevelt's friendship with the considerably younger Dr. David Gurewitsch as an affair of the heart that began in the late 1940's and lasted until she died in 1962. They carried on an extensive, often intimate correspondence. Dr. Gurewitsch accompanied Mrs. Roosevelt on her trip to India in February 1952. (*Press Information Bureau, Government of India*)

Shy at first about appearing before television cameras, Mrs. Roosevelt plunged ahead in spite of herself, recognizing immediately the potential power of the medium. In February 1950 she initiated "Eleanor Roosevelt's Weekly Forum," a roundtable discussion of social and political issues. The first topic: "What to do with the Hydrogen Bomb?" (it had just been invented). Participants were (left to right): Senator Brian McMahon; Hans Bethe, scientist; Mrs. Roosevelt; David Lilienthal, Chairman, U.S. Atomic Energy Commission; and J. Robert Oppenheimer, former Director, Manhattan Project, which developed the first atomic bomb in 1945. *(Leonard McCombe, Life Magazine © Time, Inc.)*

(Right) From the time the idea of a United Nations organization was born in late 1945, the efforts to fund and construct a permanent world headquarters began. In October 1951, Mrs. Roosevelt inspected a scale model of the complex that was by then nearing completion nearby on a site, donated by John D. Rockefeller, on Manhattan's east side.

Her United Nations duties officially over, Mrs. Roosevelt took a round-the-world trip in the winter and spring of 1952. Visiting Israel in mid-February, she met with political and religious leaders, and is here shown inspecting sacred texts. *(FDR Library)*

Scandinavia had fascinated Mrs. Roosevelt for many years: she admired the way the cultures there blended traditional with modern crafts, and monarchy with democracy. In June 1950 she took her son, Elliott, two of his children, and her secretary, Malvina Thompson, on a Scandinavian tour that began in Norway, where an FDR statue was to be unveiled. The enthusiastic reception for Mrs. Roosevelt brought out children, flags and the Queen Mother. *(FDR Library)*

Mrs. Roosevelt's hands were famous for never being idle. Through the Depression and the war, she was often seen knitting sweaters for her grandchildren or for charity. She enjoyed needlepoint as well, and perhaps nowhere more than at her good friend Esther Lape's Greenwich, Connecticut home where she was a guest on many occasions. This photo was taken in July 1951. *(Sylvia Salmi)*

Though dwarfed here by the modernist architecture in the chamber of the United Nation's General Assembly in New York, Eleanor Roosevelt's prominence at the UN was incontestable. The occasion was "United Nations Day," October 24, 1952. Mrs. Roosevelt would soon move into (nearly) full-time volunteer work for the United Nations Association, a world-wide organization dedicated to educating people everywhere about the importance of the UN. *(United Nations)*

If ever there was a "First Dog" in the White House, the Roosevelt's Fala was it. For years after Mrs. Roosevelt left Washington, the public remained charmed by the famous scottie's adventures, frequently reported in "My Day." This family portrait, with Fala's late master, FDR, in the background, was taken at Val-Kill in December 1951. *(Margaret Suckley)*

Even after her years as First Lady were over, Mrs. Roosevelt was received as if she were royalty wherever she traveled. In New Delhi, in 1952, Prime Minister Nehru and his sister held a reception in her honor attended by Indian Cabinet ministers, military personnel and other top-ranking officials. (AP/Wide World)

In late February and March of 1952 Eleanor Roosevelt fulfilled a longtime wish by touring India and neighboring countries. She tried her hand at spinning wool in New Delhi, at the Haripan Colony for refugee women. (FDR Library)

There were thousands of photographs of Eleanor Roosevelt but only one truly successful painted portrait. Artist Douglas Chandor was commissioned by Mrs. Roosevelt's children in 1949 to capture not only her appearance but her spirit. That there were many sides to this complex and endlessly active woman is made permanently clear for posterity in his work. *(White House Historical Assoc.)*

seem always to be rushing to the next thing and not really getting the full flavor of enjoyment out of the thing we are doing.

~ ~ ~

Though the international political situation, with feelings growing raw between East and West, may have been discouraging to Mrs. Roosevelt, the purpose for which the United Nations had organized in the first place buoyed her up. Like most of her other Human Rights Commission colleagues, she was willing to work extraordinarily long hours on the draft declaration simply because they all believed it was so important. (We who live in a more cynical time may find it hard to comprehend that many serious and intelligent diplomats actually did think that a declaration and a covenant to follow—an enforceable political promise to obey the terms of the declaration—could change the political and legal behavior of nations, not to mention also change a nation's moral principles if need be.) Mrs. Roosevelt is good-humored here about the pressure she and her colleagues were under as the session sped toward its pre-Christmas adjournment, but her work was absolutely serious.

PARIS, DECEMBER 9—Before we left our meeting room at 6:45 last night, our chairman in Committee No. 3 told us that when we returned for the evening session to come prepared to stay until the work on the Declaration of Human Rights was finished. Our job was to arrange the articles in their proper sequence. We were warned the task would run far into the morning.

I dashed for home because I had invited Mr. and Mrs. Charles LaFollette and their daughter to have dinner with us, telling them I would have to leave at 8:15 to go back to work. They accepted that cheerfully, realizing that everyone who works with the General Assembly is now obliged to spend long hours every day and often many nights at meetings.

As I was leaving the committee room, a gentleman stopped me and said, "I am from the Army press and we are going to start a March of Dimes campaign about the fifteenth of January. Would

155

you just do a few minutes on the radio for us before you leave—a minute and a half would do it."

So I dashed off a minute-and-a-half speech in German, being sure it was correct and that I could speak it understandably. Then with unusual firmness I managed to say that from now on until I left I could not do one thing more. He then asked me if, when I got home in America, I would do a short speech for them there, too.

I had visions of accumulated mail, of telephones ringing, of someone asking me every minute to do something, of children arriving for Christmas and all the last-minute Christmas preparations, of a hurried trip to Washington perhaps to report to the President and Secretary of State and of radio shows to be done.

I looked at him for a moment hopelessly and said, "I doubt if, when I get home, up to January 15 I will have time to breathe. But if I have time I will try to do it for you." He was very flattering but instead of feeling flattered I found myself wishing that someone would occasionally realize there are only 24 hours in a day.

Just as I thought would happen at our evening session, we had to work until after 3 o'clock this morning.

When I handed my coat to the young check girl at 8:30 last night, I said, "Perhaps you had better show me where you put it in case you will have left when I am ready to go home."

"Oh, no," she replied. "When I know it is Committee No. 3 meeting I plan to stay all night. I sleep right here with the coats. It is the worst committee we have."

~　~　~

As the work on the human rights declaration came to a close, Mrs. Roosevelt contributed whatever she could to polish the statement. But as this sardonic comment shows, she couldn't always get what she wanted.

PARIS, DECEMBER 10—I would have been delighted to see in the preamble a paragraph alluding to the Supreme Power. I knew very well, however, there were many men around the table who would violently be opposed to naming God, and I did not want it put to a [roll call] because I thought for those of us who are Christians it would be rather difficult to have God defeated in a vote.

~ ~ ~

Going home for Christmas was a great relief for Eleanor Roosevelt. Dozens of family members would gather, as they did every year, at Hyde Park for the holiday—a cheerful prospect. Yet this did not keep Mrs. Roosevelt from reflecting seriously on the domestic, everyday lives of the French people who had been her hosts in Paris during the UN session. By way of comparison, of course, she knew that life for the average person in America was better in many respects, or at least easier. The point was not to pass judgments, however; rather it was to show her readers what the lingering effects of war really are, even in a country as resilient and sophisticated as France. The final point this column makes about the psychological consequences for France of having been for several years a conquered nation would be food for thought, no doubt Mrs. Roosevelt believed, for complacent Americans who might be losing patience with the demands of the European recovery program.

EN ROUTE TO NEW YORK, DECEMBER 13—The day has come to leave and I have been trying to add up my final impressions of France.

The French people are badly off. If you walk around on a Sunday or watch them going down into the Metro you very quickly realize that most of the people you see look tired and listless. This undoubtedly comes from lack of energy-giving foods, with little sugar or chocolate or butter available. There is no milk for older people. They do have a milk ration for babies and children and that is one reason, I think, why the youngsters look fairly well. But the older people uniformly look badly.

The French have done their best to receive their guests with warmth and with their customary hospitality. When we have gone to their apartments they tried to warm them up for us and to give us all kinds of food in the lavish ways of days gone by. Only now and then by a casual sentence do you realize what they have gone through. One woman said to me as we waited for the absurd little elevator that graces the stairwells in all large French apartment houses, "It is wonderful to have the lift running again. All these flights of stairs when you carried home your potatoes and vegetables from market— that was really hard. The sacks of potatoes are heavy." Electricity is still rationed and often cut off for hours.

France is not moribund. It is just very tired and it cannot revive until the physical body has been somewhat built up. One must eat. Particularly the French people must eat, because to them it is also a necessary ritual. No businessman or woman here dashes hastily into a corner drug store and gets a sandwich and a cup of coffee for lunch. That would be a sacrilege. The French go home and sit down with their families to a complete meal. They may lose a couple of hours away from business by doing it, but they are no worse off than other businesspeople because everyone does the same thing.

France, too, was conquered. One woman, speaking of what she had been through, said she had seen the French army routed, with officers picking up their wives and children and fleeing through Paris to any place where they might find temporary safety. She said rather sadly, "It takes a long time to restore the soul of a conquered country. You are free, but you know that you have been beaten. You cringe because you have known the conqueror's touch."

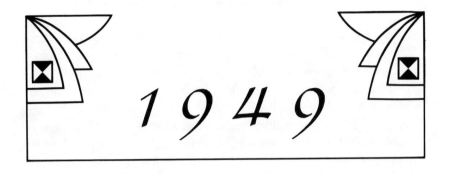

1949

$\mathcal{E}$leanor Roosevelt and many in the liberal camp, including Harry Truman, believed that the New Deal had set in motion an irreversible tide of social change in America that would once and for all bring justice and at least a minimum of prosperity to all the people. The war was seen by many as a tragic interruption in the flow of this tide of social change, but no more than an interruption. As the country settled into more normal peacetime routines, both the White House and the Congress could turn their attention more frequently to domestic, rather than foreign, affairs.

In January 1949, when Truman was inaugurated to serve a full term as an elected President, he thought he would have a better-than-ever chance to secure passage of several major legislative initiatives aimed at assuring a Fair Deal to a broader cross section of Americans. But with a Congress now heavily dominated by Republicans and conservative Southern Democrats, and lacking the political savoir faire required to garner essential votes among the legislators, Truman ended up with only a few of his key ideas being put into law. His frustration was often shared by Mrs. Roosevelt, although she was not hesitant to criticize even the President if she thought his plans were off base.

The Supreme Court led off the year with a ruling that allowed states to ban the closed shop, thus giving nonunion labor a boost. The liberal cause moved a step forward when Sam Rayburn of Texas became Speaker of the House, a post he would hold for decades. The Justice Department successfully pressed an antitrust suit against AT&T that required the manufacturing component of the giant communications company, Western Electric, to separate from its parent. The President's proposal for compulsory national health insurance continued to meet stiff resistance from the AMA, which favored a voluntary plan. Mrs. Roosevelt was less concerned about which of several proposals for national health insurance might be adopted by the Congress than she was that something be done quickly for the benefit of all Americans. She underestimated not only the strength of the AMA lobby, but the fear many Americans had developed since the war of broad, government-financed programs for social welfare such as those that characterized the New Deal.

Labor was still rambunctious; several strikes interrupted the flow of the economy but won for the workers better wages and working conditions. John L. Lewis ordered the soft-coal miners to stop work for two weeks to protest the administration's appointee, Dr. James Boyd, to the post of director of the Federal Bureau of Mines. In October 500,000 steelworkers struck for higher wages and eventually got them. Later that month the Congress raised the minimum wage from forty to seventy-five cents per hour.

One central part of Truman's Fair Deal did pass Congress in the form of the Housing Act, aimed at alleviating the critical postwar housing shortage. Ever since the end of the war, Mrs. Roosevelt had urged the Congress to appropriate more funds for inexpensive family dwellings. She received many letters from middle- and lower-class Americans, often veterans or their wives, concerning the severe shortage of affordable housing.

Secretary of State Marshall, architect of the Marshall Plan for postwar European recovery, resigned in January and Dean Acheson took the post. The Department of Defense was created in 1949, replacing the War Department. It was a year of both hopeful and frightening military events. The United States sent a missile higher than ever before (250 miles). Twelve nations signed the North Atlantic Treaty, a mutual defense pact that laid the groundwork for NATO. Mrs. Roosevelt saw this as a positive development. The U.S.-occupied zone of Germany was merged with those occupied by Great Britain and France, and on May 21 the Federal Republic of Germany was born. That month the Soviets lifted their blockade of Berlin. In late June, gambling that stability in Korea could be maintained without an American military presence, U.S. troops ended their postwar occupation of South Korea. When in October the Communist government on mainland China sought international recognition, the Truman White House refused despite the quick recognition extended to Mao Tse-tung's new government by Britain and France. The President and many in Congress were anxious about the growing worldwide strength of Communism, especially in the military sphere. In September 1949 the Soviets had achieved a breakthrough, detonating their own atomic bomb for the first time. Eleanor Roosevelt implored both nations—the U.S. and the USSR— to avoid an arms race, but her arguments were to no avail. Now America was not the only country with the dreaded atomic weapon, and the balance of power began shifting seriously again.

Mrs. Roosevelt's diverse reading habits included little if anything by the quiet Southern gentleman William Faulkner, of Mississippi, whose work was awarded the Nobel Prize for Literature in 1949. No doubt the proudest and most encouraging note of the entire year for Eleanor Roosevelt was the dedication, on the East Side of Manhattan Island, of the United Nation's new permanent headquarters. She would spend countless hours there in the years to come.

~　~　~

In one of the great understatements in the history of American politics, Mrs. Roosevelt reported her own estimation of her contribution to the Democratic Party in this brief passage in a "My Day" column. Caroline O'Day was a leader in the women's division of the New York Democratic State Committee.

HYDE PARK, FEBRUARY 3—I had what was to me an amusing request today to fill out my biography for "Who's Who in Democratic Politics." It would be a little difficult to answer the questions since I hold no Democratic office and even during the very short term which I spent in Civillian Defense I was hardly working as a Democrat. All I could say was "Widow of Franklin D. Roosevelt" and for many years

161

servant of the party in domestic affairs, as well as in a few minor voluntary jobs, such as assisting Mrs. Daniel O'Day in New York State."

~ ~ ~

Eleanor Roosevelt liked books that offered some kind of moral lesson. And she liked playing the role of prophet, the one who points out to the people that important lessons of the past have been forgotten and need to be relearned. Having lived through two horrendously destructive world wars, she was determined not to let the American public's desire for peacetime normalcy rub out its useful memory of the hell that war really is. Thus her enthusiasm for one of the more popular books of the time, World War II hero Audie Murphy's To Hell and Back. *Murphy was one of America's most decorated soldiers, with more than twenty-five separate medals, including the Congressional Medal of Honor and awards from Britain and France.*

HYDE PARK, MARCH 19—I have just finished a book which was given me when I was on the West Coast. It is called "To Hell and Back" by Audie Murphy. He had a remarkable record in World War II and holds perhaps as many decorations as it is possible for one soldier to accumulate. He has received 21 medals, including our highest military decoration, the Congressional Medal of Honor. He wanted to write this book, he says, so that we in the United States would not forget what war really means to the men who fought it. The unforgettable chapter, I think, is the last one, in which he tells of his reactions.

Some of the word pictures are ugly, some of the scenes he may never be able to forget and those who read them should not forget them either, but it is the last paragraphs in the book I want especially to remember. When Mr. Murphy was young he was told that men were branded by war. Now, with the war at an end, he thinks of all those who will never come back and wonders what he himself will do.

"My country. America! That is it. We have been so intent on

death we have forgotten life. And now suddenly life faces us. I swear to myself that I will measure up to it. I may be branded by war, but I will not be defeated by it.

"Gradually it becomes clear. I will go back. I will find the kind of girl of whom I once dreamed. I will learn to look at life through uncynical eyes, to have faith, to know love. I will learn to work in peace as in war. And finally—finally, like countless others, I will learn to live again."

Everyone of us in this country should remember that this is what many men who fought the war are now trying to do. One of our jobs is to help them to do it and, above all, to help them build a peaceful world so that other men will not have to face, first, a war and then the return to living.

~ ~ ~

Eleanor Roosevelt's father, Elliott, brother of President Theodore Roosevelt, died in 1894 when his daughter was just ten. But by then he had left an indelible impression on her, for both good and ill. They adored one another, and he called her "Little Nell." Sadly, Elliott had a debilitaing drinking problem and was sent away to Virginia— beyond the reach of easy communication. Though young Eleanor never knew why her father had gone, it was his alcoholism that took him away, a fact she later understood. Small wonder then that, although Mrs. Roosevelt was never a teetotaler herself and always had some skepticism about the Eighteenth Amendment and the Volstead Act, she was an enthusiastic supporter of any sensible programs addressing themselves to treatment of the disease.

HYDE PARK, APRIL 18—My attention was attracted the other day by newspaper stories which stated that, in the forthcoming national campaign to raise funds for the National Committee for Education on Alcoholism, one of the principal places where the boxes would appear to collect people's nickels and dimes would be in bars and other places where liquor could be bought. Impressed by this strange fact, I talked today to the vice president and executive director of the organization, Mrs. Marty Mann.

This group, she told me, was a division of the Yale Plan on Alcoholism. Dr. E. N. Jellinek, of Yale University, has stated that there are an estimated 4,000,000 alcoholics in the United States, 750,000 of whom are in the final stages of the disease. Dr. Jellinek emphasizes that it is a disease, not something which the individual can control by using his willpower. Any man or woman who can take one or two drinks and stop, even if occasionally they drink more than is good for them, is not an alcoholic—any more than the person who drinks regularly and steadily, but moderately. The distinguishing mark of an alcoholic is that, once he takes a drink, he cannot stop until he is too drunk to drink any more.

This disease is somewhat like any other allergy. A diabetic cannot eat certain things. An alcoholic is poisoned by alcohol. He knows it, and yet he can do nothing about it. Nobody thinks of urging on a diabetic the food he should not eat. Yet many of his friends will urge just one drink on an alcoholic, when just one drink is his undoing.

This national committee feels that Alcoholics Anonymous has done a wonderful piece of work, but that they cannot do the job alone. Too many people must be reached, and so the national committee is establishing clinics from coast to coast to educate the average citizen in the real nature and treatment of this disease. These committees establish information centers for guidance for alcoholics and their families; clinics for diagnosis and outpatient treatment; moderate-priced rest centers for patients requiring long-term care; and they obtain beds in local hospitals for acute sufferers.

One would naturally ask if this organization is a part of the movement against all use of alcoholic stimulants. Their answer is that they are neither wet nor dry. They believe simply in dealing scientifically with a disease. If you can't take alcohol, you stop taking it. If you can take it moderately, you are not a medical case.

The great majority of alcoholics are between the ages of 30 and 55, and five out of six are men. From the point of view of the nation this is important, because alcoholics create a public health problem and they cost the community money. The economist Benson Y. Landis estimates the annual loss of wages through this disease amounts to $432,000,000, and health authorities rank alcoholism with cancer, heart and venereal disease as a public health menace.

~ ~ ~

There is a certain poignancy in the "My Day" columns dealing with difficult social problems which remain largely unsolved forty years later. The fact that, despite the progress toward better standards of living experienced by the middle and upper classes, Americans in the lower socioeconomic class have made small advancement if any is discouraging at best. Such is the case concerning the problem of severe poverty in the slums of Washington, D.C., which Mrs. Roosevelt writes about in this column—poverty in the city's back alleys, virtually in view of congressional offices. With only minor changes in the text, this column could very well be run again in the newspapers of the late twentieth century.

NEW YORK, APRIL 22—I hope that the recent excursion of a few Senators into the old and ancient alleys near the Capitol in Washington will have a more lasting effect than previous excursions have had.

When I first went to Washington in 1933, Mrs. Archibald Hopkins, who had worked to remove these alleys from the Washington scene ever since Woodrow Wilson was President, came to get me one day and insisted that we drive through many of them. Being a New Yorker, I was impressed at first by the fact that at least here the buildings were not so high and there was a chance for a little sun and air to permeate the filth and squalor. But I soon learned just how bad these alleys were. What crime was bred there, what disease spread from there and what seeds of delinquency were sown in those alley slums.

The question has never been decided whether a human being acquires more characteristics through heredity or through environment. Nevertheless I am quite sure that human beings who live in the Washington slums are conditioned to a great extent by their environment.

The greater number of people living in the slums of Washington are Negroes. There is always a housing shortage for them; they are always being crowded into houses which have been condemned and should be torn down. It is hard to believe, but most of Washington's slums have only outdoor sanitation and sometimes the only running water available is a faucet in the yard.

From these overcrowded rooms servants go out to work in comfortable houses. Children are cared for by women whose children go to segregated schools. Poor food and poor housing make these children a prey to many diseases and as they pass through the streets, or as their elders care for them at home and then go into other homes to work, the diseases may spread.

I only hope that the things the Senators saw will stay more lastingly in their minds than the impressions which I have seen congressional groups gather before.

~ ~ ~

A great theater critic Eleanor Roosevelt was not. She sometimes seemed to miss at least part of the point about plays that have become standouts of American drama. Here, in a mixed positive and negative commentary on Arthur Miller's Death of a Salesman, *Mrs. Roosevelt brings her personal taste, favoring strictly realistic drama, to bear on a play that works only if we suspend our disbelief and accept the theater's capacity to interweave reality and fantasy, conscious and unconscious thought. Mrs. Roosevelt also had trouble swallowing the implicit indictment of middle-class life in capitalist society that* Death of a Salesman *delivers. She was too much of a resolute believer in the basic soundness of the American economy and the worthiness of the American worker to accept the play's negative view, even as a pretext for the drama. Having been all of her own adult life a stalwart mother and wife, it should be no surprise that she identified with the mother in the play.*

Death of a Salesman *was a smash box-office success, garnering both the Pulitzer Prize and the Drama Critics' Circle Award. It had an unusually long Broadway run for a deeply serious play, from February 11, 1949, through the end of 1950.*

NEW YORK, APRIL 28—Monday night I saw the much-advertised play "Death of a Salesman." It is certainly a remarkable production. The imagination shown in the scenery and in the directing is extraordinary and no one could want better acting than Lee J. Cobb brings to the portrayal of Willy Loman, the unsuccessful salesman. The rest of the cast also was excellent.

Yet I remained untouched and somewhat critically aloof. One does not hear voices at one moment and talk sensibly to the son of one's old employer a little later on. Surely, there are dreamers and there are totally untruthful people in the world, people who are untruthful with themselves, with their families and with the world as a whole. They fail everyone, including themselves, but I don't know whether one really needs a whole evening of gloom to impress that truth upon one.

There are many touches of reality in the play and, as a theatrical performance, it is something to see. But I would not choose it either as entertainment or for its moral lesson. That lesson, in more realistic style, you can find in many an American community. I think I like it better when it points to the fact that a man, if finally brought to face the truth, can pick himself up and create a different ending.

Is this supposed to be the typical American salesman? If so, I don't think it is typical. The mother was the only person who might have given some redeeming features to the boys, but even that ray of hope was not very clearly indicated. If you go to see this play, be sure you don't happen to be in a gloomy mood. If you are you will come out even gloomier than when you went in.

~ ~ ~

Eleanor Roosevelt's uncle Theodore made The White House *the official name for the President's House when he had the phrase engraved on his stationery during his residence there, although it had been so called even before British troops put it to the torch in 1814. The executive office was added in 1902, during the first Roosevelt's administration, and the east wing while FDR and his wife lived there, in 1942. In 1949 President and Mrs. Harry Truman moved to Blair House across Lafayette Square during a necessary extensive structural renovation in the course of which a steel supporting frame was built inside the venerable walls. Eleanor Roosevelt, who had lived in the executive mansion longer than any other First Lady, had some thoughts on the importance of the job and how it ought to be done.*

NEW YORK, MAY 18—I feel very strongly that, as far as it is humanly possible, the outer shell [of the White House] should be preserved. The repairs certainly should be made, but in such a way that the house should be reconstituted as nearly as possible as it has been since George Washington planned it. No new design or new house could possibly have the historic interest of this old one. The original plans were approved by George Washington and every one of our Presidents from John Adams has lived there. In spite of the fact that it was gutted by fire when the City of Washington was burned during the war of 1812, the walls stood up well and the Executive Mansion was rebuilt.

One gets a feeling for the history of one's country as one sees where Andrew Jackson kept his cows; as one looks out of the same window that Abraham Lincoln looked out of during the Civil War when he watched the retreat from Bull Run. There is an atmosphere in that old house that could not be recaptured by any modern building.

Everyone who lives in it feels it.

The President told me that he had had the woodwork, fireplaces, mirrors and chandeliers all carefully stored away and he had even had plaster casts made of the ceilings since they are among the greatest beauties of the house. There is a dignity and a simplicity about the White House that many foreigners, coming here, comment upon and which give to many of our own people who visit it a sense of pride It seems to express the spirit of American democracy.

We are a proud people, conscious of our greatness, and yet our traditions of simplicity are important to us. We want dignity but no false pomp and show. I think it invaluable to preserve traditions, whether they exist in buildings, in customs or in the things of the spirit. They are the heritage which years of history bring to a nation and they should not be lightly thrown away.

~ ~ ~

Mrs. Roosevelt says in this column that she "lived an entirely lonely life" in childhood days at her grandmother's house in Tivoli, New York. Diphtheria had killed Anna Roosevelt (Eleanor's mother) when the girl was just eight; her alcoholic father had been moved to Virginia, without her, before she was ten. It is to Eleanor Roosevelt's credit that, entitled to some bitterness about the early loss of her parents, she can still rescue as many good memories as she does from that lonely time.

NEW YORK, MAY 24—The Hyde Park Historical Association placed its first historical marker in Hyde Park Sunday afternoon. The inscription was written by Claude Bowers and placed on what was once the house belonging to Colonel and Mrs. Archibald Rogers. It is now the home of the Roosevelt School.

Since in the annals of my husband's childhood it is written that he used to have lessons in this house with the Rogers children, the Historical Association wished to place their first marker here.

I had not been in the house since it had been turned into a school. I remembered it very well in the old days when we were all children and it was often the center for young people's parties. Dances during the Christmas holidays; coasting and skating, with tea or supper at this hospitable home; and, when we were even smaller, dancing classes all through the autumn weeks, which drew children all the way from Hudson on the north and Fishkill in the south, were only some of the activities we enjoyed. Those were not the days of automobiles. We took a train down from Tivoli, where I lived with my grandmother, had our lessons and our supper and then were driven to the station and took a train home, arriving at what for us was a very late hour after another drive of five miles by horse and cart.

I was usually shy and frightened because I lived an entirely lonely life, with few children of my own age nearby. I had no ear for music and therefore danced extremely badly! My father sang well, loved music and had a real sense of rhythm. My mother played the piano and danced well. Something was certainly left out of me—at least at that early age—and what little appreciation of music I since have acquired has been acquired with toil and effort and was certainly not a gift of the gods!

Senator Estes Kefauver flew up from Washington to speak at this small meeting, which brought together the members of the Historical Association, the children of the school and their parents. Afterward I took the Senator over to see our old house and the library, but it was a hurried visit and he had to be on his way back to Washington.

$$\sim \quad \sim \quad \sim$$

A capacity for honest self-effacement was one of Eleanor Roosevelt's strong suits, and sometimes she could do it with real humor as well. The idea of appearing on television wasn't new just to Mrs. Roosevelt in 1949: it was new to almost everyone. As a medium suitable for news documentaries, television was still in its infancy. According to Eleanor Roosevelt, it took more than a little getting used to for all except the most natural of stage performers. She often had high praise for her daughter-in-law, Faye Emerson Roosevelt (wife of Elliott), of whom she was fond, but their relationship was not to last. Faye divorced Elliott in September of this year.

HYDE PARK, JUNE 27—Friday afternoon, before leaving the city, I went to see two television shows previously done by CBS for the Human Rights educational program. The UN is going to have the privilege of using these as far afield as they can obtain distribution.

Needless to say, I never am happy when I am in a television show! In the first place, I cannot remember that I am being photographed every minute and I do such stupid things as lick my lips when they get dry, which makes you look exactly as though you were sticking your tongue out at someone.

Perhaps with greater experience I will do a little better, but meanwhile I envy all those who appeared with me—they seemed to achieve so much better television manners than I did. My admiration for my daughter-in-law Faye, who does these television appearances regularly, rises every time I go on. The lights are hot and, on the whole, I think the results are none too happy for me—but for Faye they seem to be marvelous, and that is because she is really a good actress.

~   ~   ~

The Roosevelt family tree is actually more like a small forest of names. Claes Martenszen van Rosenvelt arrived in the 1640s in New Amsterdam (which became New York City and its Hudson River environs when the English took over). By the early 1700s the Roosevelts had divided into the forerunners of the two family lines most Americans know today: the Oyster Bay (Long Island) group, which produced President Theodore Roosevelt and his niece Eleanor; and the Hyde Park group, which produced President Franklin Delano Roosevelt. In the seventeenth century the Dutch patroons were granted huge estates in the Hudson River Valley. Property still in the family belonging to Sara Delano Roosevelt (FDR's mother) had been passed down from these early European settlers' estates. Thus the stamp of the Roosevelt family tradition was visible all up and down the Hudson Valley, and Eleanor Roosevelt took great pleasure in educating her children and grandchildren about their lineage.

HYDE PARK, JULY 6—Our family custom, since we are not very much given to letting our children celebrate the Fourth of July in good old-fashioned style, is to have a big picnic. So we decided yesterday, with a group of our neighbors, to go up to the place where I lived as a child, which belonged to my Grandmother Hall, and show it to the grandchildren. The house is practically falling down,

171

but the trees are finer and the view of the Catskill Mountains is as beautiful as ever.

It has gone out of the family now, since my aunt, Mrs. David Gray, sold it, and I believe since then it has been sold a number of times. No one is living there, so we disturbed no one. We stopped at the gatehouse and asked whether the road was passable and whether we would be bothering anyone if we picnicked there and were careful to leave it all tidy when we left.

All of which we did, and on the way down I thought it would interest the family to drive in and call on our cousin, Mrs. John Henry Livingston, who lives in the old Clermont house which belonged to Chancellor Livingston. Fortunately, we met her on the road, and she turned back and was kind enough to invite us in and show us the old family portraits and the interesting things in the house. There is one portrait of the early West showing Phillips Livingston and there are portraits of the First, Second and Third Lords of the Manor. They were granted 14 miles of riverfront and an acreage back of the river which spread far into what must be now Massachusetts and Connecticut.

The house was burned by the British in 1776 in the Revolutionary War and there is an old tree that for years, when I was a child, we were shown because you could see a cannonball imbedded in it. The present house was rebuilt immediately along the lines of the old house and has stood ever since, with the addition, in 1830, of one large room.

Driving home we followed as many of the old and unfrequented roads as I could remember, going past Bard College and the old Chandler place and going in to see Mrs. Lyman Delano. I could not help thinking that in many ways her old house at "Steen Valetje," in spite of being built in the Victorian era, has more real charm and sense of being a house where people have lived and really understood and loved their possessions than some houses where you have a feeling that a perfectly impersonal decorator was called in to hang the curtains and lay the rugs and choose and place the furniture. I am not very sure sometimes that the owners even choose the books and the piano. That kind of house never gives me a sense of being really representative of the personality of the people who live in it and without some feeling left by various generations a house remains a shell and never becomes a home.

The finishing touch to a pleasant day was that it began to rain as we were coming home, and we had a fairly pleasant, cooling shower. Our skies are still gray and we pray that more rain is going to pour gently down upon the parched earth, which needs it so badly in this part of the country.

~ ~ ~

The fierce competition of political interest groups was something Eleanor Roosevelt wrestled with throughout her entire public life. She took it as a matter of course that expressing her opinion was her civic duty. Inevitably following from that assumption was the sure knowledge that criticism would come flowing in from some quarter, no matter how reasonable or balanced her statements had been. On the issue of public aid to education, the 1940s and 1950s were the era of finding our way. What the country takes for granted a generation later in relying on massive amounts of federal aid to public education was then largely a new concept. Mrs. Roosevelt's predilection for viewing the United States as an essentially Judeo-Christian nation is clear in this column, but she offers a good dose of ecumenism as well. Her work in the United Nations was a broadening experience.

HYDE PARK, JULY 15—I am still getting letters from a few people who seem to think that in opposing aid from the taxpayers' money to any but public schools, I must have a particular bias against the Catholic Church. This must be because their parochial schools are more numerous than the schools of any other denomination.

I hate to continue an argument that many people think is based on prejudice, but something was written in a letter to me that seems worth mentioning.

A gentleman writes that the Barden bill was a discriminatory bill against the Negroes in the South. I have not read the bill carefully, and I have been rather careful not to say if I am for or against any particular bill or bills. As a matter of fact, I have not gone into the details of any bills.

I believe in federal aid to public education and I think it should be particularly valuable to the states of the South that do not have the income to spend as much per capita on all children, white and Negro, as should be spent. I believe that all children should have an equal opportunity for education in whatever community they live, and this holds good for the whole of the United States.

Another lady writes that I am against the Constitution, since I would deny religious education in the public schools. I did state that I thought religious education was valuable to every child, but it could not be given in the school alone. The home and the church must co-operate.

This is no real reason why every school should not teach every child that one of the important aspects of our life is its spiritual side. It might be possible to devise a prayer that all the denominations could say and it certainly ought to be possible to read certain verses from the Bible every day. It probably would do children no harm to learn to know some of the writings of other great religious leaders who have led other great religious movements.

~ ~ ~

The best entertainment for Eleanor Roosevelt was always the antics of children, her own or anyone else's. Many of the most charming and self-revealing of the "My Day" columns show Mrs. Roosevelt in her mother and grandmother role. During the summer holidays at Hyde Park and on Campobello Island she often became materfamilias to an extended family of visiting nieces, nephews, and their assorted friends. It was a family dominated by boys, and almost all of them, whether small or grown-up, were rather strong-willed. She liked poking fun at male habits of competition and scrappiness.

And the summer was a time for reflections about her own childhood pleasures, as we see in a column about her camping forays into the Adirondacks. Anyone who visits Mrs. Roosevelt's house at Hyde Park and sees the sleeping porch referred to here, with its wraparound multipane windows, will recognize immediately what a delight it must have been on a moonlit night.

HYDE PARK, AUGUST 1—When all of the New York papers put on their front pages a record of the weather, it is important news. I was brought up in an era when one was not supposed to notice temperatures. If it was hot, you were hot—and that was that. If it was cold and you were cold, that was that, and no complaints were allowed on such minor discomforts.

My grandchildren and three grandnephews spend most of their day in the water and seem to bear up well no matter what the temperature. When I was young there was some foolish apprehension as to the effect of bathing too long at a time. It doesn't seem to do anything harmful to the children of today, and they certainly seem more comfortable. Nowadays, too, we all dress more comfortably. I used to wear long black stockings and high-laced shoes. Today most of the children go barefoot. If they are really going to dress up, they put on sneakers.

Elliott bought cowboy boots for two of the small boys, aged five and seven, because they admired those worn by the children from Texas. In spite of the heat during the last two days, they have worn these boots incessantly. The youngest one, aged almost three, whom we thought too young to want cowboy boots, has insisted on wearing his rubber boots to show that he, too, had boots. Such is male vanity!

HYDE PARK, AUGUST 13—I am not sure that camping out isn't often the most delightful way to live. I know very well that when things go wrong in our modern houses—for instance, if the electricity goes off or we forget to stock up on gas for the kitchen range or my water pump ceases to function—then I really feel that to live in the country with so many things that have to be looked after is a nuisance.

I wish, at such times, that I was back in the Adirondack camp I used to stay in many years ago when we cooked on an outside fireplace and fetched our supplies in a canoe when the lake was smooth enough to cross it. We slept under a lean-to with a blanket

175

spread over pine boughs and had a dancing fire to watch as we dropped off to sleep.

The moon has been shining down on me these last few nights out on my sleeping porch.

It is a glorious full moon and if there is any truth in the old wives' tale about people being moonstruck if they sleep in the moonlight, my two little dogs and I certainly should be moonstruck.

The only effect that I have discovered, however, is that the brightness wakes me up and I lie and drink in the beauty of the night. Then I look over and see two pairs of bright little eyes and two pairs of ears cocked up watching me, as if saying, "What are you awake for? Do you notice something we don't? What's going on anyway?"

And then we all go to sleep again.

~ ~ ~

Herbert Hoover had been swept out of the White House in 1932 by FDR's promise of a New Deal that would put the economy back on its feet and guarantee a minimum of financial security to the common man. It took eight years in the White House to accomplish even a portion of the goals the President and his first cabinet laid out for themselves during the famous initial hundred days. Many of those, generally on the conservative side, who argued before FDR came along that government ought not to take on financial responsibility for the working man were still pressing that argument long after the New Deal was officially installed by legislation in such institutions as Social Security and Unemployment Compensation. Herbert Hoover was one of them. Mrs. Roosevelt had carried the banner of the New Deal as robustly as anyone, and she was not too tired of defending it to respond to the former President's criticism yet again.

HYDE PARK, AUGUST 15—Ex-President Herbert Hoover on his birthday announced that he thought we in this country were on the "last mile" to collectivism. President Truman, when asked to comment on that statement, smiled and said he thought perhaps it was a slight exaggeration. The really important thing for us to think about, of course, is whether as individuals we are actually not taking our full responsibility—whether we are letting other people decide too many things for us and are turning over to government things that we should do ourselves.

One newspaper, in discussing Mr. Hoover's statement, cited Social Security as a good example, arguing that in the old days children would have been responsible for their parents, with individual or group charities being responsible for many of the things done under Social Security. Strangely enough, the newspaper did not mention the fact that in the old days the individuals themselves would have been putting away money for their old age—and, as far as the present plan is concerned, that is actually what they are doing. The present plan is more secure because today the government receives their money and is back of it; and as long as the government is stable, they are sure of their old age insurance. They will not go through the tragedy of putting their money in a sock and then losing the sock or having it stolen, or of putting it in a bank run by individuals whose bad judgment sometimes made the bank fail.

I do not think we have really changed the basic obligations in this case. We have simply made it a responsibility of government and thereby a little more secure for the individual. The same thing can be said in answer to the question of whether the blind and the handicapped should be taken care of under Social Security or by private charity. If it is well done through government, as it should be, we are more secure and the cost to the individual is no greater than when he had to do it through private charities.

~ ~ ~

In a marvelously articulate and well-argued column, Mrs. Roosevelt took up the cause of freedom of speech and at the same time managed to criticize the Communist ideology and American intolerance for black people. Few writers of her generation, or any other, could walk a philosophical tightrope with as much finesse.

Paul Robeson was the son of a slave. Recognized when young as unusually bright, he was admitted to Princeton University, where he became an all-American football star in 1917–1918. While the sports world had lionized him, the profession he chose—the law—had no place for him even after a highly successful law school preparation. Embittered, his political thinking shifted far to the left and his interest in Soviet-style Communism grew strong enough eventually to draw him and his family to Moscow and a new life there. Robeson had meanwhile become a widely admired actor and concert singer in America during the 1920s and 1930s, with starring roles in several major plays and musicals—The Emperor Jones, Show Boat, The Hairy Ape, Porgy (the original play, later to become the opera and film, Porgy and Bess), Othello—and several concert tours in Europe and one in Russia (1936). When the war came he returned to the United States and often mixed political monologues with his concert programs.

HYDE PARK, SEPTEMBER 3—A great deal of feeling has been aroused by the riots that took place in Peekskill, New York, at a meeting sponsored by the Civil Liberties Union. I, myself, cannot understand why anyone goes to a meeting at which Paul Robeson is going to speak unless they are in sympathy with what he is going to say, since by this time everyone must be familiar with his thinking. I have been told that what I once experienced, namely, seeing him turn his concert into a medium for Communist propaganda, is his constant practice, so whoever goes to hear him must know what to expect. They might well want to hear him sing, in spite of knowing that he would sing certain songs that they might not like, or at some point, talk in a way with which they might not agree. If so, in this country, it is their privilege to go to hear him and leave. I think if we care for the preservation of our liberties we must allow all people, whether we disagree with them or not, to hold meetings and express their views unmolested as long as they do not advocate the overthrow of our Government by force.

It seems to me that peaceful picketing of such a meeting is also an unwise gesture. I can well understand why veterans want to show their displeasure, but I think there are other ways of doing it. They can hold a meeting and see to it that their speakers are as well reported as those at any other meeting. They can see that the press carries refutation of whatever arguments are given at any meeting with which they disagree, but I do not think they need fear that the average American is an easy prey to the Paul Robeson type of propaganda.

I believe the average American should realize that rioting and lawlessness—even when we can prove that they were, as some people are trying to prove in this case, incited by some Communists—are still not good propaganda for democracy in the world.

We in the United States should, I think, make it very clear that we disagree with and disapprove of many views of Paul Robeson, but it is well also for us to remember that Paul Robeson left this country and took his family to the USSR until the coming of the war. He wanted to find something he did not find here. He was a brilliant law student and could not find a job in any good New York firm staffed for the most part by men and women of the white race. In other words, he could not be a lawyer, so he became a singer—a gain for art—but perhaps there was some bitterness in his heart, brought about by the fact that there was no equality of opportunity for educated men of his race. He did not want his boy to have the same experiences. Others might feel the same way. In the USSR he was recognized as an educated man, as an artist and as an equal. We disapprove of his speeches, but we must also understand him and above all other things, we must be jealous to preserve the liberties that are inherent in true democracy.

~ ~ ~

By late 1949 Mao Tse-tung had succeeded in unifying sufficient support from various factions in the sprawling Chinese territories and throughout the intricate web of Chinese interest groups, including the military, to declare his revolution a fait accompli. The Nationalist Chinese, under Chaing Kai-shek, had battled Mao during a protracted civil war that was both ideological and military to no avail. Mrs. Roosevelt did not have any neat formula to offer to the Chinese to move them closer to truly democratic revolution. One could only watch and wait.

179

En Route Home from Atlanta, September 10—If the Chinese people as a whole are going to be democratic they will have to get together. This is no recent civil war. This is a war that has been going on for a very long time. China is too big a country, it has too many people for any other nation to be able to fully control unless they wish to invade and control by force.

The Communistic theories are those of a dictatorship and it may be that for a time and on a partial basis they may control certain areas of China. But if the people of China do not become convinced Communists, not even the dictatorship sponsored by Communism will really run a stable government for the whole of China.

I have a feeling that China is slowly emerging into a new and strange era. An unsettled situation may be theirs for a long time, but I doubt if we can do more than remain the friend of the Chinese people and be ready, when signs of stability emerge, to help them in any way that it becomes apparent might be useful.

~ ~ ~

No charity was closer to Eleanor Roosevelt's heart than the March of Dimes, sponsored by the National Foundation for Infantile Paralysis. She had nursed FDR through his own bout with the crippling disease and had learned how difficult life could become, on a permanent basis, for anyone who did not recover or did not have access to proper treatment. She took up the banner of the polio campaign many times in her "My Day" columns.

Hyde Park, September 13—This is a busy time of the year, with children going back to school and people just coming back from vacations, so we are apt to overlook many things that ordinarily would strike us as important.

None of us, however, can forget that we have had and are still having one of the worst epidemics of infantile paralysis that ever struck this country. It is so bad that the National Foundation for Infantile Paralysis is asking everyone during this week to make another contribution instead of waiting for the usual March of Dimes drive. Funds are very low and we are told that money will be needed, which is not now in hand, for the rest of this year.

Up to August 27 the number stricken had climbed to over 20,000, and medical authorities think we will have at least 40,000 cases by the end of the year. In 1948 the total was only 28,000.

Fortunately for us, we know now that more than half, perhaps as many as 75 percent of the total number of cases will not be permanently disabled. However, the expense of giving the early treatment is the same for the mild case as for the serious one. There is no immediate diagnosis that differentiates between a mild and serious case.

Last week the national headquarters of the National Foundation sent out $438,353 to chapters that had run out of funds, and it is likely that similar financial help will be needed for the next two or three months. The Foundation is asking for $14,500,000 from the people of the United States to be used entirely for epidemic service and the care of patients until the January, 1950, March of Dimes replenishes the funds of the organization.

I think that, having just been to Warm Springs and seen patients of every age—one almost a baby, many little children, some older children and adults—I feel more keenly than I might otherwise about the need for care, and care of the very best kind, to bring every patient back to maximum activity. We are fortunate that so many cases in this epidemic year have been mild ones and many sufferers have little or no paralysis. All of them, however, must be carefully watched in the early stages and one cannot fail to give the best of care just because the money is not available. That is something the people of this country will not permit, I am sure.

Therefore, I hope each and every one of us will feel a responsibility to give an extra contribution at this time. We may even add a little, specifying that the Foundation shall put the extra sum into a fund to intensify the research in some of the institutions which give promise of making real advances in discovering the cause and cure for this dread disease.

~ ~ ~

Later Native American political activists might find a column such as this one patronizing because Mrs. Roosevelt several times uses the expression "our Indians." And it does sound like an open letter to readers other than the Indians themselves, though why she might have excluded them is not clear. In any case, the plight of the Native Americans—in this case the Navajo and the Hopi—was often her subject. She found it unconscionable that Native American cultures were being toyed with for political and financial reasons by congressmen and state legislators who merely wanted whatever votes could be secured by facilitating land acquisitions for white businessmen. Mrs. Roosevelt linked the credibility of American foreign policy directly to the issue of consistency in American domestic policy in the area of civil rights—a viewpoint that had become a recurrent theme in her writing.

NEW YORK, OCTOBER 5—One of the Soviet attacks on the democracies, particularly the United States, centers on our racial policies. In recent months the Russians have been particularly watching our attitude toward the native Indians of our country. So, the question of what we do about our Indians, important as it used to be for the sake of justice, is enhanced in importance now because it is part of the fight which we and other democracies must wage, day in and day out, in perfecting our governmental household so that it will not be vulnerable to attack by the Communists.

For that reason our country as a whole should understand what is going on at the present time in Congress in this connection. This particular little plot, shall I call it, has to do with the Navajo and Hopi. There are 11 Hopi pueblos, surrounded by Navajo country. The Navajo number about 65,000 and are the largest Indian tribe north of Mexico. The Hopi represent the most perfect flowering of pre-Columbian culture from the Rio Grande to the Arctic.

For purposes largely of publicity, because it was not really necessary, the Interior Department drafted a bill to authorize a rehabilitation program. This bill re-authorized already-authorized appropriations, and the interested public and the Indians gained an impression that the bill actually appropriated $90,000,000 for their needs. It did nothing of the kind. The hope was that it would create public interest and thus stir the appropriations committee in Congress to appropriate some very much needed money.

The bill was approved by voice votes in the House and the Senate and sent to President Truman. Even if it is signed by the President, funds must still be appropriated to put the bill into effect.

I certainly hope President Truman will veto this bill. One provision of it would place all Navajo and Hopi Indians under the state laws of Arizona, Utah, New Mexico and Colorado. Only a few minor exceptions in the matter of land law and property taxation were made; nothing was said of water rights; and without any exceptions the Navajo and the Hopi are placed under the jurisdiction of the state and local courts.

For a hundred years it has been the U.S. policy to allow Indians their own tribal, customary law. Under Section 9 of this new bill we will interfere with all the things that are important to them—their religion, their art, their self-governing arrangements. The very things that those who study Indian life consider most important, this bill would destroy.

There is a constant effort going on to transfer Indian property to whites, and one of the most successful ways in the past has been to disrupt the Indian social system. Between 1887 and 1933, through land allotments, we transferred 90 million acres of the best Indian land to whites. This was largely done by the method of persuading or compelling the individualization of tribal properties.

In 1934, under the Indian Reorganization Act, land allotments were stopped. Now there is still another bill up for consideration, called the Butler–D'Ewart Bill. This authorizes any Indian individual, if declared competent, to sell his equity regardless of the consent of the co-owners and, of course, strikes a body blow at all Indian corporate holdings. The intent is similar to the Indian Omnibus Bill of 1923 which Albert D. Fall nearly succeeded in getting enacted.

There are many other things that are being done in Congress at the present time and which the public knows little or nothing about.

Often the Indians themselves and the welfare groups that are trying to watch legislation for them know nothing about what is being done by the conferees in Congress.

Are we indifferent to the way our Indians are treated? If not, we had better let our representatives in Congress know that we do not like the present trend of legislation.

~ ~ ~

Eleanor Roosevelt was above all things a resolute optimist. In the Nobel Prize for Literature acceptance speech delivered by William Faulkner in 1949 were words that aptly sum up Mrs. Roosevelt's own philosophical attitude: The key virtues, the novelist said, are those "old verities of the human heart" among which are courage, honor, forbearance, patience, compassion, and endurance. Faulkner also said that he believed, despite the new atomic threat to civilization, that mankind would not just survive but would prevail. His words might well have served at the dedication ceremonies of the United Nations Headquarters in New York where Eleanor Roosevelt found a new infusion of hope and confidence for her work and for the world.

NEW YORK, OCTOBER 26—The ceremonies at the dedication of the cornerstone of the new United Nations building on Monday were very impressive and very simple. Radio stations broadcast the messages to the far corners of the earth, and it was a curious feeling as you sat there and realized that people in such distant parts of the world were listening to the same words and visualizing the scene as well as their backgrounds and experiences would allow them to do.

It was rather windy and gray as we first sat down and looked up at the tall, as yet unfinished, administration building towering over us. But the sun was soon out, giving one a feeling that the clouds breaking and the light spreading throughout the sky was symbolic of the actual way in which this home of the United Nations would see peace opening up for the world as a whole in the future.

The bands from several New York City government departments played extremely well throughout the whole morning. I admired, as I always have, the efficiency with which the Secret Service scattered throughout the crowds and had eyes everywhere and carried out their duty of protecting the President. He was greeted by great and enthusiastic crowds as his open car sped through New York City followed by a long line of closed cars. We knew the minute he reached the site because we could hear the cheers that went up from people at the entrance. The only disappointment of the day was that Mrs. Truman was not well and could not come with the President.

After the ceremonies were over we all went up to Gracie Mansion for a luncheon given by Mayor O'Dwyer in the President's honor. It was a gay and friendly affair. The musicians played as though they enjoyed it, and as a result the guests began to feel in the mood to join in with the musicians, till even political enemies were singing songs joyously together!

At four o'clock the President left to take a plane back to Washington. As I was driving home I could not help thinking that perhaps many of us who were fortunate enough to see these ceremonies had witnessed a dramatic moment in history, marking the beginning of the United Nations being actually firmly established in a permanent home, well on its way to being the mediator of all serious disputes for years to come.

~　~　~

No one who had lived through the Depression could ever forget the horrors of the great dust storms on the plains and prairies, where hundreds of thousands of acres of good farmland were literally blown away: The topsoil broke loose in dry periods before new crops could take root to hold it down. Nor could anyone forget the floods that caused major erosion in many river valleys before adequate dams had been built to control the overflow in seasons of heavy rainfall. It was a Roosevelt family tradition to be intensely concerned about protecting the natural environment, a tradition dating back to the conservation policies of Theodore Roosevelt when he was President. Eleanor Roosevelt's enthusiasm for new legal measures requiring lumber companies to

*restore the forests they cut down was in line with the lessons of the
Dust Bowl and the well-established Roosevelt family values.*

HYDE PARK, NOVEMBER 14—News of a recent Supreme Court
ruling has pleased me more than anything I have read in a long time,
since it seemed a step forward in the field of conservation. The
ruling, by upholding the power of the State of Washington to
compel persons engaged in commercial logging operations to reforest
cut-over areas, reaffirmed the concept that man is the trustee of the
land for the general welfare.

Announcement of this decision was made by Fairfield Osborn at
the annual meeting of the Soil Conservation Society of America,
and strangely enough on the very same day I received from him the
report of the Conservation Foundation, published July 1, 1949. This
corporation was formed to "promote conservation of the earth's
life-supporting resources, animal life, forests and other plant life,
water resources and productive soil," and its report should be read by
every American citizen, for it deals with subjects of vital importance
to our ultimate survival.

~ ~ ~

Alan Paton's haunting novel, Cry, The Beloved Country *(1948),
about intractably difficult racial relations in his native South Africa,
attracted widespread favorable reviews and brisk sales in the United
States and Great Britain shortly after it was published. The musical
play Mrs. Roosevelt saw,* Lost in the Stars, *based on the book, was
thematically just to her liking: a political and moral drama in which
compassion and courage are shown to be qualities that can build
bridges between people of entirely different status and background.*

NEW YORK, NOVEMBER 19—Wednesday night was a very pleasant
one for me, for after dinner at a little restaurant where the food was
excellent we went to see "Lost in the Stars." Perhaps I should say
"hear" as well as "see."

This play, written by Maxwell Anderson, is based on Alan Paton's novel, "Cry, The Beloved Country." The production was directed and supervised by Rouben Mamoulian and he has done a most extraordinary job of stage setting. The sets merely suggest the situation and leave so much to your imagination that you can really hold the atmosphere of the play much more clearly than if he had attempted to put it realistically before you.

I did not think I would ever like Todd Duncan better than I liked him in "Porgy and Bess," but he is really wonderful in this. So is Leslie Banks, who plays Mr. Duncan's opposite number as the white man. When Mr. Duncan made his speech about the white race in South Africa I almost thought I was listening to a speech made in the Paris General Assembly last year in Committee 3 by one of the delegates from that country.

The music in the play is haunting. Todd Duncan's song "Thousands of Miles" and his prayer and "The Little Grey House" still stay in my mind along with many others. Perhaps reading the book, which gives a more complete picture of the whole problem, will make it difficult for some people to enjoy the play. But I was grateful for the beauty of the play, for its tragedy and the inescapable problem that it sets before us so vividly.

~   ~   ~

The question of whether the Allies would ever be able to trust the Germans again plagued foreign-policy thinkers in the years following World War II. On the one hand, the practical demands of economic life and political interaction meant that some rapprochement was necessary: Germany would not disappear from the map and would indeed become a significant market again. On the other hand, fear of Nazism and distaste for the evils it represented led many in government to believe that no former Nazis should ever be allowed to hold positions of authority again. Moreover, as the Soviets exerted increasing power in all their Eastern-bloc satellite nations the potential threat to the West loomed ever larger, and Germany was almost the only available buffer between East and West. How then to steer the middle course between these extremes of accommodation and resistance to Germany's internal redevelopment? Eleanor Roosevelt urged watchful caution but also placed some hope in the prospects for educating younger German people in the ways of independent thinking and thus in the art of democracy.

NEW YORK, DECEMBER 14—Many of us in this country are disturbed by the persistent reports that Nazis were being placed in many important positions in Germany. And I think it is a good time to examine the whole situation.

Those of us who have known Germany and the Germans for a long time (and my knowledge of that country goes back 60 years, as I went there as a little girl) have a rather long perspective on the character of the German people. They like authority. They have been accustomed to direction and to being told what to do in every phase of their existence. I have never been in a country where the signs are more completely explicit. They do not say, "Please do not do thus-and-so"; they say "Verboten," pure and simple.

As a result of all this, there has grown up in Germany a system of class. Any little government functionary had certain little responsibilities and certain authority. He was looked up to by all his neighbors and as you went higher up he was shown even greater respect by the people.

You do not change the character of a people overnight. They may not have liked the Nazi regime. But they accepted it because it represented authority. Now, as they get control of their own affairs, they are going to put back into places of authority the people whom they are accustomed to have manage their affairs, whether in the economic, the governmental, the educational or the religious field.

The people in Germany who stood out by themselves in opposition to authority are rare indeed. We must realize, therefore, that as we give more authority to the Germans we are going to find back in positions of trust more people who were in those positions during the Nazi regime. Some of these leaders may have become convinced of the evils of the Nazi government. We may, through our efforts at education, help to educate some of the younger people in democratic ways, and if there is enough exchange on the student level some

188

young people may become convinced of the value of a democratic and free country.

~ ~ ~

As American as apple pie, but more interesting: such were the tasty treats concocted in a national baking contest Mrs. Roosevelt attended in New York and reported to her "My Day" readers as though she had been a fly on the wall on their behalf. A very high percentage of her readership were housewives and thus could identify immediately with the winners in the baking contest. Never known for a discriminating palate, Eleanor Roosevelt nonetheless could recognize and report a delicious story with good humor and an eye for telling detail.

HYDE PARK, DECEMBER 15—I went to a luncheon on Tuesday in New York City at the invitation of Philip W. Pillsbury, president of Pillsbury Mills, which was advertising on a grand scale but at the same time had a very healthy human touch about it. It was the finals of the national recipe and baking contest at the Waldorf-Astoria that brought women from 37 states, the District of Columbia and Alaska to New York on a trip financed by the Pillsbury company. They were a very happy and excited group of people.

There were $1,000 awards in six categories for the best bread maker, cake maker, cookie baker, etc., but it was for the three big awards that every woman sat on the edge of her chair waiting to find out who the lucky one would be. Those who got the six awards in the various classes were happy, indeed. But I think Mr. and Mrs. Pillsbury must have felt quite proud when they gave out the other prizes, because it is given to few people in this world to give such great happiness to other human beings.

It is a pleasant thing in itself to have the journey and the fun of a baking contest in the Waldorf, and every woman did her baking in a General Electric stove, which she will take home with her. As a by-product, Mrs. Ethel Hansen, from Anchorage, Alaska, who has been a missionery there, saw her brother from Hartford, Conn., whom she had not seen in 36 years. That in itself must have been worth the trip, and more, to her. It must be exciting, too, to see some of your favorite radio people in the flesh, instead of just knowing their voices over the air.

The really tense and moving moment came when Mr. Pillsbury and I went down to the little platform in front of the raised dais where we had lunch and the announcement of the prizes was begun. Third-prize money—$4,000—went to Mrs. Richard W. Sprague, of San Marino, Calif. Her winning entry was named "Carrie's Creole Chocolate Cake." She was asked what she would do with the money and answered: "Well, the baby is paid for but there is still the mortgage on the house."

Then came the announcement of the second prize—$10,000. That went to one of the few unmarried contestants, Miss Laura Rott of Naperville, Ill. Her entry was "Mint Surprise Cookies." I was assured by those who sampled them as they came out of the oven that though they might look like ordinary cookies they tasted like your dream of something highly delectable. Miss Rott was speechless. She could hardly stand up and she had no idea what she would do with the money. She never thought of having so much money at one time in her hand.

Finally came the announcement of the $50,000 prize. It went to Mrs. Ralph E. Smafield, of Detroit, Mich. Her entry was "Water-Rising Nut Twist," and we were each given a bite. It certainly is delicious. Tears were in her eyes as she was asked what she was going to do with her prize. She did not hesitate: "We will have a home of our own at last." Her husband is an electrical engineer. A home of their own seemed to be a dream which she had long cherished.

This is a healthy contest and a highly American one. It may sell Pillsbury flour but it also reaches far down into the lives of the housewives of America. These were women who ran their homes and cooked at home; they were not professional cooks.

I almost forgot to say that three men got the trip to New York by qualifying and one man won with an entry which he called "Quick Man-Prepared Dinner."

~ ~ ~

Though she speaks here with graceful charm about her decision to sit for a portrait to satisfy her children, there was more than common modesty or humility behind Mrs. Roosevelt's long resistance to meeting their request. From childhood days on there were those in her family who encouraged in her a self-image of being the Ugly Duckling. As a married woman in public life she was frequently criticized for the plainness of her clothes, the inappropriateness of her flower-bedecked hats, the shrillness of her speaking voice. Despite a warmth of spirit that many found irresistible and a smile that most would agree could light up a room, Eleanor Roosevelt was never celebrated as an American beauty. Her willingness, finally, to sit for a portrait was no doubt a triumph not so much of her children's persuasiveness as of her own self-acceptance, even with her lingering reservations.

HYDE PARK, DECEMBER 16—I might as well own up to the fact that to please my son, Elliott, I have broken all my vows and finally am sitting for a portrait done by Douglas Chandor. He did a wonderful portrait of my mother-in-law when she was an old lady. And while I hope that this portrait of me will be kept from public view until after I am dead, I have to acknowledge that he is a remarkable painter and that my grandchildren will find in me much more that is pleasant and agreeable to look at in an ancestor than really exists! One must look on a portrait as something to make future generations feel that they do not have to be too much ashamed of their forebears.

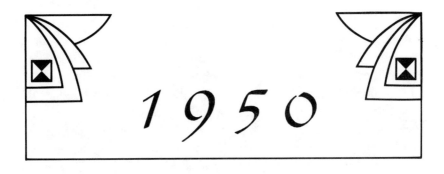

1950

*T*ension at home, conflict abroad: 1950 was not a good year for the United States, and Mrs. Roosevelt's "My Day" columns were necessarily full of bad news and plainly angry opinions. Since 1945 at war's end, America had poured almost $25 billion in aid and loan credits into other countries. But the postwar world was no friendlier for all of it. In January President Truman initiated the Civilian Mobilization Office, a sign of America's continuing fear of Soviet attack. Truman also announced that the U.S. was at work on the hydrogen bomb, presumed to be the next right step in what was by now irreversibly an arms race. Eleanor Roosevelt had serious reservations about these developments.

In February Senator Joseph McCarthy of Wisconsin stunned the nation in a public speech accusing the State Department of harboring Communists. At the time many people were convinced or at least scared into believing him. A Soviet consular officer was found guilty in March of espionage against the United States: perfect kindling for McCarthy's growing fire. The Supreme Court evidenced its own fear of political subversion by upholding the controversial Taft–Hartley Act requirements that union leaders take an oath indicating they were not Communists. Mrs. Roosevelt consistently labeled McCarthyism's rabid hatred of Communism as dangerous and even insane while maintaining her staunch dislike and distrust for Soviet Communist politics. On the other hand, her acceptance of the more benign forms of socialism deepened as she visited several of the socialist-oriented Scandinavian countries in the late spring.

When the Korean conflict (never officially a war in American

193

constitutional terms) broke out in late June, with North Korean troops invading South Korea using Soviet military equipment, the case against the Soviet Communists was sealed. The UN Security Council (minus the boycotting Soviet representative) moved immediately to authorize armed intervention to save South Korea. Truman responded by sending the Navy to blockade the Korean coast and the Air Force and Army to lead the way in the UN's battle on land. General Douglas MacArthur was appointed commander of all UN forces. Former Secretary of State George C. Marshall became Secretary of Defense during this crisis. Late in July the Senate Foreign Relations Committee reported that Senator McCarthy's February speech had had no basis in fact, but the damage was done, and years would pass before the McCarthy witch hunt for alleged Communists was over. In September Congress passed, over Truman's veto, the Internal Security Act, requiring all Communists to register with the government and authorizing their detention in case of a national emergency.

The Korean Conflict, or War, was enormously frustrating to Mrs. Roosevelt and to many other observers of American foreign policy. She had placed such high hopes in the UN as a means to establish world peace that to see another war break out, so soon after World War II ended, was profoundly disillusioning. Eleanor Roosevelt used her "My Day" columns to educate her readers about the rather complicated history of Russian-Chinese-Japanese-American involvement in Korean affairs.

Throughout much of 1950, on an almost daily basis, Mrs. Roosevelt confronted the UN Soviet delegates, with whom she found it increasingly difficult to work. And, except for the Scandinavian trip, a visit to family and friends in California, and a short vacation at the Roosevelt's home on Campobello Island, her UN job kept her busy in New York most of the time.

During the early fall the UN troops made steady progress in Korea, recapturing Seoul; reaching the 38th Parallel, which divided the two Koreas; and penetrating beyond toward the North Korean capital. Then an unanticipated additional enemy appeared on the battlefront: The Chinese Communists joined the North Koreans and,

194

toward year's end, drove the UN force into retreat. By now it was clear this was going to be a protracted struggle. General Dwight Eisenhower took a leave of absence from his post as president of Columbia University to assume command of NATO. Truman declared a full national emergency to facilitate his military strategy. General MacArthur urged that we attack mainland China.

In November, two Puerto Rican nationalists staged an unsuccessful assassination attempt on President Truman—who escaped unhurt, though a guard was killed, as was one of the assailants. It was a time in which almost no one felt entirely safe.

It bears saying here that during these years of Eleanor Roosevelt's public life as reported in "My Day," actually from December 1947 onward, there was a parallel private life in which there were developments that never made it into the newspaper. Although she would occasionally effervesce in "My Day" about the antics of her grandchildren and from time to time would publicly mourn the loss of a loved one, Mrs. Roosevelt played other cards in her private deck very close to her vest. One such card was her relationship with David Gurewitsch, for whom and from whom—much to her own surprise—she found love. Joseph Lash observes: "Eleanor was sixty-three when her quenchless desire to love and be loved settled on David Gurewitsch. Her letters to David lack the passionate intensity" of others she wrote earlier in her life, "but they were love letters. She was fifteen years older and a figure now in history, which made even more remarkable her ability to shake free of convention and upbringing to love a younger man. He was forty-five."

Gurewitsch had been a longtime friend and was the physician of the former First Lady's friend Trude Lash, the biographer's wife. Sadly, Dr. Gurewitsch had himself been stricken by tuberculosis and had been told to go quickly to a sanatorium. Having trouble getting a plane ticket to Switzerland, he appealed to Trude Lash to ask Eleanor Roosevelt for help, which she delivered. Mrs. Roosevelt and Dr. Gurewitsch took the same plane to Geneva and remained in frequent contact by letter and visiting from then on until she died in 1962. Her correspondence to Gurewitsch tells an interesting tale of an older woman whose previous marriage and public life had made it impossible for her either to find comfort with a disloyal husband or to seek escape through divorce or open displays of anger but who now would come alive again in her heart.

~ ~ ~

One measure of Eleanor Roosevelt's status as a voice of authority was the fact that she found herself, in her word, "deluged" by questions about where the world might be heading in the second half of the twentieth century. Many of her "My Day" readers must have thought of her as someone so well informed and so well connected that crystal-ball-gazing would come naturally to her. In a clever way Mrs. Roosevelt dismissed all these questions about specific events yet to happen in the future. Instead, she took the occasion to remind her audience of something that had been a frequent theme in "My Day" over the years: that resolving to work for peace in the world was the most important step toward the future anyone could take and that such a peace begins with individuals in their everyday relationships.

HYDE PARK, JANUARY 2,—I have been deluged in the past few days by requests to give my views on what will happen in the next 50 years as regards peace; to review the most important happenings and accomplishments by people in the last 50 years; to forecast the work that will be done and to give the names of those I think most likely to accomplish it, etc., etc., ad infinitum.

I am no prophet and I dislike trying to project my thoughts into the future to construct the kind of world which probably would have an influence on the next 50 years. It might be good and it might be bad.

The old-fashioned habit of making New Year's resolutions is one still practiced by many Americans. When I was young the resolutions were not often too serious on New Year's Day. The serious ones waited to come when Lent was upon us and the children were told to give up candy for that season or to give up some favorite dessert, which to us seemed a very real and serious sacrifice.

Today these things seem very small to me, but the New Year's resolution remains and grows more important year by year. One cannot ask for specific things for oneself or for one's children or one's friends. But one can and should ask, I think, to be given the qualities of mind and heart and spirit which will make it possible for us to live better in this world, to serve our country with greater efficiency, and in our own little corner, wherever we may be, to advance the cause for which we work. This should be not only at home but in the world as a whole.

One of the questions most frequently asked is: "What can I do to help bring peace into the world?"

It seems to me that New Year's is a good day to try to think that question out. Surely, we can do nothing outside of our own sphere of influence, and that sphere is not likely, for the most part, to touch directly the field of government or world affairs. Nevertheless, if we have eyes to see, we can so live in our own surroundings that we will pull our friends and our community to a greater sense of obligation to make democracy succeed—in order that it may help to bring about peace in the world.

It is true that the Communists say we are attempting to impose our will on them by keeping them in constant fear lest we are going to attack them. That can only mean that they know that they might attack us and, therefore, are afraid of what may lie in the back of our minds.

I do not know how we can persuade them that our desires lie in the direction of peace, but at least we need do nothing which would substantiate their suspicions. Little by little they may come to trust us more and believe us. In the meantime, if we devote ourselves to improving our own democracy we will give them less and less cause to find fault with us and make it more and more apparent that democracy has everything that Communism can offer. Everything plus freedom, which to us, means a great deal.

~   ~   ~

Mrs. Roosevelt took up the question of civic responsibility again in her January 3 column. This time she happened to be talking about the duPont family, which had been prominent in French politics and military affairs well before the late eighteenth century, when its members began to settle in the United States. Industrialists from the beginning (at first in woolens and later in a wide range of chemical products), the duPonts built an empire almost without parallel. The Roosevelts had given most of their family's best talent and energy to the world of politics, but the duPonts had found many other ways to contribute constructively to the public good. For generations they had been philanthropists and military leaders; one, Henry Algernon, had been a Senator. The duPonts had even given something precious to the Roosevelts: daughter Ethel duPont married Eleanor Roosevelt's son Franklin, Jr. in June, 1937. Mrs. Roosevelt's message was clear. From those to whom life has been generous in abundance, life—the community and the nation—expects generous contributions in return.

HYDE PARK, JANUARY 3—I notice that 632 members of the duPont family celebrated the 150th year that the family has been established in the United States. As a family, they have certainly done a great deal for the advancement of the country. The country, however, has also given them the wherewithal with which to work. One hopes that they, like so many other families who can look back over a great many generations established in this rich country of ours, will now be concerned with preserving—through careful conservation of our natural resources and through the use of their laboratories and inventions for the benefit of the nation as a whole—the same type of opportunity for future generations which their ancestors enjoyed. When families grow in number and wealth, they exert great influence and power and have a responsibility to carry their share of the country's responsibilities. Today, the United States of America carries heavy responsibilities, and every citizen who has received much from this country must feel the need to give much in return.

~ ~ ~

There is a charming discontinuity in Mrs. Roosevelt's column about visiting her son John's family in Los Angeles. The first half of the column reads as though it were a letter to a friend about the kinds of

*domestic and familial activities anyone of any background or social
status might be concerned with: the kids, their schools, their clothing,
the weather. But then it's off for lunch to Romanoff's, the pricey place
where Hollywood's elite, the movie stars, gathered to see and be seen.
The tables were turned on Mrs. Roosevelt, however, in a flattering
way that day by one Humphrey Bogart—in whose eyes, apparently,
Eleanor was the real star.*

Los Angeles, January 18,— Here in the city of Los Angeles the
usual winter rainfall already has exceeded the average mark. My first
two days have been beautiful ones, with blue sky and little wind. The
grass is green everywhere and the flowers are in bloom. I wish we
might have had some of the rain in New York about which they
complain here. Then we would not be so short of water.

Here they are accustomed to measuring their water supply, and I
was interested to find that in my son's house in Pasadena there is a
regular monthly bill for water, and the gas bill comes at the same
time. Gas furnaces seem to be a convenient method of heat here and
they only turn them on in such sections of the house as they feel
have need of greater warmth. In many rooms there is no central
heating and often just a small open fire will be all that is needed to
take off the winter chill. I can well see, however, that when the good
weather goes back on them, they are not equipped to be warm in the
way that we are at home in the East.

For the children, though, this climate has many advantages. Little
boys wear their overalls the year round, and I went with a friend of
mine to take her little daughter, my godchild, to nursery school this
morning. The sweater set, which I had sent her for Christmas, was
all that was needed; no gaiters or arctics and heavy coats.

Nevertheless, my grandchildren think of snow and ice in the East
as something highly enjoyable. I think if they were given a choice as
to whether they would come to visit in the summer or winter they
would choose winter because their only contact here with snow is up
in the mountains on an occasional trip.

My son, John, took Anna, Miss Thompson and me to lunch
yesterday at Romanoff's and I had the pleasure of seeing a number of

the famous Hollywood people—Walter Wanger; George Jessel; Freeman Gosden and Charles Correll, of "Amos and Andy" fame; and Humphrey Bogart, who flattered me greatly by bringing me a copy of my book, *This I Remember*, to sign. I could not help thinking how many of my youthful acquaintances would have thrilled to see so many people whom they enjoy on the stage and screen and radio actually in the flesh.

~ ~ ~

For one who repeatedly disclaimed any authority or expertise as a drama or music critic, Eleanor Roosevelt gave a substantial amount of attention in "My Day," to reviews of plays and concerts. Here are two more, one showing us again how little she liked the obscurities of modernist drama, in this case in the T. S. Eliot play The Cocktail Party. *Eliot's success as a poet, though here he was often misunderstood too, was far greater than his success as a playwright. The second performance had a more straightforward political theme, something Mrs. Roosevelt felt she could sink her teeth into. She had high praise for Gian-Carlo Menotti, the author, whom most Americans know for his Christmas drama* Amahl and the Night Visitors.

HYDE PARK, MARCH 24—The other night I went to see T. S. Eliot's "The Cocktail Party." The first act, I felt, stated rather well the problems of a certain kind of marriage, but somehow the doctor, who acted as a kind of super-FBI man, never made much sense and the almost slapstick humor bewildered me rather than clarified for me the serious part of the play.

I came out not knowing what the play was really supposed to make me understand. I don't usually find plays difficult to understand and thought perhaps I was too far back to hear the lines clearly, so I certainly am going to buy the play and read it. Perhaps, however, many of us like to be bewildered, and if we don't understand the author's meaning very well we decide he must be doing something extremely clever!

New York, April 5—I am no music critic but I thoroughly enjoyed the performance last night of "The Consul," the new musical drama by Gian-Carlo Menotti. Through the first two acts I literally lived in Magda Sorel's' emotions. Vera Bryner played the role and I thought it was not only rare theater but wonderfully moving music and a fine performance. Somehow the last act moved me less. Whether the fantasy broke the impact or what it was, I do not know. It was still fine but I was not living it any more.

This is a wonderful achievement for Mr. Menotti. He is young and I know how much more lies ahead of him. Marie Powers was wonderful, and though I was sorry not to hear Patricia Neway, of whom I have heard wonderful things, still I cannot say that I felt the slightest lack in Miss Bryner's performance.

All in all, I think it is an evening no one will quickly forget. There is food for thought in the Consul's office. How horrible to live in a world of papers! Human values count for so little and machinery for so much. It is a truthful picture of totalitarianism, with secret police and psychological torture, all unrolling before your eyes. Pray God it never comes any nearer than the stage.

~ ~ ~

April 1950; Eleanor Roosevelt was sixty-six and a half years young. The following column speaks for itself of her vitality, her high energy, her sense of momentum. Few people half her age could cram as much activity into a day and still have resources left in the evening, indeed the late evening, to continue being productive or charming or both.

New York, April 27—The visit of the President of Chile Gabriel Gonzalez Videla and his charming wife to Hyde Park the other day was an informal and very pleasant occasion. From the time I greeted them, as they walked from the library to my husband's grave, through the visit to the old house, the recording for the Voice of America on the front steps, and finally to the library, the whole party seemed interested and unweary in spite of the whirlwind pace of events arranged for them since they arrived in the United States.

Ambassador Herman Santa Cruz drove with me in my little new car, which I have not yet mastered very well, as I led the official cars through the wood road to my cottage. I was apologizing for the holes left by the winter frost and the spring mud and to console me he remarked: "Many roads in Chile are like this."

I had tacked the flags of our countries on my door and the President at once noticed his own flag. In spite of the fact that we are somewhat crowded in my little cottage when we are a large party and we cannot eat out-of-doors, everybody seemed relaxed and at home. I had a warm feeling about this party, as though it really had created a greater sense of friendliness between the representatives of our two countries.

After my guests had gone to visit their old friend, Mrs. Olin Dows, Miss Thompson and I drove down to New York City, arriving in time for me to attend a meeting of the United Nations Day Committee at 6:30.

After a hasty bite of dinner there was a Wiltwyck School Board meeting at 9 P.M., which, wonder of wonders, ended at 10:30. We are having our usual troubles, reaching the month of April without having raised enough money to cover our summer expenses for Wiltwyck.

A special meeting will be called to consider how this money may be raised. While we have put forward great efforts this past year and have greatly increased the list of subscribers, our budget has gone up but still falls short of increased costs. There is much work to be done for these little boys who still find trouble getting started in life and land in police courts and then in Wiltwyck.

On Tuesday I reached Lake Success in time to do a recording for the YMCA before our morning Human Rights Commission meeting opened.

We started our discussion on implementation of a Covenant of Human Rights, but after a number of preliminary speeches, which took us halfway through the afternoon, we found that the commission was anxious to have a little more time for preparation of this subject. Therefore we postponed further consideration until next

Monday, when it was agreed we would take it up and conclude our work on it.

Then we went back to drafting Article 18, as, during my absence on Monday, Article 17 of the Covenant on Freedom of Information had been completed. Later in the afternoon, I looked in for a brief moment at two meetings that were going on—one in the Economic and Social Council and one in a large conference room.

Then I hastened back to New York City and a brief half hour at a brilliant and crowded party given on the Starlight Roof of the Waldorf-Astoria by Laurence Rutman, editor and general manager of United Feature Syndicate. Newspaper people from all over the country were there and I felt a little bewildered as I was engulfed by the crowd and realized that I would have difficulty in locating my host in that sea of faces.

I got home in time to change and eat dinner before going across the street to the Broadway Tabernacle for the annual banquet of the Lemuel Haynes Congregational Church. There I was presented with an award, and an added thrill was hearing Carol Brice sing. She has a beautiful voice.

From there I went to Hunter College, where they were holding a meeting in the interest of the activities carried on at the Inter-Faith Houses which are named after my mother-in-law. There I saw the most interesting and graceful dances presented by a young Indian student from Bombay. There ended a very full "My Day."

~ ~ ~

Realpolitik: in the world of negotiations, debate, and behind-the-scenes deal-making, power is what talks; the social graces are not the most important element. At the UN committee meetings, however, delegates were in some sense caught in a nether world between private diplomatic negotiations and public performance for the benefit of spectators and news reporters. Occasionally a committee chairman would make a gaffe or read the political situation wrongly. Here Mrs. Roosevelt, sitting in just such a position of responsibility, confesses her mistakes. She set high standards for herself, but she must have trusted that her "My Day" readers would understand that even the best tightrope walker sometimes falls off his precarious perch.

NEW YORK, APRIL 28—The day in the Human Rights Commission yesterday was not very peaceful, and I think it was largely because I started the commission off all wrong in the morning.

I did not intend, of course, to offend the honorable delegates or to be discourteous. But I was away on Monday and for some inconceivable reason I got it into my head that the speeches on a resolution presented by the delegates had all been made by the proponents of the resolution. This resolution asked the General Assembly to bestir itself and write a Covenant on Freedom of Information at its next session.

The United States had an amendment to propose. First, we had a suggestion that we drop the resolution, which, I must say, I had little hope of having anyone accept. Then our amendment was to substitute a very much milder last sentence to the resolution to the effect that nothing which the Human Rights Commission had done on freedom of information prevented the General Assembly from proceeding to draft a covenant if it desired.

Then I made the speech on our amendment at the opening of the session without letting anybody else speak first and the result was that I hurt everybody's feelings and made them all feel injured for the rest of the morning. I apologized profusely because I knew only too well how stupid I had been. But one can never undo stupid things of that kind once they are done, nor can one change the way people feel about them.

~ ~ ~

Who wouldn't like to find a way into mental distraction while visiting the dentist? Mrs. Roosevelt did just that (and found her subject for a column) by looking out the dentist's window and contemplating the steeplejacks at work on a rising skyscraper within her view. Throughout her life in and around government, she often expressed not just political sympathy for working men and women but also her deep respect for the skills they practiced, to no particular applause from any admiring audience, day in and day out.

Eleanor was getting ready for a trip to the Scandinavian countries with two grandchildren in tow. As usual when she traveled, this trip would be a combination of diplomatic appearances and social meetings.

NEW YORK, JUNE 5—Friday was the usual "day-before-you-leave," when you try to remember all of the things you have forgotten to do and do all the things you should have done beforehand. What always takes me longest is getting thoroughly cleaned up before I start. Feet, teeth, hair and nails—all have to be attended to; and the older I grow, the more necessary I realize this care is and the less interest I have in it because the results seem so unsatisfactory!

While my teeth were being attended to, I sat looking out an 18th-floor window at a group of workmen at their tasks on the steel framework of a new building under construction. Some manipulated the big cranes, and opposite my level were men putting the girders in place. How much we usually take for granted about the work of our fellow human beings! Somehow I had always thought of these huge skyscrapers as they are when finished and had never before seen the skilled work and calm courage that goes into putting up the framework. Just walking across from one beam to another is an amazing acrobatic feat of balance, with sure death below if you lose your head for a minute. The workers don't wear belts and are not hooked to anything, yet they behave just as though theirs was any ordinary occupation with the ordinary risks which all of us take in our daily work.

I have long known what it means to be a miner, and I can well understand the responsibilities and risks of a pilot or of the men in the army and navy in various branches of the service. But here were men doing work that goes on day in and day out and is part of our daily lives, and I had never given a thought to the extraordinary skill and physical ability required to carry it through successfully. I was overcome at my own lack of imagination and understanding; but I shall be grateful to these men in the future, and have a better understanding of what this kind of work requires.

~ ~ ~

Five years after FDR's death the peoples of Europe were still occupied with their efforts to commemorate his contributions to revitalizing the world's economy during the Depression and to saving the world's democracies from totalitarianism during the war. Eleanor Roosevelt recognized that the praise lavished on the late President was really meant to be shared by all Americans who had shared in these tasks.

OSLO, JUNE 9—The crowd yesterday waiting for the King and the royal party to arrive for the ceremonies of unveiling the monument to Franklin D. Roosevelt was large and enthusiastic. As I stood listening to our national anthem, I realized anew what a beautiful site has been chosen for this statue. It stands over the quayside looking down the fjord. The speeches were fine and warm and I think there was a full realization by all the people present that this statue symbolizes their gratitude not to one man alone, but to the people of the United States of America, to President Truman and Congress. And to the ideals for which they stand—continuing to give cooperation and support to attain peace and justice which men in the United States military services fought for during the late war, side by side with their allies.

~ ~ ~

In Copenhagen Mrs. Roosevelt saw something that would no doubt have pleased William Shakespeare greatly: an open-air production of Hamlet *in the castle of the moody Dane. The* Old Vic Company *of London was one of Britain's best, and seeing Michael Redgrave in the title role was indeed a rare pleasure by anyone's standards. "My Day" columns like this one gave Eleanor Roosevelt's American readers a chance to travel with her to exotic places and events.*

COPENHAGEN, JUNE 19—We had a most delightful drive out to the Montebello sanitarium, where the whole party, including the Ambassadress and her husband and children, dined with Mr. and Mrs. Robert Megidoff.

This sanitarium is in a beautiful spot, and from the porch you can see the roofs of the Castle of Elsinore. We drove there immediately after dinner, and in the great courtyard watched a performance of "Hamlet" by the members of the Old Vic Company. Hamlet was played by Michael Redgrave and Ophelia by Yvonne Mitchell. Although the setting is beautiful, it must be hard on the actors, who have to project their voices in the open air. They did it magnificently, however, for every word was distinctly heard.

The courtyard was crowded with people from many countries, all of whom had the same idea I had—that to see "Hamlet" given in such surroundings would be a real experience. The big light in one of the towers flashed its message to ships at sea, and it was so light they did not have to turn on the floodlights until the second act. In the interval between the two acts, we went up in the castle to a great room which looks down on the court. There we were given coffee and wonderful Danish pastry. I cannot remember an evening which I have enjoyed more thoroughly, and I hope it will be a great experience for our two young travelers.

~ ~ ~

The most momentous event of 1950 took place in June when the North Koreans invaded South Korea, crossing the 38th parallel on June 25th. This column, however, is Eleanor Roosevelt's public eulogy for her elderly cousin Susie, Mrs. Henry Parish, also her godmother, who had looked after her as a child.

NEW YORK, JULY 12—Late Sunday afternoon at Hyde Park I got the news that my cousin, Mrs. Henry Parish, of New York City and Llewelyn Park, N.J., had passed away. She had been ill for a very long time. I had spent last Thursday in Orange, N.J., but had only been able to speak to her for a very few minutes. She had no close family ties and since I was her godchild she befriended me when I was young and I have always been deeply grateful to her and saddened by her long illness.

As far as she is concerned I feel that it is a release from both pain and monotony. There will be friends and relatives who will wish they had been able to do more for her in the last few years, but that was made impossible by the nature of her illness, which practically isolated her from those who wanted to be with her.

I shall never forget how kind she was to me through my early life, taking me in when my mother was ill and died; taking me in again when my little brothers had scarlet fever; inviting me to stay with her in the days when my life held none too many enjoyments.

She was extremely strict, and her husband, Henry Parish, who was the most angelic person, used to have to intercede for the younger generation when they did not live up to the high standards which his wife thought we should achieve. We were all devoted to him and as I look back on it, for a childless couple, they were wonderful in what they did for various young people in the family and for the children of their friends.

Since Mr. Parish's death a number of years ago, Mrs. Parish's life has been more lonely and more restricted by illness. She adored Mr. Sumner Welles, whose mother was one of her best friends, and I know that he will be happy that his visit to her last spring was the one thing that gave her real pleasure. I can only be thankful that I returned from abroad in time to go down and spend the day in Orange, and that I am here now to carry out her last wishes, which were all carefully given me many, many times.

When one grows old as she was, the mind seems to dwell on the past and on what will happen after one's own departure from this world. She was concerned about the turmoil of the world. It seemed to her that everything was deteriorating and in many ways her anxiety for all the individuals around her was because of her anxiety for the world as a whole.

All one can say is that peace is with her now.

~   ~   ~

The late 1940s and the 1950s laid the groundwork for the great civil rights battles of the 1960s. It took many small steps, or what a later generation might view as small steps, to build up the momentum that would eventually produce a Martin Luther King, Jr., the Freedom Riders, and Supreme Court decisions outlawing all school segregation. Mrs. Roosevelt seemed to recognize, while it was happening, that the momentum would build slowly, and she used her "My Day" column to praise what she felt were positive contributions to the struggle.

HYDE PARK, AUGUST 18—I received a letter the other day from Mr. Joseph D. Lohman, of Chicago, who is secretary of the National Committee on Segregation in the nation's capital. The letter carries very heartening news as regards the fight for civil liberties in this country. He tells me that the courage of the President and the Secretary of the Interior in running, on a nonsegregated basis, the swimming pools in the District of Columbia, has proved successful. This has resulted from the careful planning and training of the police, Park Service personnel, and the organization and cooperation of the community groups. Mr. Lohman points out that St. Louis without this careful planning had difficulty, but that nevertheless Judge Rubey Hulen of the United States District Court has handed down an opinion which ordered the city of St. Louis to refrain from segregating their pools.

It is heartening to find democratic principles being firmly established in the nation's capital and in such big cities as St. Louis. Each time an accomplishment of this kind is brought about, it has a far-reaching effect. It would not be so important if the effect was only in our country, but it will reverberate around the world and be of value to us in every country where the population is largely of another race and color.

~ ~ ~

In a kind of lazily rambling way in a late August column Mrs. Roosevelt, reporting from Campobello Island, touched on half a dozen topics almost as though she were chatting with friends. Her readers

*knew she could just as well write a tightly argued piece on a single
subject, with plenty of well-documented information, but here we find
her relaxed and playful yet still not entirely unobservant of social
problems even when they seem to cloud over an otherwise sunny
vacation day.*

CAMPOBELLO ISLAND, N.B., AUGUST 25—I have not driven a great
deal since I arrived on the island. In the years when I spent long
summers here we always walked or went by boat so I find it hard to
remember to use the car; besides, when one has driven across the
island to Herring Cove and up to the head harbor end of the island,
one has been about everywhere that one can go by car, whereas by
boat there are endless trips to take. One can go up the St. Croix
River to Calais, or stop at St. Andrews and see the fashionable world
in the big hotel, and buy handwoven rugs and tweeds in the cottage
industries shop which has flourished for many years. By now one can
probably get some English china and pottery, which was not available during the war and is still not too plentiful in England itself. One
can travel in a little boat among endless islands up the coast of
Newfoundland, and even out to Grand Manan, and all the way
around Campobello Island itself, joining the fishing fleet if one wants
to fish.

The seining of a weir here is one of the sights no stranger should
miss, for it takes one back to the days of the Bible as one watches the
fisherman pulling up the seine and filling their dories with fish. One
can stay in American waters and find endless picnic spots up the
Denny River which flows down to the west of Eastport, as the St.
Croix does on the east.

There is a little Indian village north of Eastport where the Indians
still sell some of their baskets and other wares in the town, but on this
visit I have not been to Eastport.

I am no happier about the way the Indians have been treated in
this part of our country than I am anywhere else in the United
States. Had we done a really good job it seems to me that our
Indians today would be educated; there would be no need of
reservations; they would be fully capable of taking their places as

210

citizens, and the tribes would have had full compensation for the lands they owned. Our inability to work out this small problem satisfactorily and fairly is one of the real blots on our history.

We don't seem to be able to deal with dependent people, and that is why I have always been anxious to see us admit Alaska and Hawaii as states. Once they are an integral part of our country we will have a completely different attitude toward them and their inhabitants. They will be fully represented in Congress and no other state's interests will be more important than theirs.

~ ~ ~

It was not just for his work as a representative of the United States in the UN and as secretary for special political affairs there that Ralph Bunche was awarded the Nobel Peace Prize. He had had a distinguished career long before Harry Truman appointed him to the UN job. Bunche was a professor at Howard University for twenty-two years; he collaborated with Gunnar Myrdal on a groundbreaking sociological book, The American Dilemma, *about race relations; and he served with the Office of Strategic Services during the war. Blessed with superior negotiating skills (always valuable in a world where conflict seems endemic), Bunche had been chief UN mediator in Palestine in 1948. (Nor did the Nobel award push him into retirement. Bunche worked in the UN until 1970, contributing to the mediations in numerous international trouble spots. Without question his example of professional competence and high character belied all claims that black people could not contribute to public life as effectively as whites.)*

NEW YORK, SEPTEMBER 28—One of the most gratifying things that has happened in the last few days is the choice of Dr. Ralph Bunche as the winner of the Nobel Peace Prize. No one deserves this recognition more. His patience and fairness, his refusal to be drawn either to one side or the other are what laid the foundation for peace in the Near East and made possible the negotiations that are still going on.

211

Dr. Bunche accepted the award with modesty, saying that he was a servant and a representative of the United Nations and had acted under their orders. But, of course, the success of any policy is due largely to the man who carries it out.

This action of the Norwegian Nobel Prize Committee is very significant because it brings before the world the fact that the color of your skin has nothing to do with your ability to accomplish results in your chosen field of endeavor. That is something we need to take to heart in our country and remember when the next Congress faces the President's program on civil rights. Our Congress has taken the responsibility of turning this program down and yet the passage of civil rights measures in this country would be one of the greatest victories for democracy as against Communism that we could achieve.

~ ~ ~

In other circumstances Eleanor Roosevelt might have become a teacher of what years ago was called "civics" and later usually referred to as "social studies." In some sense her entire political career was characterized by a continuous effort to keep before the public one simple lesson: that democracy is not a spectator sport. It requires active participation by the electorate to have any chance of working successfully. Many "My Day" columns took up this theme.

On a more subtle level, Mrs. Roosevelt had some avant-garde ideas about how to reform the American style of campaigning. Some of her suggestions were still being debated forty years later. Probably no other woman in American political life has ever been directly involved in so many local, state, and national campaigns as Eleanor Roosevelt. The fact of FDR's death in no way made her withdraw from presidential campaigning. She was soon to be drawn into helping Democratic presidential candidate Adlai Stevenson. (In her last years she was courted by the party's fastest-rising star, John F. Kennedy.)

NEW YORK, NOVEMBER 2—I think we need to change completely our type of campaigning, and there is one thing we can borrow from the British. Because BBC is owned by the government, the govern-

212

ment allots radio time to the candidates of all parties running and it is done on a completely fair basis. I wish that same thing could be followed up in newspapers and advertising of all sorts and that, in addition, a sum of money could be given every candidate to cover the needed educational services which should be the basis of any campaign in a democracy.

It is important for the people to be educated as to their candidates' qualifications and as to the issues and beliefs of the various parties.

In a democracy it should be part of the obligation of every voter to obtain this amount of knowledge before an election, but the knowledge must be available and it must be available for everybody. The next obligation is to make sure that we vote. If we don't vote, then we cannot complain when the power of the government gets into the hands of a few, sometimes corrupt, individuals.

The average citizen of a democracy does not fulfill his obligations on Election Day. He must try to follow the record of those for whom he voted. He must write them now and then and make them feel that he is an interested citizen, watching day by day how his business is being conducted.

This is our business, whether it is what happens in our local community, or in our state, or in our nation, and now even if it is what our delegates stand for in the United Nations. All of this is our business.

You do not directly elect your representatives in the United Nations, but indirectly you do. Your representatives in the Senate ratify United Nations' appointments and there is no reason why you should not follow with care the people who do your job in the UN. You belong to a nation that carries a heavy burden of responsibility in the UN and for that reason you should make sure that here, too, you fulfill your obligations.

~ ~ ~

Any threat on a President's life is serious, not to mention a real attack. Having been for twelve years the wife of a President who, though he was loved, was also intensely hated gave Eleanor Roosevelt

213

plenty of opportunity to think about how vulnerable any President is. When two Puerto Rican nationalists tried to kill Harry Truman, Mrs. Roosevelt saw the occasion as warranting some reflection on the political foolishness of such violence and the courage of those who are regularly exposed to this random danger.

The Puerto Ricans who staged the attack were disgruntled over the failure of their nationalist party to win public support for independence. By this time the island, which had been a U.S. territory for most of this century, was well on its way toward the commonwealth status it achieved in 1952. (Puerto Ricans had been granted American citizenship in 1917.)

About a month after the attack on Truman, Mrs. Roosevelt herself received a death threat. She was incredulous about why anyone would take her seriously enough to justify such hostility. But being identified as a spokesperson for the liberal left made her a likely target for a crazed person with a different political orientation.

New York, November 3—I was coming away from a French broadcast, which I had just done with Professor René Cassin and the delegate from Czechoslovakia on the question of the inclusion of the economic and social rights in the First Covenant of Human Rights, when I was told of the attempt on President Truman's life.

In a short time they brought me another bulletin as I sat in Committee 3, giving a pretty fair description of what had happened. Finally, the rumor came through that the two men who staged this dramatic attack outside of Blair House were Puerto Ricans who belonged to the nationalist party. That same party was responsible for the bloodshed in Puerto Rico this past week. It is quite evident that some people on that little island have not yet learned to use the ballot instead of bullets.

It is highly regrettable that it should be any group of Puerto Ricans. They made their own decisions as to the type of government they wanted, and though it may not have pleased everyone on the island, they should at least have been willing to live with that decision until it was possible to make another through orderly processes.

It gives the whole country a black eye when they first try to stage a revolution and then try to attack the President of the United States. Sometimes one wonders what are the mental processes of people of this kind. Even if their ridiculous plot had succeeded it would have made no difference in Puerto Rico and they themselves would have died just the same.

Any President of the United States, or any ruler of any country, or any public official who holds a position of great responsibility and power, must face the fact that they run this type of risk. Usually it is someone with a grievance, whose mind is slightly unbalanced, who attempts to take the life of another, feeling that this person is responsible for his particular difficulties.

I used to think when my husband was President whenever we went anywhere that there was nothing in the world that could prevent a bullet from finding its target. That is, if the one who might have fired it had no objection to being captured and punished. The Secret Service men are most watchful but they cannot cover every window in every building when one stops for any reason on a trip.

I thought occasionally they were rather rough with people who were just trying to touch the President or hand him some flowers, until I discovered that a bunch of flowers could conceal a bomb. And if you get near enough to touch the President, you were near enough to do him bodily harm.

My husband never gave it much thought and a man like President Truman, who is able to get about quickly, probably gives it even less thought, but the Secret Service give it much thought. They probably will give it more thought during the next few weeks and the poor President's life will be made miserable.

These two would-be assassins were evidently stupid as well as fanatical. But perhaps an incident such as this does no real harm, for it makes all of us more alert and more aware of the risks that have to be faced daily with complete calm by so many of our public servants.

~   ~   ~

The civil rights struggle began to mix with medical and scientific progress when the Red Cross took a stand against labeling blood according to the race of its donor, a practice it had followed for years. Mrs. Roosevelt's "My Day" column was used in this case to trumpet this news to the nation as a way to make the ethical point about racial equality.

NEW YORK, NOVEMBER 22—That was certainly a very welcome piece of information given out by the Red Cross yesterday.

In the future the blood donor cards will no longer designate whether blood given is white, Negro or Oriental. The Board of Governors announced this decision. Scientists have been urging this for some time, since it is a well-known fact that human blood is all alike, regardless of race.

This discriminatory practice created too much bad feeling during the last war, and it has carried over to the present. All of us should be relieved to know that at last one of our greatest relief organizations will be free of this particular type of discrimination.

~ ~ ~

With discouraging events in Korea, with the fear of Communist subversion sweeping the land at home, with the Pentagon at work on ever deadlier weapons, and with an ugly civil rights struggle shaping up now to last for years, the end of 1950 was a gloomy time. The Roosevelts had received sad personal news as well when Anna's ex-husband, John Boettiger, committed suicide at the end of October. Joseph Lash records Mrs. Roosevelt's reaction: "Is there nothing I might have done to help poor John? What dreadful things can happen when people fail each other. I did try to offer him friendship, but what good did it do?" Mrs. Roosevelt had the task of informing her daughter.

No wonder, then, that the final "My Day" columns of the year had a sense of onrushing darkness and a surprising chill, like a wintertime late afternoon.

Hyde Park, December 20—Some of us feel, as we live through these days, that in a curious, haunting way we know each step of the way. We have lived it before, not only once but perhaps twice if we are old enough to remember the prewar years of World War I as well as World War II. All of us feel that the collective intelligence of mankind should be able to save the world from suicide, and yet nothing seems to indicate that such is the case. We follow the path of the years gone by and we feel a little of the inevitableness of the Greek tragedy.

1951

*W*ith the Korean conflict at the heart of the matter, America spent much of 1951 focusing its attention on developments in the Far East. Mrs. Roosevelt was a frequent commentator. War abroad always does damage to the economy at home, and one result of the Korean military engagement (of which the United States carried the largest burden for the UN) was that price controls once again became necessary. Congress authorized a price freeze and President Truman instituted it on the first day of the year. The President wrestled with another national railroad strike in 1951, this one lasting twelve days and winning most of the workers' demands.

Good news from the Korean battlefield came on March 14 when UN troops recaptured Seoul, the capital of South Korea. By this time the United States had built up its military strength worldwide to 2,900,000 men and women, twice what it had been before the Korean war. The courtroom was another dramatic battlefield in 1951. After a highly controversial trial, Julius and Ethel Rosenberg were convicted of passing nuclear weapons secrets to the Soviets and, in April, were sentenced to death. Part of the pressure on the jury to convict the Rosenbergs no doubt arose from the fear in the land about Communist subversion. McCarthyism was rampant, and the military news from Asia suggested that Chinese Communism might be just as dangerous to American interests as anything the Kremlin might dream up.

In 1951 Mrs. Roosevelt tried numerous times to disentangle the many threads of opinion about the linkage between Communism

219

abroad and Communism at home using the "My Day" columns as
her podium. She remained resolutely suspicious of Communism
of the Chinese variety, under the revolutionary leadership of Mao
Tse-tung, and supported U.S. efforts to contain it within Chinese
borders. At the same time she became even more disgusted with the
paranoid psychology of McCarthyism that, by now, had wrecked
a great many people's careers and reputations while turning up
precious few truly subversive Communists.

General Douglas MacArthur, commander of UN forces in Korea,
found himself on a collision course not only with the enemy
but also with his own Commander-in-Chief. The General argued
publicly that in Korea "there is no substitute for victory," while
the President was preparing to enter negotiations for a truce—a
cessation of hostilities with no clear winner. By mid-April the
President had had enough from MacArthur, whom he recalled
and then replaced with General Matthew Ridgeway. MacArthur
remained popular at home among those who shared his fear of the
Chinese, and Congress itself gave him the extraordinary forum
of a joint session to state his case for expanding the war against
the Chinese. Mrs. Roosevelt gave President Truman her full support
in the MacArthur affair though she admired the General greatly.
She recognized the necessary pre-eminence of the president and
also advocated a truce as soon as possible. No doubt her continuing work for the UN, which took her to Geneva again in
April, reinforced Mrs. Roosevelt's sense of urgency about ending
the Korean War through negotiation rather than with military
hardware.

In June the Supreme Court handed down two decisions backing
the government's right to keep track of Communists. The military
continued to expand: The draft age was lowered to eighteen and a
half and the required service lengthened to two years. By July the
truce talks had begun, at Kaesang in Korea, the UN negotiating
with the Chinese Communists. Meanwhile a weather and financial
disaster struck the Mississippi River basin in July when a massive
flood spread over parts of several states, causing a billion dollars'
damage.

Years after World War II had ended in fact, a formal peace treaty with Japan remained unsigned; this was remedied in September 1951 when forty-nine nations signed a treaty with the Japanese. The United States claimed the right to maintain permanent military bases in Japan. Mrs. Roosevelt went to Europe again in the fall for the UN, this time to Paris. (The UN headquarters was still under construction in New York.) During her visit to France she made side trips to Geneva and Brussels and in the latter city attended a conference on spirituality that had a deep impact on her ideas about peace.

The critical importance of cooperative political and military security was reflected in the passage by Congress in October of the Mutual Security Act, which funneled $7 billion in aid to selected countries whose politics the United States felt it could trust or influence. These dollars were sent abroad in a different spirit than were the millions appropriated as immediate, emergency postwar aid to displaced persons of all political stripes.

Technological advances for Americans in 1951 included initiation of the first transcontinental dial telephone service, and the first electricity to be created by a nuclear-powered steam generator sparked through test wires in a government laboratory in the mountains of Idaho.

~ ~ ~

There was a sense in which it was possible to believe that Mrs. Roosevelt would go on forever at the same fevered pitch of political and social and familial and journalistic activity. Her "My Day" columns could leave readers breathless, considering the amount and variety of work and play in her life. But more important, Eleanor Roosevelt's spirit, or at least her public guise of confidence and determination, inspired people to think of her as almost immortal.

HYDE PARK, JANUARY 2—I have just had an amusing anonymous letter, and I am going to reproduce it here because I think it is a good note on which to start the New Year. My correspondent writes:

"My dear Mrs. Roosevelt: Don't you think it is a mistake to refer to yourself as a very old lady? How do you think a person eighty years old reacts? The impression is a poor one. One does not think of you in any age bracket, but as a self-disciplined woman . . . so please in the future forget your age and just be yourself. No need to sign this. My answer will come if in your talks you just speak as Eleanor Roosevelt—the Invincible. Thank you."

I want to thank this anonymous correspondent because it had never occurred to me that it would be discouraging to anybody when I said I was a very old lady. I realize there are many older people. Perhaps, therefore, my correspondent is right, and I will heed this warning. I wish I were "invincible." That means you have no weak moments, but I am afraid there are very few of us these days who don't occasionally have them.

~ ~ ~

At this point in American history surely the most misunderstood war so far was the Korean conflict. For one thing, although thousands of American lives were lost or damaged by the fighting and millions upon millions of dollars were spent on it, the United States never formally declared war on anybody. For the first time the United States was fighting as one power among many (though certainly the largest) under the United Nations banner. Then too, the Korean conflict was a military mare's nest set in a part of the world few Americans had ever heard much about, let alone visited. There were few cultural and economic ties to that part of the globe to justify American involvement in the conflict.

George F. Kenan of the State Department had a year or so earlier introduced a term that would help shape American foreign policy for a generation: containment. By which he meant that while we could not expect to overcome Communism and drive it out of political business, its roots already being too deep, we could at least keep it from spreading elsewhere in the world beyond its present borders. Hence the rationale for the fighting in Korea. Insofar as the Korean conflict represented an ideological battlefield on which Chinese and

Soviet Communism could struggle against Western capitalist democracy, it was the perfect laboratory experiment to test Kenan's containment theory.

Mrs. Roosevelt served a vital national purpose in several attempts through "My Day" columns to explain to her readers just how we had ended up in an undeclared war in Korea.

HYDE PARK, FEBRUARY 2—I have come to the conclusion that the nation as a whole has a very short memory. A number of people lately have asked me how we happened to be in Korea and why did the President start the war there? These seem to me almost impossible questions.

Anyone remembering back to the last war should know that the Japanese occupied Korea, and when we conquered Japan, we took the country over from them. They should also remember that Russia came into the war as our ally against Japan some months earlier than had been expected. It was originally understood at Yalta that the Soviets could not fight on two fronts, but would come in just as soon as the war in Europe ended. Instead of that they came in ahead of schedule, perhaps because they felt they must guard their Asiatic interests.

In any case, when we took over Korea, Russia quite naturally claimed a part of the responsibility and an arbitrary line was set up—the 38th Parallel. North of that was Soviet responsibility, south of that was ours.

The United Nations was asked by us to supervise a free election in South Korea. Syngman Rhee, while out of the country during the Japanese occupation, had been constantly agitating for Korean freedom. Since this was the first election participated in by the Korean people, it is perhaps understandable that they voted for this man whom they considered the leader for Korean independence. I am told that under him some steps toward a free and democratic government have been taken.

On the other hand, the Soviets refused to allow any interference and set about militarizing the North Koreans. When they were ready, they invaded South Korea. The South Koreans resisted. Immediate-

223

ly our President asked the United Nations to take action. It did so promptly, and the call went out for volunteers to enforce the UN stand against aggression.

This is the history of how we happen to be in Korea and how this whole situation came about. And this is why, having branded the North Koreans as aggressors, we also had to brand the Chinese Communists as aggressors. Whether you are a big or a small nation, aggression must be called by the same name.

If the Russians had not been the ones responsible for the North Koreans' preparation, one might hope that the Chinese had suffered anxiety in seeing us so near their Manchurian border. But I am quite sure the Soviets know that we are a peace-loving people and the Chinese Communists know it, too. Had they listened to what we said—and believed us—they would know that we had no intention of invading China, that we are only anxious to see Korea a peaceful country with a government the people themselves have chosen.

That is our aim today and the aim of the UN. I hope it can be carried out.

~ ~ ~

Arthur Koestler's 1940 novel Darkness at Noon *garnered glowing reviews and sales success as a Book-of-the-Month-Club selection before it was adapted for the stage. Like many of the most moving books in the genre of prison literature, this one tells a harrowing tale of mind-bending manipulation by repressive authorities and the parallel triumph of a resilient human spirit—in a prisoner convicted of a crime he did not commit. As a Hungarian, Koestler had experienced such repression first hand, under the aegis of Hungarian and Soviet communism. Mrs. Roosevelt admired the play greatly, in part because it addressed issues of freedom and control that all the citizenry of a democracy must think about carefully.*

HYDE PARK, FEBRUARY 8—Monday night while in New York City I went to see Claude Rains in "Darkness at Noon." I rarely have been to a play that gripped harder. Sidney Kingsley has done a wonderful piece of dramatic work in the adaptation of Arthur Koestler's novel.

It is not a pleasant play to sit through and yet you are tensely attentive every minute. You never want to hear the phrase "The end justifies the means" again, or listen to the hollow excuses that the "work" must go on regardless of the suffering of a few individuals or groups here and there. Mr. Rains' acting is superb; in fact, the whole cast is very good.

The atmosphere of terror that exists in the prison, in the office, in the girl's home, seems unreal—and yet you know how very real it is. You wonder at the cruelty that you see growing in the people who practice it. Then you remember Ilsa Koch, for instance, and realize that people either become callous or they go mad, and that callousness is part of the instinct of self-preservation that is so deeply ingrained in all of us.

This play should make many of us Americans more aware of the need for preserving our liberties and not giving up any one of them in the hope of being saved from Communism. Our only defense against Communism is to keep our freedoms.

~   ~   ~

Despite the emotional distance between Franklin and Eleanor Roosevelt that developed over the years, there were ways in which each remained passionate about the other. On her side perhaps the most important was her respect and deep admiration for his liberal political philosophy and his ability to show people how to overcome their fears and apply themselves to the tasks at hand. Thus, facing the worrisome scourge of McCarthyism with its exaggerated fears of Communist subversion, Mrs. Roosevelt believed the nation needed frequent reminding that American democracy was strong and quite capable of defending itself—if only people would rise above their fears. To deliver the message, she borrowed rhetoric from her husband.

NEW YORK, FEBRUARY 16—The Lord meant us to pray when we are frightened and when we feel the need of help. None of us in ourselves can feel that we have the wisdom and courage to meet the happenings in our ordinary daily lives, much less to meet those in the troubled world of today. But there are many verses in the Bible that would remind us what strength there is in faith. And instead of encouraging fear, I would encourage our representatives to have faith in our great destiny which is now shaping up.

The leadership of the world is no easy undertaking and it will not be adequately met by fear. It must be met by strength and objectiveness. We ended World War II with great military strength backed by an enormous productive capacity. We made a very rapid transition to civilian production and stood the strain on our economy in an extraordinary way. We were too quick in throwing away controls; we were too quick in giving up our military strength. Therefore, now we are having to accept more sacrifice than we might otherwise have had to make.

To feel, however, that the people of the United States cannot understand the need, cannot accept the responsibility of leadership, cannot meet the sacrifices and also the goals of production and even the regimentation, if necessary, is to show little faith either in God or in ourselves.

I would not look for a Communist under every bed. I would believe that the vast majority of our people believe in their republican form of government and their democratic way of life. I will accept the fact that we have to improve and constantly try to give benefits to more people within our own nation, but I will not believe that the terror and poverty of Communism and their faith in materialism instead of in God can win in the struggle in which we are now engaged.

~ ~ ~

Eleanor Roosevelt was no sportswoman. She was neither athletic herself nor interested in big-league sports, and her life was simply too full of other activities and commitments. But when a betting scandal in college basketball surfaced, Mrs. Roosevelt jumped to the defense of the importance of athletics in education. Her argu-

ment favoring the decommercialization of college sports fell on deaf ears.

HYDE PARK, FEBRUARY 22—None of us can help but be shocked to find that boys have been bribed to throw basketball games. But I feel that the men who did the bribing deserve the severer punishment because they were willing to make money out of young people to whom they were offering a very serious temptation.

Many boys who are working their way through a university have to work very hard. Many of them not only feel the pressure of meeting their own expenses, but sometimes things are happening at home which make it truly difficult not to have money to help out.

I can see the temptation that it might be to many a young person, though I must say some of these boys seem to be old enough to know better. I am rather glad that college games will now, in great part, be taken out of Madison Square Garden.

When you are in college, sports are a vital part of a man or woman's activity. They build health and they give young people good, strong bodies and the ability to use them skillfully.

In addition, we have always thought of sports as an aid to character-building. The old saying that many battles were won for Great Britain on the playing fields of Eton did not come about because of physical development alone, but because of the spirit of fair play, the teamwork, the ability to stick even in the face of defeat developed there. All these things are valuable assets to education. They go by the board, however, the minute there is cheating in a game just as an honor system is of no value if boys cheat in examinations.

Perhaps we have allowed our college sports to become too commercialized. Big gambling was possible on the results of these games and so the gambler tempted the players. Intramural sports are good, but I think it will be a pity if, because of the weakness of a few boys, we wipe out all intercollegiate sports.

I have never liked the practice of the alumni subsidizing good players and thus attracting athletes to college regardless of their mental attributes. But I do realize that the GI Bill of Rights has enabled many young people to go to college who might otherwise not have had the opportunity for an education. Therefore, I am very anxious that some way be devised by which boys who show ability in school shall have an opportunity to attend college regardless of their financial status.

We cannot afford to waste brains in this country. They are becoming more important to us every day. And surely financial position should not bar young people from the education which can give them positions of leadership in our nation in the future.

~ ~ ~

The Adventures of Fala! *It's a wonder that Walt Disney never made an animated film about the nation's First Dog, the Roosevelts' Scots terrier. Perhaps it was a case of early spring fever that got into the old dog and led him into an all-night ramble in the woods. He never explained himself, but Mrs. Roosevelt shared the family reaction— worry and then relief—with "My Day" readers.*

HYDE PARK, MARCH 23—Since there are so many people who are interested in Fala, I must report that he gave his family a very bad 24 hours one day last week.

I took all the dogs walking before breakfast in the woods. Just as we reached the point where we always turn homeward, all three dogs made a dash after something they saw scurrying along the ground. Up and over the rocks and away through the hemlock trees they went. I called and called and called in vain. Anyone who has Scotties will understand the strange way they have of proceeding on their own business regardless of how much training they have received.

They must have been wrapped up in this chase, and there was spring in the air as well.

As I walked on in lonely contemplation toward home, Frannie, remembering her four puppies at home, came helter-skelter out of the woods behind me and accompanied me sedately the rest of the way. But there were no signs of Fala or Tamas.

When something like this happens I always think of Dorothy Canfield Fisher's story of the old grandfather who took his grandson to the county fair and nearly died as a result. Nevertheless, when they returned the grandfather still had a gleam in his eye which said the excursion was worth it!

At about 3 o'clock in the afternoon, Tamas came dashing home, tail in the air and a look of great triumph on his face. When I demanded to know where he had left Fala he looked around rather indifferently and showed no signs of wanting to lead me to his grandfather. Usually they come home together when they go off together, so I really worried and pictured poor old Fala falling down a hole, or drowning in a pond with no one at hand to pull him out.

All of us scoured the woods, calling him until dark. I sent around to my near neighbors asking if they had seen him. And we spent the night waking every little while to go to the door to call him.

In the morning Miss Thompson called the pound, but no Scottie had been brought in. We put an ad in the Poughkeepsie "New Yorker" and I was about to appeal in desperation to our local radio station when the guard at the Franklin D. Roosevelt Library called up to say that a small boy, living at least three miles away, had got his father to bring him over with Fala. The boy said Fala had spent the night with them.

I went for Fala at once and he didn't seem particularly pleased to see me. Miss Thompson remarked that he was probably bored with us and wanted a change of scene.

In the late afternoon a lady called me on the telephone from this same road and said that she brought Fala in and fed him. So he didn't even suffer the pangs of hunger. Now he's paying for his mischief, though. I don't dare let him off the leash, so he has to walk beside me instead of being able to make excursions into the woods and chase various animals.

~ ~ ~

Mrs. Roosevelt's political thinking was a generation or more ahead of its time on various issues. In several "My Day" columns she examined the issue of illegal aliens, particularly those coming into the Southwest across the Mexican border. As usual she sought to pose the problem with a balanced view of the competing interests, here involving the needs and concerns of both American laborers and the aliens themselves. (The investigations by the Labor Department she called for went on until the mid-1980s, when new immigration laws were passed to clean up the mess while still trying to protect workers' and employers' rights.)

NEW YORK, MARCH 27—Yesterday I read of an investigation made by a "New York Times" correspondent, Gladwin Hill. He told of the million Mexican workers who slip across our border every year. They know of our high wages and seek to escape the unemployment and low wages at home. They are illegally in our country and they swell the ranks of low-cost labor, which at the same time depresses wages of the American worker.

Many of the Mexicans come only as seasonal workers, but some of them remain in hiding in the country, traveling as far north as the Canadian border. They add to the school problem, the illiteracy problem and the health problem.

Supposedly we have an agreement with Mexico as regards Mexican labor when it enters this country, but a certain percentage of those coming north escape this arrangement. And though most of us resent the accusations made by the Soviet Union that we have slave labor in this country, the accusation may be not far from the truth where some of this group are concerned. Therefore, we should be aroused to demand an investigation by our Labor Department into this situation in the Southwest.

Where regular wages go as high as they have in parts of the country for farm labor and ordinary labor of different kinds, it is not surprising to find employers willing to take on hands without asking too many questions if the demands are not too high. There is the possibility, too, that those in this country illegally may be forced to work for any pay on the threat of being turned over to the authorities. We should be grateful to Mr. Hill for having drawn this situation to our attention and I hope it can be investigated.

~ ~ ~

Sometimes statements we make about others we mean unconsciously to apply to ourselves as well. Such may well have been the case when Mrs. Roosevelt quoted in her "My Day" column from a booklet about Léon Blum (1872–1950), a French statesman she admired greatly. Blum had a long and distinguished career. He was a deputy in the French National Assembly during most of the 1919–1940 period. Promoting a program of pacifism and economic development, he joined the radical Socialists and Communists in the Popular Front in 1936. He was premier of France from 1936 to 1938, then was arrested in 1940 by the Vichy (German Occupation) government and imprisoned until the war's end. Blum then became a special ambassador to the United States and returned to France to serve as head of the provisional government in 1946 and 1947.

These details may explain his political importance but, to Eleanor Roosevelt, Blum was something more: a man of character and conviction who lived life to the fullest.

NEW YORK, APRIL 7—Madame Léon Blum has sent me a little pamphlet which she wrote for the first anniversary of her husband's death. I wish it could be published in this country and read by many people, for we need the type of courageous, quiet leadership that Léon Blum gave to so many people during his life.

I want to give you a few sentences, which I will try to translate here: "He had made up his mind to be an optimist. . . . He never was afraid to appear in the wrong. . . . The desire to appear to be right never made him rush to a conclusion."

Finally, these sentences: "The best among us sacrifice our lives, want to make life an act of devotion; the bad sell their lives; the

231

neutrals drag out their lives; others burn up their lives; just a handful refuse to live. The very rare are those who accept their lives. He accepted life."

~ ~ ~

General Douglas MacArthur caused a major stir when he overstepped his bounds (according to President Truman) and began issuing statements about how U.S. foreign policy in the Far East should be conducted. Within days the General's position—that we should expand the war in Korea to include military action directly against the Communists in mainland China—had polarized the American political scene. Mrs. Roosevelt sided with those who thought that the military should fight and the Congress and the President should set foreign policy. Others at the time, however, lionized MacArthur. He was, after all, a hero from World War II. Some believed MacArthur had his eyes on either a Cabinet position in an anticipated Republican administration soon to replace Truman or even on the presidency itself. It was the season, after all, for candidates to toss their hats into the ring.

Mrs. Roosevelt chose to refocus the discussion on the policy rather than the personality issues. Just what should America be thinking about the Communist Chinese?

NEW YORK, APRIL 9—I have a very great admiration for General MacArthur as a soldier and, from all I hear, he has been a good administrator in Japan who has made some wise and far-reaching reforms. I feel that this country owes him a debt of gratitude for the part he played in World War II, and I hope when he comes home he will be received with the honors due one of the great American generals of that war.

I cannot feel, however, that a commanding general in the field, particularly when he commands for a group of nations, should take it upon himself to announce the policy that in his opinion should be followed in the area of the world where he commands troops. I cannot speak for any other citizen of the United States, and I know there are Representatives in the House and in the Senate who are in complete sympathy with the things that have been said lately by General MacArthur—but, for myself, I am unhappy about them.

As a citizen, I have two great concerns at the present time; first, that the United States policy and the United States troops should continue to support the United Nations in an effort to show the world clearly that aggression by any nation is going to be withstood by the UN as a whole. Second, my concern is that we, as a nation, should do all we can to bring about a peaceful world. We will not help in that direction if any overt act, or anything said by responsible officials, is taken by Communist China as an excuse for charging that we are aiding and abetting aggression against the Communist Chinese government or against USSR-controlled territory in Asia.

Why should we, at this juncture, ally ourselves with any portion of the Chinese people? Whatever difficulties now exist in China must be settled by the Chinese people themselves. It may be they can settle their difficulties without further internal strife. Certainly that is a solution much to be desired. But that we should in any way support a government that could not remain in control of the Chinese people because it was unable to bring about a unified government or the reforms that would give the people hope of a better life in the future seems to me a mistake.

Again we seem to be lining up on the side of reaction simply because we cannot approve of Communism, which is on the opposite side. I think we would be justified in refusing to recognize the Communist Chinese government for some time. In any case, I would think we could not recognize them until they did represent all the Chinese people and had proved their ability to accept the requirements that go with becoming a member of the United Nations. If the Chinese people as a whole live under a Communist regime, I think that regime will either have to satisfy some of their needs or it will cease to be acceptable to the people. Chinese people are a patient people and heaven knows they have lived with civil war a long time. But, having made up their minds to get some reforms, they will be critical, I think, of any sham reforms and will be quick to resent anything which gives them reforms only in name and not in fact. To accept the suggestions made for our foreign policy by General MacArthur would seem to me to put us in a very equivocal and undesirable position.

~ ~ ~

The European Economic Community, long known as the Common Market, moved haltingly toward a truly integrated economy after the Schuman Plan was worked out in 1951. Robert Schuman, a French politician, had served in the National Assembly since 1919, was minister of finance in 1946 and of foreign affairs between 1948 and 1952 and prime minister between the cabinet posts. Schuman's idea was to encourage Franco–German rapprochement by linking the economies of the two recently warring countries. His plan resulted in the establishment of the European Coal and Steel Community in 1952, and Schuman became the first president of the European Parliamentary Assembly. Mrs. Roosevelt favored the plan because, in the marketplace, international cooperation rather than selfish competition stood the best chance of assuring the fragile European peace.

GENEVA, APRIL 25—It is quite possible that the signing of the Schuman Plan treaty by the six European foreign ministers may prove to be one of the greatest turning points in history.

The treaty pools the coal and steel production of France, West Germany, the Netherlands, Belgium, Luxembourg and Italy. After the pact is ratified by the member governments, they are bound to surrender their sovereignty over their coal and steel industries to a supranational body for the next 50 years.

This agreement forms an economic basis on which an organized Europe can be planned. It eliminates coal and steel tariffs and creates a single market for these products for 160,000,000 people. It forms a foundation in Europe for the political community which already has begun to grow and function through the Council of Europe.

234

Without the strength and perseverance of Mr. Schuman, whose name the treaty bears, this would never have been an accomplished fact. It would have remained in the area of those things which are good ideas but which no one ever had the courage and forcefulness to push to conclusion.

We can be proud that the United States helped to bring this plan to reality. The next five years will be difficult years since inefficient industries will have to be shut down and new industries started. Capital will be needed from us. But as this economic basis becomes solid in Europe the chance of future wars gradually will be eliminated, and there is a hope that in time the old hates will vanish and a federation of Europe, as strong as the federation of the United States, will bring greater prosperity and security to all peoples.

~ ~ ~

From time to time Eleanor Roosevelt simply saw things as funny, particularly when at least part of the joke was on her. Never vain about her appearance, she could easily laugh at the way television seemed to require so much fussing over one's make-up and note that different cultures—American, British, French—did this fussing in rather comically different ways. Mrs. Roosevelt and her son Elliott were in Geneva, where she was attending a UN session.

GENEVA, MAY 5—It has been amusing to me to put on television make-up and to see the other guests, both men and women, being made up in France and in England. We were all given much heavier make-up in France, and the lights must have been warmer there because the bald-headed gentlemen were watched over by a pretty little make-up girl who ran out in the intervals between filming to wipe off their heads and powder them again.

In London the make-up was even lighter than at home. I asked a young woman who did mine whether she did not get a little weary putting stuff on people's faces. She said she didn't, that every face was different and it was something like creating a new picture each time.

The last two nights we have been doing radio interviews here in

Geneva. Elliott and I have been doing our questions and answers on things which have come up here and it has been fun seeing the different methods used. The first night there was a break in the tape or something. Anyway, suddenly the lights began to flicker and the strangest noises came out of the loudspeaker and it sounded as if an irate little animal would shortly land in the middle of the table.

~ ~ ~

Among the issues in the "My Day" columns of this period of United Nations work was the question of whether the United States ought to pass an Equal Rights Amendment to the Constitution to guarantee fair treatment of women. For a long time Eleanor Roosevelt opposed the idea of a constitutional amendment because in her opinion the biggest offenders were the states themselves, with discriminatory laws. She felt the state legislatures should clean up this business. By mid-1951, however, Mrs. Roosevelt had seen enough foot-dragging by the states and had learned enough in the UN Commission on the Status of Women to recognize that an amendment would probably be necessary. She began an educational campaign through her column.

Educating the nation on women's rights was one thing; educating her grandchildren was something else. Mrs. Roosevelt found playful ways to instruct them on weighty matters, in this case by reading to them from the children's stories of Rudyard Kipling.

BOSTON, JUNE 16—Kipling has gone out of fashion more or less, whereas when I was young it would have been almost impossible to find a child who did not know "The Jungle Book." It is a rare thing nowadays to find a child who does. But on the afternoons when I am home some of my grandchildren gather around at five o'clock in the afternoon and I read aloud. The other day we read "How Fear Come" from "The Jungle Book."

Some of my contemporaries will remember from that story of a few of the rules of the jungle, as taught by old Baloo, the brown bear.

236

These particular rules apply to the wolves, but as I read I could not help thinking how well they applied to us all. For instance:

"As the creeper that girdles the tree-truck the law runneth forward and back,
"For the strength of the Pack is the Wolf and the strength of the Wold is the Pack."

Isn't that a pretty good picture of why we should have a United Nations and why each nation in the UN should look to its own contribution? The success of the organization depends on what each member is and can contribute.

I could not help looking at my small fry with a smile as I read:

"Wash deeply from nose tip to tail tip; drink deeply, but never too deep."

And then again:

"When Pack meets Pack in the Jungle, and neither will go from the trail,
"Lie down till the leaders have spoken—it may be fair words will prevail."

So, even in the law of the jungle the value of conversation before action was recognized.

And here again is one of the human rights expressed as the law of the jungle:

"The lair of the Wolf is his refuge, and where he has made his home,
"Not even the Head Wolf may enter, not even the Council may come."

So the right of privacy and the ownership of property was one of the laws of the jungle! Kipling even made it clear that in the jungle you could not be completely selfish. Here it is:

"If Ye plunder his Kill from a weaker, devour not all in thy pride;
"Pack-right is the right of the meanest; so leave him the head and the hide."

In other words, if you can get it, you can take the major part. But don't take everything or you may regret it later. And now for the last verse:

"Now these are the Laws of the Jungle, and many and mighty are they;
"But the head and the hoof of the Law and the haunch and the bump is—Obey!"

~ ~ ~

She was in a playful mood again when writing the next column, about men's fashions. Mrs. Roosevelt had been mocked so many times by fashion critics who said her own clothes left just about everything to be desired that one might think she would never dare to venture into the fashion field as a social commentator. But not so. Clearly, in Eleanor Roosevelt's opinion, it was time for men to shape up.

NEW YORK, JULY 13—After watching the red fezzes and costumes of the Shriners now in convention here, I have come to the conclusion that somewhere in the male make-up there is a desire to make their costumes a little more interesting and to allow them to express themselves better through their clothes.

I never have understood why every member of the male sex had to dress in the same way. I always liked to look at pictures from the era when our gentlemen wore breeches of beautiful materials and colors, long silk stockings and beautiful shoes with a variety of buckles. Coats and waistcoats rivaled any lady's finery and, if they so wished, men wore powdered wigs tied with gorgeous ribbons.

How they came to be so restrained later on I don't know, unless the difficulty of obtaining this finery in the early days of this country was too great. Perhaps the Quakers and some of the other religious sects had a quieting effect.

I'd like to see our gentlemen follow the rules of nature that govern our animal friends. Almost always the male animal is the showoff while the female remains demure and is less startlingly clad. Perhaps someday we will have the courage to strike a good medium and let the men have a little self-expression in their clothes.

~ ~ ~

Another column with a double subject; sometimes Mrs. Roosevelt couldn't resist building her "My Day" columns out of apparently unrelated blocks. Here we see a plug for a political novel that soon became required reading for many high schoolers, George Orwell's Animal Farm. *It would have been easy enough for "My Day" readers to guess whether Mrs. Roosevelt would like this book because it tells a tale in which totalitarian government is satirized and shown to be contradictory to the yearning for freedom in the human breast.*

Her second subject was the praise her husband had received from Dutch friends in a letter to the President's widow that had touched Mrs. Roosevelt deeply.

HYDE PARK, AUGUST 15—Have I ever mentioned George Orwell's little book, "Animal Farm"? The other day I read it in more leisurely fashion and enjoyed every word.

There is a quiet satire and humor in the animals' behavior and "Revolution and the Pigs" which is quite delightful. I think everyone would not only enjoy but profit by reading this little book.

Some Dutch-Americans, Mr. and Mrs. H. P. Van Walt, have been visiting us. They had written me that they wanted to spend a day here in Hyde Park, to see the house and library. They were among the most charming guests I ever had the pleasure of welcoming. Everyone who showed them around told me of their appreciation and enjoyment.

A letter came today from Mrs. Van Walt and I think that what she says represents what many people feel who come here. As it is the kind of tribute that would make anyone happy, I am going to quote it.

"During those years he was not only president to us. He was in a very deep sense a father; and it was as a father that we mourned him.

239

He interpreted America to us. It was through him that we first began to yearn for citizenship.

"Perhaps the strongest thought we brought away with us was this. That tens of thousands of Americans and more, are better men and women today, finer citizens, because of that twelve years when he guided us; and that we shall go on trying to be worthy of it."

Could one ask for a better way to be remembered? It seems to me that this is the way all of us would like people to feel about our influence after we have left this world.

~ ~ ~

"Sacrifice for the good of others and count your own blessings as abundant" might have been the basic rule of thumb for a life well lived in Eleanor Roosevelt's terms. Hence her surprise at the trouble the Red Cross continued to have in obtaining enough donated blood to meet emergency needs. Here we see her step onto the podium and lecture her fellow citizens.

NEW YORK, SEPTEMBER 26—It is astounding that the newspapers have to keep on urging the people to respond to the appeal by the Red Cross for blood. There must be plenty of people who could take a half hour off, even at lunchtime, and go into a center and do this little chore. It is not painful and it has no aftereffects.

I used to go regularly during World War II until the unfortunate day when I went as usual and an embarrassed attendant asked me if I had not had my sixtieth birthday a few days before. When I replied in the affirmative and still did not understand the implication, she looked more embarrassed and said, "You can no longer donate blood."

Giving one's blood was quite the easiest service that one could render. And today I cannot understand why the desire to help the wounded, whether in Korea or in cases of accident anywhere, does not inspire every person able to do so to give their blood regularly.

240

~ ~ ~

There was no more committed, articulate defender of the New Deal than Eleanor Roosevelt. Some historians argue that by the time the U.S. entered World War II, the American experiment with a mixed socialist and capitalist economy was necessarily over, but the debate continues. Mrs. Roosevelt makes an interesting argument in this column: that the New Deal may have seemed somewhat radical at the time but in fact served rather conservative purposes. It did this first by calming fears of an imminent workers' revolution and then by getting people back to work under circumstances similar to those they had known before the stock market crash in 1929 and the ensuing Depression, although supported now in part by a bigger role for government. Who else but Eleanor Roosevelt could get away with defending FDR in conservative terms?

NEW YORK, OCTOBER 5—Occasionally I get a letter from someone who feels that in this country we have lost the old virtues of standing on our own feet, of realizing that we have to work for what we get, of being honest in our relations with one another.

This feeling often is attributed to the fact that under the stress of economic disaster people began to look to their government for aid because they themselves were unable to meet the desperate situations in which they found themselves.

Most of the people who write me seem to have forgotten that the businessmen who had striven to find answers to the economic problems up to 1932 had not succeeded in keeping down a wave of foreclosures on farms in the middle part of this country. Thus, many of our farmers were made completely desperate. Factories were closing everywhere, railroads were hardly receiving freight enough to run a full train at any time during the 24 hours, and the economic wheels of our country were practically at a standstill. So much so that many a man who always had operated honestly and expected to ask nobody's help found himself offering his business to his government.

The "dangerous and socialist" schemes that came into being at this time were designed primarily to try to prevent such conditions from ever recurring. The people whose farms were saved, the people who did not lose their homes, the people who found work on government projects until the factories could begin to open again—all these people were not made dependent. They were simply kept from revolution against our government.

When you stand in line in the street for a cup of coffee, you rarely feel that your government is a successful one. I would like those who feel that the people of the United States have been rendered soft and dishonest by the things the government has done for them to remember that there were a good many parts of this country in 1933 where a revolution could have been engineered by almost any enterprising person. And that condition was brought about by the conservative, orthodox business methods that prevailed under the experienced men of business under President Herbert Hoover and his very able Cabinet.

These very people who complain to me that under the almost 16 years in which this country was under the administration of the Democratic Party and who believe that this fact is responsible for all the shortcomings that they now see in various parts of the country are putting the cart before the horse. The Republicans, perhaps because of circumstances beyond their control, but still while they were in office, brought this country to a condition where only drastic measures could keep us from complete disaster. These measures were applied in cooperation with the people of the country, who worked hard to make them succeed.

I cannot believe that the people of this country, by and large, are less honest today or have less independence and moral fiber than they had in the days gone by. We hear today of every shortcoming in public office, in business, or among our youth. Perhaps in the old days these things would not have been so easily discovered or so quickly exposed, but I am glad that we expose them and that they inspire us to work harder as citizens to make an even better record in the future. We have shown that we are no weaklings; we have tried to devise ways of preventing a recurrence of conditions that existed up to 1932.

242

~ ~ ~

On Eleanor Roosevelt's political scorecard, Senator Robert Taft, a
Republican, already had more than one black mark by the time he
announced he would run for President. His co-sponsorship of the
Taft–Hartley Act, which put numerous controls on unions to the
advantage of management, convinced Mrs. Roosevelt that he was no
friend of the constituency she most readily identified with—the liberal
working men and women of the country. And so, it was up on the
soapbox again for her when Taft began making claims that only his
line of thinking could save the nation from socialist wrack and ruin
under the misguided Harry Truman. One can imagine Taft's followers
wincing when this "My Day" column appeared.

NEW YORK, OCTOBER 20—One of the really interesting announce-
ments of the last few days was that made by Senator Robert A. Taft
concerning next year's political conventions and the presidential
election. And, like all candidates, he exuded utmost confidence
when he stated: "I will be nominated and elected."

How anyone knows so far ahead what a convention will do or what
the citizens of the country will decide is difficult for me to understand. But I suppose Senator Taft's backers have counted noses and
think they have a sufficient number of votes in the convention to
defeat all comers, including General Dwight D. Eisenhower and
Governor Earl Warren, and that after that there will be clear sailing.

It is interesting to have a statement from Senator Taft that he will
restore "liberty, integrity and sound judgment" to the councils of the
nation. It seems to me there are a good many men who are now
included among those who counsel, who think they have liberty and
integrity. Sound judgment is always a matter of opinion on decisions
taken after the results of the judgment are available.

Senator Taft is going to carry on an active campaign and not make
the mistake made by Governor Thomas E. Dewey when he ran for
the Presidency. The Senator's platform seems to be condensed in the
three following points:

1. Opposition to what he called "socialism and excessive spending of the New Deal on the domestic front." This has a familiar ring, but it doesn't mean much until you really sit down and put into words what you are going to do away with. Would it be old-age pensions, Social Security, unemployment insurance, an effort to improve housing, care for the handicapped or the blind? Just what are you going to consider as socialistic and stop spending on it?

2. Criticisms of the Truman administration's "fatal mistakes" in foreign policy, including the war in Korea, the "building up of Russia," and "other disastrous occurrences due to their judgment." We will hope that the Korean War will be at an end before Senator Taft is called upon to correct these "fatal mistakes." If not, he will have something difficult to handle. I would like to have explained to me just how he feels Russia had been built up and what are the disastrous occurrences he refers to before I can get a picture of what he is planning as our foreign policy.

3. "Restoration of honesty and integrity in government." I think there is no candidate who would not make this last statement. All are for honesty and integrity in government, but the Senator will have to depend on others besides himself to make good on this promise—and that is where the best of intentions sometimes fail.

Senator Taft's answer to the question, however, put by the reporters as whether he would welcome Senator McCarthy's backing was that he would like to have the Senator with him. This makes one wonder about this honesty and integrity with which he hopes to surround himself.

~ ~ ~

Eleanor Roosevelt did not have a graduate degree in anything, let alone art history. But she did have enthusiasm for the arts that traced itself back to childhood education in England, to travels in Europe and visits to the great museums. Stealing a little time to see once more the Louvre in Paris while working feverishly there with the UN Commission on Human Rights, she found inspiration enough to remind her readers of how uplifting the sheer beauty of a great work of art can be. The ship on whose prow the statue "Winged Victory" would have ridden would have sailed the ancient Greek waters of the northeastern Aegean Sea.

PARIS, NOVEMBER 8—I was able to spend an hour in the Louvre the other day, the first time in a good many years, so I decided to go in up the stairs that lead past the statue of the "Victoire de Samothrace." Standing on the prow of a ship, this figure of a woman is one of the most commanding and beautiful imaginable. You can almost feel the wind blowing around her and the spread of the wings is an inspiring sight.

We walked slowly through the rooms with the early Italian paintings, stopping to look at some of the lovely Madonnas and being intrigued and amused by the Mona Lisa smile.

Seeing these pictures again after so many years made me want to go back to Florence and Rome and see some of the others that I have not seen for an even longer time.

The part I really like the most about some of the early Italians, such as Fra Filippo Lippi, is the little formal landscapes that form the background of the pictures. The flowers stick up like little spikes and sometimes the human figures are bigger than the background, but there is a charm in those landscapes that always holds me enthralled.

What masters of color they were! Somehow we never use gold or blue or red in modern paintings as well as they did in those early days. Perhaps as they painted largely for churches there was a sense of dedication to the service of the Lord and the secret of some of their success may lie in that dedication to the spiritual as well as to the art.

I doubt if any of those early artists were really paid for the work they did. I think most of them worked for the love of the art. You look at some of the early Gothic churches, such as the one in Senlis, which was badly damaged by the war, and you wonder how long it took a man to carve one of the figures around the door.

~ ~ ~

What of the spiritual Eleanor Roosevelt? There was family loyalty to the Episcopalian church in Hyde Park, where generations of Roosevelts had worshiped, but one doesn't get a sense of true spiritual engagement or enthusiasm from her comments about attending services there. She did believe deeply in the power of prayer, and during both the Depression and the war when so many national and international problems seemed unsolvable, Mrs. Roosevelt often encouraged her readers to pray for their leaders and for those who were in great need.

While in Europe in 1951 she was invited to a conference in Brussels at which spirituality of a different sort was the topic. A gathering of religious leaders and thinkers from the university and artistic worlds of Europe, the meeting focused on how an individual's spiritual development could affect, for better or worse, his or her action in the world. It is only a short step from this basic question to one of Mrs. Roosevelt's own longtime beliefs—that peace in the world begins with peace in the individual's heart. Though we see her here standing steadfastly within her own Christian tradition, she is at the same time ecumenical in recognizing that other religious practices may lead humankind in the same positive direction.

PARIS, NOVEMBER 22—I think I should say that the membership of the group [the spiritual conference in Brussels] was highly intellectual. It was composed of university professors, teachers, ministers of many faiths, philosophers and representatives of such religious groups as Bahai.

I think Europe is a more fertile ground than the United States for this type of intellectual and spiritual research. The organizers of this group, I think, feel that the intellectual approach is not a good one; that it must be a purely spiritual approach on the part of the individual. But there were certainly a great many people at these meetings who could not divest themselves of their intellectual capacities.

The one thing that I would fear is that people who become enthusiasts are apt to see in everything that happens to them a corroboration of the things which they wish to believe. To be sure, therefore, that you are not imagining something because you wish it to be true is very difficult.

For instance, if I desire guidance in a difficult decision, and I have done everything possible to prepare myself to receive guidance, might it not be possible that subconsciously I would accept what was my own desire rather than any direct communication from God? Take another instance: If someone were not completely honest, or even if they fooled themselves because they had a desire to do something or not to do it, they could hide behind a feeling of guidance which really was only an expression of their own desire.

Again it seems to me that there is the chance that we were given our intelligence and our gifts as a part of God's plan, and it might well be that each and every one of us should develop our faculties to the best of our ability, that we should seek information from others. In fact, we should explore all avenues that would help us to meet our own problems.

This is not saying that we would feel able to decide without God's help. But the deep religious feeling of many people will not, of necessity, mean that on each action that they take they feel direct guidance from God. Rather, it may mean that what they have learned and the effort they have made to live, if they are Christians, according to Christ's teachings, will have so molded their characters that unconsciously they will do the Lord's will. These people may need contact with their churches and they may not have exactly the type of guidance that the organizers of this movement feel is essential.

I think I believe that the Lord looks upon His children with compassion and allows them to approach Him in many ways. I am glad to have had the opportunity of association with the group at Brussels—it was a rare privilege—and it is a wonderful thing in these times to feel that people are devoting themselves to the growth of spiritual strength and capacity. But I do not think that anyone can feel that there is only one way, since what may meet someone's needs may not of necessity meet another's needs. And one must even beware of too much certainty that the answers to life's problems can only be found in one way and that all must agree to search for light in the same way and cannot find it in any other way.

~ ~ ~

The Commission on Human Rights pushed itself to finish as much work as it could on its Covenant of Human Rights before all the delegates were to return home for the year-end holidays. There were many technical points to hammer out, each requiring careful negotiations about wording and intentions, but the broad issues were clear. Having completed the year before a draft of the Declaration of Human Rights, a statement in principle, the commission had this year concentrated on how the principles might be enforced. In the absence of an international police force run by the UN, and wishing to avoid tainting the high principles of human rights with the darker implications of armed enforcement, the commission decided to write a covenant. Any nation signing the covenant would have promised in front of all the world to uphold the Declaration. The covenant was the closest the UN could hope to come to giving the Declaration the powerful status of international law. Mrs. Roosevelt used many of her "My Day" columns to keep her readers apprised of the progress being made on the covenant and of the hurdles it faced.

PARIS, DECEMBER 13—We are progressing slowly in Committee 3! We are still going through a general debate on human rights problems. The point that we in the United States delegation hope will be decided first is whether there shall be one covenant containing all human rights or whether there shall be two covenants presented simultaneously, one containing civil and political rights and one economic and social rights.

But in the course of the debate many other questions have been covered. People have touched on the federal-state clause, on the right to own property, and mention was made of the rights of the family, which had only been touched on in the present draft of the covenant by mentioning maternity and child welfare. Some delegates think these rights of the family are deserving of a separate covenant.

Finally, a number of delegations have presented an article that they desire included in the covenant which is to read: "All peoples have the right to self-determination."

It seems to some of us rather narrowing to put such an article in the covenant, since the principle of self-determination is recognized in the Charter of the United Nations. It is a living principle today, applicable to all member nations. Such an article in the Human Rights Covenant, we fear, might be restrictive rather than broadening. So we are suggesting an amendment that we hope the sponsors of this suggested article may accept.

Twenty-six speakers put their names down to speak in the general debate Monday and Tuesday and yet we had to adjourn nearly an hour early both days because there were no speakers ready. This seems to me a sad waste of time when time is the most precious thing that any of us have.

1952

*N*ot many years so truly represent the end of an era as does 1952. There were changes in Eleanor Roosevelt's life this year which made it seem to her a clear turning point as well. When in January Dwight David Eisenhower announced that he would accept a draft to run for President on the Republican ticket, it was the beginning of the end of a twenty-year period of continuous Democratic dominance of the White House. Though there was much campaigning still to come, in a sense the dice had already been rolled. The country was ready for a change, generally in a more conservative direction. "Ike," as Eisenhower was called, would fill the bill. Mrs. Roosevelt, as a thorough-going liberal, naturally supported the Democratic candidate, Adlai Stevenson; however, even she had such deep respect for General Eisenhower that she made no dire pronouncements about the fate of the country should he become the next president.

But Harry Truman had twelve months of chief executive work still to go. In January he reached an accord with the once-again prime minister of Great Britain, Winston Churchill, in which the United States promised never to initiate an atomic bomb attack on Europe without British consent. Late in the month, the Korean truce talks stalled, much to everyone's frustration.

Always on the go, Mrs. Roosevelt began 1952 in Paris, where the UN was continuing to meet. In the early spring she travelled eastward on her first round-the-world journey, making stops in India, Nepal, and other countries over a three-week period. By late April she was back in New York to take up her UN work once again.

McCarthyism was headed into its heyday. Eleanor Roosevelt's reactions to what she saw as the scourge of McCarthyism grew stronger and more hostile as she condemned the red baiting and character assassination techniques of Senator McCarthy and his congressional colleagues on the House Un-American Activities Committee. The Supreme Court ruled in March that people termed subversive could be barred from teaching in the public schools; by October New York City had begun a purge in which eight teachers, alleged Communists, were dismissed. Also in March Senator William Benton of Connecticut tried to discredit Senator Joseph McCarthy's earlier attacks on the credibility and patriotism of the Foreign Relations Committee and the Pentagon by claiming that McCarthy had used Hitlerite scare tactics. McCarthy countered with a suit (for slander, libel, and conspiracy) against Benton. Benton hit back with a move to have McCarthy expelled from the Senate. Who won? Neither Benton nor the nation won: In the November elections he was defeated by a pro-McCarthy challenger, while McCarthy was re-elected. Anti-Communist foreign policy hard-liners were pleased when George Kennan, architect of the containment policy, became ambassador to the Soviet Union.

Harry Truman, who had experienced some health problems, announced at the end of March that he would not run again for President. Meanwhile, Truman's problems with organized labor continued. The President ordered a federal takeover of the steel mills in Youngstown, Ohio, to avert a strike. In a landmark case, the Supreme Court ruled unconstitutional the government's seizure of the mills, thus severely limiting the power of the President. The federal courts also denied the steel companies' requests for restraining orders, and in June 600,000 workers walked out in what was to be an expensive month-long strike. Later in the summer, railroad owners regained control of their lines, which had been under Army jurisdiction because of labor-management disputes since August 1950.

At their convention in Chicago in July the Republicans nominated Eisenhower (with Senator Richard Nixon, for Vice President) on the first ballot in a spasm of party unity. Their platform: balance the budget, reduce the national debt, retain the Taft–Hartley Act (this last plank was cold comfort to Senator Taft, who tried hard to get the nomination himself). The Democrats, split, took three ballots to settle on Adlai E. Stevenson (with John Sparkman as vice-presidential candidate). Eleanor Roosevelt admired Stevenson greatly as an intellectual, a liberal, and as Governor of Illinois. At the same time she believed Stevenson lacked certain essential qualities necessary to a presidential candidate, particularly campaigning skills. Stevenson asked Mrs. Roosevelt to make every public appearance with him and for him that she could: He knew that her endorsement would be required to carry the election. However, Mrs. Roosevelt's status as a UN delegate prevented her from much active involvement in the race.

In late September, Nixon delivered his melodramatic "Checkers" speech, an emotional self defense in the face of allegations about an illicit campaign slush fund. While that speech cleared up very little, the Supreme Court was clear on several new decisions. The justices rejected the appeal of their death sentence by Ethel and Julius Rosenberg and reaffirmed a lower-court ruling barring segregation in interstate rail travel. The Rosenberg trial evinced strong reactions from conservatives and liberals alike. Mrs. Roosevelt avoided taking a stand on the question of the defendants' innocence, though she respected the courts' decisions; nevertheless, she did come out against the death penalty in her "My Day" column.

Mrs. Roosevelt made one more important trip in 1952, at the request of outgoing President Truman. Chile was to inaugurate a new president of its own, and the former First Lady carried Truman's and the nation's good wishes to Santiago. This unofficial role as ambassador was one more indication of how highly esteemed Eleanor Roosevelt had become.

With a popular general about to assume the presidency, the year ended on a military note. In November the United States successfully tested the first hydrogen bomb, blowing up a tiny atoll in the Marshall Islands. John Foster Dulles, whose foreign policy ideas fueled the arms race for years to come, was nominated to be Secretary of State. In an attempt to break the stalemated Korean peace talks, President-elect Eisenhower, long familiar with Army life on the front lines, went to Korea but did not bring home the hoped-for news of peace. Even the literary world seemed hooked on the military theme in 1952: The Pulitzer Prize went to Herman Wouk's *The Caine Mutiny*, a gripping novel about the paranoid lunacy of a naval commander drunk on his own power, obsessed with a rigid battle plan.

Writing in her "My Day" columns, Eleanor Roosevelt reminded her fellow Americans that McCarthyism represented just such a madness in its insistent search, often in entirely wrong places, for alleged subversives who usually turned out to be innocent.

~ ~ ~

Mrs. Roosevelt returned to Paris, where she was continuing her UN work, and wrote a broadly idealistic column about converting the American economy (and others) to full-time peacetime production. Ever since World War II had forced a complete mobilization of all U.S. resources and effectively put the country back to full employment, a debate had gone on about whether entering the war had been the only way out of the Depression's prolonged economic slump.

Paris, January 4—Occasionally over here somebody says to me: "What will happen if peace comes? We are all geared from the economic standpoint for a war economy. It would mean economic collapse."

Many of us who have a habit of looking backward as well as forward remember people who came home after traveling in Germany before World War II. They would tell with great admiration of the fact that there was no unemployment in Germany, that everyone was working, that conditions, on the whole, were very good. But these conditions were brought about almost entirely by Hitler's preparation for war.

Now, many people in Europe feel a certain analogy between prewar Germany and the United States of today and wonder if, rather than face an economic collapse, certain people in our nation would not rather have war.

Of course, this is utterly ridiculous and unnecessary. Those of us who know the needs of the underdeveloped areas of the world today are conscious of the fact that there is a need for production that will go on for many, many years. When it is possible, the production for defense can be quickly changed to production for peacetime usages.

This cannot happen, however, unless there is a blueprint and unless a decision is taken now as to the steps that will be followed when we reach the point where we feel we can face the Soviet Union on an even basis.

That day we should be ready to enter into worldwide development, which probably could be started now but probably cannot get into full swing until less money has to be devoted to defense preparation.

We should know how and what we will produce, where we will place it, what we will get in return for it and how we are going to develop a permanent peacetime economy, moving according to priority from one section of the world to another until we have a well-balanced international economy.

This requires thinking and planning on a world scale. I am sure that it should be done within the United Nations or, in any case, in close cooperation with the UN. A well-thought-out plan needs us to increase the heights of freedom and higher standards of living, but only if we have the imagination and the brains of the people who have built great enterprises in their own sections of the world, proving their ability to achieve greater benefits for the whole world.

Only the unimaginative could ever ask the question: "Do we have to have an economic collapse if our defense preparation comes to an end?"

We should face a peaceful world not only without fear but with great joy at the realization that the creative powers of many people can be let loose for good instead of being directed toward developing the type of goods that are essential for defense but which bring no return on the economic level. When these goods for defense are used in war they are destroyed and a chain of destruction is started, instead of a chain of constructive development such as peacetime activity can produce.

~ ~ ~

*Sometimes the nation needed disciplining, thought Eleanor Roosevelt.
Unpleasant as it was to be the disciplinarian, Mrs. Roosevelt never
shirked what she believed to be her duty. Many times what pushed her
into this role was her moral outrage at another instance of American
racism. To set the following case in perspective, we need to recall that
only after World War II did President Truman issue orders desegre-
gating the armed forces. Here we see evidence of an act of noncompli-
ance in a blatant insult to a dead black soldier and his family.*

PARIS, JANUARY 14—I cannot overlook one piece of news which has
been in our U.S. papers of late—namely, the story of the long
wrangle as to whether a Negro veteran, Pfc. Thomas Reed, can be
buried in a certain cemetery in Phoenix, Arizona. It is understood
that his father was willing that the effort should be made to gain for
him the right of burial without being in a segregated plot, and we can
well understand why his father would be willing to make this effort.
Pfc. Reed fought in Korea for all of the free world, for its freedom
and protection from aggression. The bullet that killed him might just
as well have killed a white boy, and neither the colored nor the white
boy would have died only for his own race. Somehow it saddens one
greatly, as one works for freedom and human rights throughout the
world, to have these rights flouted in our own United States.

~ ~ ~

*The British political philosopher Edmund Burke, in a letter on the
French Revolution, wrote "The only thing necessary for the triumph
of evil is for good men to do nothing." Mrs. Roosevelt had read
about evidence of high levels of citizen participation in voting and
campaigning in India, which she would soon visit. Even in remote,
undeveloped, illiterate India, the degree of participation in democracy
put Americans, who were more casual about their political responsibilities, to shame. In this column, Eleanor Roosevelt gives a not too*

*subtle reminder to her fellow Americans: If you value democracy,
exercise your right to vote; there is no excuse not to.*

PARIS, FEBRUARY 6—I was particularly interested in a story here
reporting the voting of certain wild tribes in India. I had been
wondering, as perhaps so many people in the United States might
have, why it should take so long to go through this process in India.
This story cleared this up, describing how many of the Indian tribes
from deep in the jungle had marched miles to reach the polling
booths and how others had left the worship of their Babylonian gods
in order to travel long distances to worship the god of "vote."

We cannot get out more than 51 percent of our vote at home, if I
recall the statistics correctly, and yet whole tribes in India can trek
through jungle and over desert with drums and flutes, leading
processions to cast their ballots. Think what this must mean for the
campaigners!

We think it is quite a task to cover a state by car and make
speeches to our constituents. How would we feel about making our
way through tiger-infested jungles to make stump speeches and later
to vote!

Perhaps someday it will be the Indian people who will be teaching
the rest of us how to use our precious secret ballot, which we are
inclined to take so much for granted and even to neglect.

~ ~ ~

*En route now around the world, making stops in more than a dozen
nations and often acting as an unofficial UN–U.S. ambassador,
Eleanor Roosevelt indulged herself in playing the role of travel writer.
The three-week period from which these typical columns come was
filled with the sights, sounds, and smells of exotic places. In these
far-off lands it was often the working-class people whose dignity and
demeanor impressed Mrs. Roosevelt most. She took great pleasure too
in spreading American culture wherever she could. The image of doing
the Virginia reel to Pakistani music in the first of the next two
columns must have raised many a smile among "My Day" readers.*

New Delhi, March 1—Many of the people of this area are refugees; many of them are just poor people; but some of them are leading a life they would not change. For instance, we saw one of the hill tribesmen who had spent the winter down in this warmer area and was on his homeward trek. He had probably lived on the sand in one of those odd little round huts they build with bent bamboo ribs and which open out like a folding basket to hold up the outside. The front is open and the family cooking goes on the outside. The inhabitants need only mats to lie on at night and their animals are herded around.

For transportation everything is loaded on donkeys, and the other travelers we saw who were on their way back to the hills were trudging single file over the roads that led there.

The faces of the people are extraordinary and their carriage is regal in its dignity for both the men and women, the women carrying large burdens on their heads.

We returned in time for a reception given at the Ladies Club in Lahore. Then I spoke to a group of students at Lahore University and later attended a large women's dinner at which some of the younger women did folk dances for me. And in a very few minutes I taught them the Virginia reel, dancing it to their own Pakistani music.

Bombay, March 11—The flowers are beautiful here and from the veranda outside our room one looks straight across the ocean not to Spain, as my husband used to say as he stood on a beach in Campobello Island, New Brunswick, but to Arabia.

So far India means color to me—brilliant color in cotton saris, in silk saris, and in beautiful embroideries so vivid that perhaps at home they would look out of place. Here, however, they fit into the landscape. The birds can be heard at all hours; the parrots chatter; and there is one bird that cries like a baby. I thought at first I must be hearing a jackal but I have discovered it is a bird.

It is far more tropical here and warmer than in New Delhi but still very comfortable. We actually spent this morning being very lazy. I had my hair done, then we went shopping, and later we drove along the shore and looked at the sailing boats since I wanted to see the sails unfurled. I got out of the car and watched the loading of these small boats, which engage in coastwise traffic. Most of the boats have two sails, one of which is enormous.

We drove through a slum area on the way back and saw many huts built of straw matting along the pavements. These huts are occupied by gypsies, other nomadic tribes, or anyone who wanted a temporary home in pretty uncomfortable surroundings but nevertheless cleaner than one would expect. The streets are cleaned by people using little straw brooms—just a few sticks tied together—and the sweepers scrape up every bit of dirt into tin containers.

~   ~   ~

Though the dateline was Katmandu, high in the Himalayas, the next column concerns events in New Delhi, India, where Mrs. Roosevelt found herself being overprotected by her hosts. She had been invited to visit India by U.S. Ambassador Chester Bowles, a longtime and much-respected friend. She had been sent out on this round-the-world tour also, in part, by Secretary of State Dean Acheson. The schedule of meetings, visits to important sites (not necessarily tourist sites but schools, hospitals, and so forth) and appearances at dinners, receptions, and parties was exhausting for a sixty-eight-year-old woman. More than once, Joseph Lash recounts, Mrs. Roosevelt slipped into a depressed mood and wanted to quit. Her friend David Gurewitsch was traveling with the Roosevelt entourage, and there were some moments of impatience with him as well. But the vast crowds who turned out to see Mrs. Roosevelt—including hundreds of Indian and Pakistani peasants who knelt in the street as she passed—inspired an aging and fatigued international heroine to carry on.

In New Delhi, faced with the possibility of an angry confrontation with disgruntled Communist university students, Eleanor Roosevelt insisted she could handle it and did just that. No doubt the students quickly realized that Mrs. Roosevelt sympathized with their disillusionment about poor employment prospects and with their restlessness under the the lingering repressive effects of former British colonial rule.

259

The students' Communist affiliation neither frightened nor impressed her.

The Katmandu column also shows Mrs. Roosevelt's concern for Indian religious beliefs as she tries to clear up an error made in a column about Gandhi's death and funeral.

KATMANDU, MARCH 26—I have just learned that I was in error earlier this month when I called the memorial to Gandhi in New Delhi his tomb. This was incorrect as, according to custom, his body was cremated and the ashes were buried in the Ganges. The Indian name for the memorial we visited is Samadhi. It was ignorance on my part and stupid acceptance of Western ideas that made me make this mistake. I am most grateful to have it called to my attention, for I know it must have seemed very stupid to anyone who knew the Indian customs.

In the afternoon I received a degree at a special convocation at Allahabad University. I had accepted an invitation to the Students' Union right after the convocation and at lunchtime an open letter was read, which had been written by some of the Communist students and signed by a number of others who were probably only dupes. The authorities were rather worried for fear that I would be treated discourteously but I protested I could handle any group of young people. They insisted, however, that I refrain from attending the large meeting of students.

Then I invited those who had written me the letter to come and see me, and I was prepared to receive up to 100 members of the union out on Mrs. Pandit's lawn afterward. Unfortunately, a delegation came to ask Mrs. Pandit why the meeting with the Students' Union had been canceled. Among them was the vice president of the union who was one of the foolish boys who had signed the open letter.

Mrs. Pandit told them that the open letter was foolish and discourteous. They were so annoyed they staged a demonstration, demanding that she come out and apologize. Finally, I went out and talked to them and promised to go to their meetings, which I did.

They gave me a very nice welcome and presented me with a framed scroll. Then I made another lecture.

It is quite evident that these young people are frustrated, unable to find work to do, and brought up in a tradition of British education which provides them with a good classical education but rather little in the way of practical learning that they can use today to serve their country more effectively.

I hope that after my meeting with them the incident was closed.

I thought the university was a delightful spot and I am very glad to have a degree from there and I hope all universities in India will think over their predicament and try to make such arrangements that the boys will find it easier to get jobs and also have the kind of education that serves the present needs of India.

~ ~ ~

When one of the most devoted Hyde Park family workers died after fifty-five uninterrupted years of service on the estate, Mrs. Roosevelt knew she had to be at the funeral to pay her respects and that she would eulogize the man in her column. In her mind, such a loyal employee had become family in all but the biological sense.

Eleanor Roosevelt also attended a funeral of another sort this spring at Hyde Park: The Roosevelt family dog, Fala, died of old age. She buried him near FDR in the Rose Garden. Her son Elliott, recounts biographer Joseph Lash, said later, "She had not wept at Father's burial, but the tears came this day. I had never seen her openly give way to grief before. . . . In lamenting the end of the scottie, Mother wept for his master."

NEW YORK, APRIL 18—Instead of going to the Human Rights Commission meeting on Wednesday morning, where the work up to now has been moving slowly, I took the train to Hyde Park to attend the funeral of Mr. William Plog, who had worked for my mother-in-law and then for my husband as superintendent of the Hyde Park place. Mr. Plog stayed on when we turned the place over to the government and continued to do the flowers in the house, just as he had always done them for my mother-in-law, and to superintend the gardens, particularly the rose gardens which he had always loved.

It is rare that someone works in one job for nearly 55 years. Mr. Plog was 30 years old when he came and 84 when he died. He was a faithful and loyal employee. He had seen my husband grow up from a young boy and he was always fond of him. I was glad that I could be at the funeral and that my cousin, Mrs. Theodore Douglas Robinson, was at home and able also to go to the funeral.

Fifty-five years is a long time to be associated with anybody as closely as one is with those who live on the same place. Mr. Plog will be missed very much because he was active almost right to the end. At 84 it probably is fortunate, though, when one has to die, to do so without suffering or too long an illness. The men who worked with him were devoted to him, for he was a good and kind person. It will seem very strange to me to go over to the old place and not see his familiar face and hear his warm and friendly greeting.

~ ~ ~

America Firsters were isolationists between the two World Wars who believed that no matter what European ties our culture might have, we owed no debt of responsibility to help Europe defend itself against the scourge of totalitarianism. To Mrs. Roosevelt this was a morally reprehensible position. Equally unacceptable in her view was the idea of impugning the patriotism of an American hero like General Eisenhower. Such insinuations of Communist sympathies were rife in the emotionally charged atmosphere of McCarthyism, and they made Eleanor Roosevelt wince in embarrassment for her country.

NEW YORK, APRIL 19—I wonder if many of my readers noticed that an organization that seems to stem somewhat from the old America-Firster group was formed the other day to prove that General Dwight D. Eisenhower is closely associated with Communists. This type of thing is becoming so ludicrous that each time it happens we should point it out and say to ourselves: "How stupid can we be? Is hysterical fear turning us all into morons?"

~ ~ ~

The Diary of Anne Frank became a phenomenal best-seller and went from book to successful play. Mrs. Roosevelt had read the book in manuscript form and recognized its importance, not just as a powerfully emotional true story but, more to the point, as a useful political sermon, warning us to safeguard our democratic rights. The diary was published initially in German in 1947 by Otto Frank, Anne's father. A German-Dutch Jew, Anne and her family spent more than two years in an Amsterdam attic hiding from the Nazis who had occupied the country. Discovered, she and the others hiding with her were sent to concentration camps, where Anne died of typhus.

NEW YORK, APRIL 22—Last winter in Paris I read the manuscript of a book, which I have just received in bound form, called "The Diary of a Young Girl" by Anne Frank. It is the story of a child who went through the invasion of Holland and all the fears that Jewish people had to live through at that time. It tells us simply and vividly what it was like.

I think it is well for us who have forgotten so much of that period to read about it now, just to remind ourselves that we never want to go through such things again if possible. Her story ended tragically. She died in the concentration camp at Bergen-Belsen. This diary should teach us all the wisdom of preventing any kind of totalitarianism that could lead to oppression and suffering of this kind.

~ ~ ~

In 1952 her UN Commission on Human Rights work brought Eleanor Roosevelt face to face with Third World delegates whose countries were starving for cash to invest in their feeble, sometimes primitive economies. Though she may sound here a bit simplistic in response to these delegates' pressure for guaranteed capital support, she nonetheless articulated well the fact that for investment in the Third World to work at all, it must be arranged so as to be advantageous to both the giver and the receiver. Also, here, we catch a glimpse of the inner workings of the UN Commission Eleanor Roosevelt chaired with what most observers labeled a remarkable aplomb.

NEW YORK, APRIL 24—The sins of the past are rising up to make life difficult for us today in many ways! In the Human Rights Commission last Monday one of the most evident examples came to light. The delegate from Chile presented an article to be attached to an article already passed in general terms on the right of self-determination. This article stated that the right of people to self-determination included the economic right to control all of their natural resources and not to be deprived of their use or their means of existence by the action of any outside power.

The article was loosely drawn and could be interpreted in many ways. Therefore, as it was for inclusion in a legal document, the United States was opposed to it. I recognized at once, however, the reason why this article received such immediate consideration from all the underdeveloped countries sitting around the table. All those who have to borrow capital were in favor of it.

The reason came out in private conversations. One after the other told me how contracts had been made and natural resources granted for development, and then either they were left undeveloped or developed for a short time and closed down to meet some world situation and keep the price of some article at the desired level.

People would be thrown out of work under these circumstances; royalties would not be paid to the government, which would result in higher taxes for the people.

I pointed out that all these abuses could be remedied by better contracts; that the difficulty they had labored under was unfair and unsafe contracts, but that an article phrased in the way they were proposing would result in no capital being available for development. No nation is going to risk its taxpayers' money outside its own country if there is no regard for contractual agreements, and no group of private individuals is going to feel that they can risk their money or their clients' money without proper safeguards.

One recognizes the evils that underdeveloped nations were trying to correct, but one also fears that they are cutting off their sources of future supply for development.

For those of us who take a serious view of the obligations imposed by a covenant drawn in treaty form, such articles as this create great obstacles. It may be possible to make reservations, but what amounts practically to confiscation of property of foreigners without compensation being legalized by a treaty is going to be extremely difficult for a great many nations to accept.

~ ~ ~

When Eleanor Roosevelt was really seriously upset about something, she took time to do her homework well, to think carefully, and then to write as long and as complex a statement about it as her "My Day" column format would permit. This must have been the case with the next column, which lays it on the line: McCarthyism's nasty habit of insinuating guilt by association, in its ever-widening Communist witch hunt, had to be stopped. The mere idea of alleging that Mary Bethune was a Communist sympathizer convinced Mrs. Roosevelt that Senator McCarthy, if not the whole country, was going mad. Eleanor Roosevelt feared the consequences.

Mary McLeod Bethune was a Southern educator who, in Mrs. Roosevelt's mind, had two distinctions to her credit right at the beginning of her career: She was a woman and she was black. She founded a college for black women in Daytona Beach, Florida, in 1904 that eventually became the co-ed Bethune–Cookman College of which she was president for twenty years. An important member of FDR's New Deal team, Bethune served the country as Director, Division of Negro Affairs, in the National Youth Administration (1936–1944). In Mrs. Roosevelt's opinion, Bethune was a true American heroine.

New York, May 3—A few days ago I read a newspaper account here that shocked me. A group of people, evidently without much knowledge, had so frightened a school organization in Englewood,

265

N.J., that the school rescinded an invitation to speak which it had extended to Mrs. Mary McLeod Bethune.

It seemed to me so preposterous that I waited day by day to see if they had reconsidered, apologized and invited her again to come. But I have seen nothing further, and I cannot let this incident go by without protesting such treatment of an elderly woman who is a leader among the American colored citizens and loved and admired by all American citizens who know her.

Mrs. Bethune is probably a little older than I am. She really worked for her education, and when she had obtained it, literally on a shoestring, she founded a college in Florida to help Negro people. Hundreds of people have helped her because one could not meet her and not recognize her sincerity, her deep and simple Christianity. She has built up this university.

She has headed and worked for the Negro Council of Women, and made it into a strong organization. She has the gift of getting people to cooperate with her. She is the kindest, gentlest person I have ever met.

She lent her talents to the federal service in the National Youth Administration during my husband's administration, and there are countless other positions and responsibilities that she has taken and filled with honor both for her country, for organizations and for individuals. She is the last person that I can imagine any thinking person would believe to be a Communist.

This is again that pernicious thing that we are allowing to bedevil us: guilt by association.

She is accused, I believe, of having gone to Communist-front organizations to speak, even of having belonged to some of these subversive groups.

If she did belong to any, I am sure with her keen mind she soon discovered something wrong and was not a member for long. If she went to them to speak, she undoubtedly did them good. Mary McLeod Bethune would meet the devil and confront him with Christ and I would feel quite sure that she and Christ would triumph.

If it were not so sad to have respected and beloved American citizens insulted and slighted, it would be funny. But those of us who have loved and known Mrs. Bethune for many years must speak up in her defense. If we do not, then this country of ours is in danger of curtailing the liberties for which our forefathers fought.

I still believe that people should be considered innocent until they are proved guilty under the law. I still think that a life of work and service should carry some weight against the idle accusations of a group of extremists.

I know the danger of Communists in this country, and I know the subversives can do us harm. But it does us much more harm to tear down the fabric of justice and fairness and trust in our fellow human beings who have a life record to disprove an idle accusation.

Let us hope that this possibility, having been drawn to our attention in this little magazine, will never actually come to pass in America. There are moments when I listen to Senator McCarthy and hear about an un-American activities committee when I wonder where our freedoms are going and hope that the academic tradition, which is perhaps one of the strongest in this country, will save us from the kind of complete conformity which kills originality and truth.

~ ~ ~

Anyone who takes great cultural institutions like Lincoln Center in New York City or the Kennedy Center in Washington, D.C., for granted should pause to consider what grand efforts and how much time were required to create these institutions and to lay the bricks and mortar. Mrs. Roosevelt was in on the ground floor in the campaign to create a Washington cultural center. She had no idea it would take more than a decade, would just be nearing completion when she died, and would eventually bear the name of an as-yet-unelected President who himself would have died by an assassin's bullet. But Eleanor Roosevelt did know that a society seriously needs its arts just as a child needs its play. Thus, culture was high on her political agenda.

NEW YORK, JUNE 6—There is a bill before Congress to build in Washington, as a national war memorial, a great cultural center, to include a theater and an opera house, as well as the Smithsonian Gallery of Art, which had been authorized by a 1938 act, but for which public funds were never appropriated.

Our national capital could become a very great cultural center and its influence could be felt in every other great city of the United States if we did something of this kind. We have in Washington representatives from all the countries of the world.

We could have there a center that would encourage modern art in all its branches. We might develop a place where young artists could feel they would receive a sympathetic and understanding opportunity. To do something of this kind would prove to the older nations of the world, which are now turning to us for economic and military leadership, that we have come of age and also have much to offer in the way of leadership in the cultural field.

~ ~ ~

A great many organizations asked Mrs. Roosevelt to give them some attention, even a brief mention, in "My Day." Not only was the column distributed to scores of newspapers by the United Feature Syndicate, but it also found its way abroad in English and in translation. To have your group's pet project or key problem discussed in "My Day" was to have received the best possible public relations help. And if Mrs. Roosevelt gave you her enthusiastic support, it could be like a gold coin dropping in your lap. Or at least such must have been the thoughts of Mrs. William Olmstead, who was seeking contributions to support a group of American libraries in France.

We see here again Eleanor Roosevelt in her role as ombudsman, acting principally out of a sense of noblesse oblige to promote better international relations. No cause was too small for her, even if it meant soliciting contributions of twenty-five cents each.

NEW YORK, JULY 19—The other day I had a letter from my friend, Mrs. William B. Olmstead, Jr., who is the American representative of the American Library in Paris. This library also has branches in

Roubaix, Toulouse, Rennes, Montpelier and Grenoble. She has been trying for the past year to form groups of Friends of the American Library in Paris in as many communities as possible in the United States. She hopes that these friends will send American books and magazines to France.

The library has for sale at 25 cents apiece some double cards and envelopes. These cards show fine collotype reproductions of etchings by Samuel Chamberlain. They are views of France which anyone who has traveled there would be glad to have as a reminder of his trip. Their purchase represents a contribution to the work of the library.

We all know what an effort our government is making through the U.S. Information Service libraries to create better understanding between us and the many countries of the world. But Mrs. Olmstead's undertaking is just an added way in which we can help in France, where we have historical affiliations and where it should be very easy to build better understanding and good will.

~ ~ ~

Mrs. Roosevelt was taunted for years by right-wingers for her association in the 1930s with the American Youth Congress, a dissident left-wing organization of intellectual students and recent college graduates who believed the American system—both political and economic—had failed them. FDR and the First Lady, as well as several members of the New Deal Cabinet, recognized the students' disillusionment as painful for the young people and dangerous for the country. Some members of the AYC were indeed Communists, and some were Communist sympathizers. Eleanor Roosevelt did attend AYC meetings and did make financial contributions to the group. Eventually she detached herself from it when its program moved too far to the left—and when public opinion against her participation forced the White House to reconsider its value. Whether her involvement was sensible may be debatable; whether her motives were sincere and patriotic (as she explains them in this next column, which turns into a bitter denunciation of McCarthyism) is not.

Hyde Park, August 29—I have a rather interesting letter from a lady today and I would like to answer it in my column. She says: "In view of your past record of sponsoring organizations with Communist leanings, some of which even booed your late husband, I cannot conceive of your making a speech against a red-blooded American like Senator McCarthy. He has earnestly tried to free our government of Communists. What have you done in that line?"

First, I would like to point out that I have not as yet made a speech against Senator McCarthy.

The only organization I ever sponsored which had any degree of Communist control was the American Youth Congress in the early thirties. There was a very good reason for working with those young people and the bulk of the membership was not then, and was never later, Communistic.

A group among them were Communists then and perhaps may have remained so—that I do not know. But I would like to remind people in general and especially my correspondent that this was a particularly difficult period for young people.

They were coming out of college in great numbers and finding no jobs. Democracy was failing them and many of the most intelligent thought Communism would solve their problems.

Sooner or later many of them found out how intolerable Communist control was and they became better citizens of our democracy than ever before. They did not inform against their former colleagues, they simply gave up Communism and went to work as citizens of our democracy.

They were the more valuable because they knew what was wrong with Communism and they understood and cherished the democratic form of government and the democratic way of life.

Back in the thirties, however, these young people—even those who booed the President—needed friends. They were rude, true, but also desperately unhappy and frustrated. It was fortunate that the White House understood this.

My devotion to my country and to democracy is quite as great as that of Senator McCarthy. I do not like his methods or the results of his methods and I would like to say to my correspondent that I think those of us who worked with young people in the thirties did more to save many of them from becoming Communists than Senator McCarthy has done for his fellow citizens with all his slurs and accusations.

I know the danger of Communism. I know it perhaps better than many other American citizens because for nearly five months of every year for the last six years, I have sat in meetings with the Communist representatives of the USSR.

I despise the control they insist on holding over men's minds. And that is why I despise what Senator McCarthy has done, for he would use the same methods of fear to control all thought that is not according to his own pattern—in our free country!

~ ~ ~

When Harry Truman declared he would not run for President in 1952, the field for Democratic Party nominees was thrown wide open for the first time in twenty years—since 1932 when FDR drove Republican Herbert Hoover from the White House. Everyone knew that Mrs. Roosevelt would have strong feelings about this year's crop of candidates, but she had made it clear that she would do little if any campaigning. As chairman of the UN Commission on Human Rights she wanted to remain disengaged from the hurlyburly of American domestic politics. At the UN, she believed, a delegate, especially a committee chair, was responsible first to humankind, then to his country, and only then to his own political party.

But there was another set of reasons why Eleanor Roosevelt had surprisingly little to say about the presidential election in 1952. Within her family, political enthusiasms were sharply divided. During the primary election campaigns, son Franklin Jr. worked for Governor Averill Harriman of New York; son James supported Senator Estes Kefauver of Tennessee; Eleanor liked Adlai Stevenson. At least these candidates were Democrats. Son Elliott, privately, and son John, publicly, favored Eisenhower, the Republican. And so Mrs. Roosevelt welcomed an excuse to keep hands off. The worst of it, for Adlai

271

Stevenson, was that Eleanor Roosevelt seemed to damn him with faint praise. She had every respect for his intelligence and his platform, but (as the next two columns show) she did not believe he had the requisite amount of what a later generation would call charisma to lead the country effectively.

Stevenson was regularly labeled by his opponents and even by the liberal press as an egghead, meaning in the slang of the time a cool intellectual, rather aloof from the common people. Eleanor Roosevelt's model president was one Franklin Delano Roosevelt. Like Stevenson, FDR was a clever, well-educated man. But he had a warmth and a joie de vivre that charmed and reassured the people in ways that Eleanor Roosevelt thought Stevenson never could. She gave the Illinois governor her more or less passive support and offered him a few lessons about practical politics—through her "My Day" column—but that was about all she did. Eisenhower overwhelmed Stevenson in November, and the Democrats were gone from the White House after a long, uninterrupted reign.

HYDE PARK, SEPTEMBER 4—I understand that Governor Adlai Stevenson accepted the idea that he and General Eisenhower have a debate on a nationwide television hookup but that the general declined. This must mean that either General Eisenhower or his advisers feel that Governor Stevenson can outtalk the Republican candidate.

Perhaps he can, and certainly he is making a very good impression in all of his major speeches. He has wit and humor, charm, restraint and intelligence.

But these things alone will not win the presidential election for the Illinois governor. He must find out how to have the people feel that he is talking to them individually and that they must listen or they will miss something that really affects their daily lives. This is a gift that can be cultivated, and the candidate who achieves this close relationship with most of the people in his audience probably will win on Election Day.

HYDE PARK, SEPTEMBER 13—As the two presidential candidates tour the country I really wonder whether we can count on people as a whole listening to or reading in full their speeches. If they do, they cannot fail to be impressed, I think, by the fact that there are more real issues being discussed in Stevenson's speeches than in General Eisenhower's.

This is probably because Governor Stevenson is more personally familiar with the domestic questions in the country, having been governor of Illinois and being in active politics for some time and with a family background that would have led him to the study of day-by-day political situations.

They might feel, however, as I do, that occasionally the Governor is a little academic. Please remember, Mr. Governor, we are usually sitting down after a long day's work to listen to you in our living rooms. We want to feel that you are visiting us, that you have something which you want us to know about in order that we may help you. We don't want to be talked down to; we just want you to tell us very simply what your problems are and what you face in the great task you are asking us to help you meet by voting for you in November.

~ ~ ~

By 1952, Richard M. Nixon had made loyal friends and lifelong enemies through his work, while a Representative in Congress, for the House Un-American Activities Committee. Eleanor Roosevelt held him accountable for his contributions to the rise of McCarthyism. But Nixon was Eisenhower's choice for Vice President, and that carried some weight with Mrs. Roosevelt because basically she respected the General.

Beyond this, the issue raised in Nixon's famous "Checkers" speech (the name derives from the Nixon family dog, a political gift the Senator swore he would never give back) was the matter of setting appropriate levels of salaries and expense accounts for public officials. Nixon defended himself on television against well-substantiated claims that he had a hidden slush fund of campaign money in an expense account. His speech was a bravura performance, if one believed that an emotional public confession of personal financial details and spending habits counted for anything. Mrs. Roosevelt thought it unseemly and unnecessary. Ahead of her time, as usual, she cut to the nub of the issue: Public officials running national campaigns and serving in high office needed a salary boost to keep them from relying on hidden, privately donated funds beyond the public's scrutiny.

HYDE PARK, SEPTEMBER 24—I must say something today about the subject that has certainly caused a great deal of excitement in these past few days—the discovery that Senator Richard Nixon, the vice-presidential candidate of the Republican ticket, has been using an $18,000 expense fund raised by his California supporters.

Listing his personal resources and expenditures in order to clear himself of any possible personal accusation of the misuse of these funds seemed to me to be a mistake. It is not proper to require men in public office to list their private assets and account in detail for all their expenditures.

What is required is that where a man is a public servant he should not receive money from sources which, no matter how respectable, may bring some undue influence to bear. These friends might expect some return for their gifts at a given point where their own interests are concerned and a public official who had received money, no matter for how good a purpose, would perhaps find it difficult to vote according to his conscience against the wishes of people who had been upholding some special interests of his.

This whole question points up, I think, the need that we must pay higher salaries to senators, representatives, judges and executive officers in both state and federal positions. In many cases salaries are such that a man cannot live on his salary, so he must engage in business or receive some outside assistance.

For a nation like ours this does not seem right. Allowances should be given to public servants for entertaining where it is necessary and to cover such expenses as are considered legitimate to their position and for travel. Their salaries should compare favorably with the salaries in other occupations of importance. Merely stating that serving the government brings a man opportunities in the future and some renown in the present is not the proper way to safeguard our public interest.

It would not be right, it seems to me, to think that Senator Nixon had in any way felt that this fund was something he should not accept. He probably reasoned that these were men with whom he saw eye to eye and anything they desired he would desire and there would be no conflict at any point.

That reasoning, however, will no longer satisfy the public, I am sure. The people know the weakness of human nature and the pressures which personal interests make some people bring to bear on public officials. Therefore, the standard of what should or should not be done by men in public office is getting higher and higher in an effort to eliminate the possibility that improper pressures will become effective.

The suggestion I have made is the only one, it seems to me, that would make it more possible for a man in public life to carry on his work efficiently and feel utterly free from any outside pressures.

~ ~ ~

In 1952 Mrs. Roosevelt found herself under some pressure from the Democratic Party to endorse John F. Kennedy, then a Representative from Massachusetts, for a Senate seat. Kennedy was more than sufficiently attractive as a candidate. However, for Mrs. Roosevelt, supporting him meant striking a blow at another distinguished, articulate public servant, the Republican incumbent, Senator Henry Cabot Lodge. Senator Lodge came from a Boston Brahmin family with roots as deep in the Colonial American past as the Roosevelts'. And, like Eleanor Roosevelt, Lodge was a fervent supporter of the UN.

Kennedy eventually won Mrs. Roosevelt's favor and support after talking politics with her over a cup of tea at her Hyde Park cottage. The young congressman had made a pilgrimage there to ask for her help, as though coming to Court to ask for the Queen's blessing. But only four years later, after successfully gaining the Senate seat, Kennedy would fall out of favor with Mrs. Roosevelt because in her view he remained insufficiently outspoken on the question of censuring Joseph McCarthy in the Senate as a way to dissolve the insidious power of McCarthyism.

NEW YORK, SEPTEMBER 27—While in Amherst I had the pleasure of meeting Congressman John F. Kennedy for a few minutes. He is campaigning vigorously for the Senate seat against the present incumbent, Senator Henry Cabot Lodge.

Mr. Kennedy has been a Congressman for six years and in the State of Massachusetts I think they should know him well enough to realize that he has certain very good qualities that should recommend him for election to serve in the Senate. It is important, I think, that these young, courageous representatives who have had experience in the House move into the Senate and bring into that body some of the influence of youth.

~ ~ ~

Mrs. Roosevelt never let up in her campaign for civil rights for all Americans. The "My Day" column was used many times to expose cases of particularly virulent racism that she felt simply had to be addressed both legally and morally. The next column asks its Caucasian readers to imagine what they would feel like if, while traveling abroad in a country where the dominant population was not white, they were denied medical help because of their race. Anyone who took the point to heart would immediately see the absurdity, Mrs. Roosevelt hoped, of denying to black people in America the medical assistance they might need at a hospital simply because they were black.

NEW YORK, OCTOBER 17—I have just received from the Southern Conference Educational Fund, Inc., a most interesting pamphlet entitled "The Untouchables." It deals with the question of segregation in hospitals and the difficult situations that arise when hospitals do not accept all sick people but put limitations on their service.

The Southern Conference Educational Fund is a Southwide, nonprofit organization with headquarters in New Orleans. The little prospectus sent out with the pamphlet states that "it is dedicated to the fight against racial segregation and discrimination in all fields of social endeavor."

Through pamphlets and publications, conferences and opinion polls, the SCEF seeks to achieve a more equitable sharing of our democratic heritage. Its funds come from voluntary contributions from some 3,000 individuals throughout the country. "The Untouchables" is one of its pamphlets. Ben Shahn has contributed the illustrations and layout as a gesture of his concern with the great social problems the pamphlet discusses. The text was written by a native Southerner and a former New Orleans newspaperman, Alfred Maund.

No one could look through this pamphlet without being deeply troubled that such things as it describes should happen anywhere in the United States. Some of the instances it mentions go back many years, but also detailed are some occurrences of recent years that seem fairly shocking.

For instance, on "August 27, 1950, three victims of an auto accident were denied beds in Breckinridge County Hospital, Hardinsburg, Kentucky, because the establishment had no facilities for colored people." They were left lying on the floor of the emergency room for three hours, their wounds were untended, and the only medication given them was morphine. One of the men died on the floor, and, ironically, his family later received a bill for "services rendered." The others were removed to Louisville General Hospital, where they eventually recovered. One sustained partial permanent paralysis as a result of a broken back.

Also, in February, 1951, an 18-year-old boy suffering from sugar diabetes died after being refused admission to the Akron, Ohio, City Hospital.

These two stories would make sorry reading for any American finding himself in the Near East or Asia. Suppose we white people were taken ill in those areas of the world and this type of segregation were practiced against us. Yet, that would be the normal and natural thing to do, according to some standards, because we would be in the minority, since two-thirds of the world's people are colored.

The picture is changing, however, in the South. As of last February, the Kentucky state senate passed by unanimous vote a bill forbidding all licensed medical institutions to deny care to any person on the basis of color or creed. In at least six cities similar citizen's movements combating Jim Crow medical care are under way.

It is such organizations as the Southern Conference Educational Fund that will really bring about the changes all of us hope for—not only in the South but throughout our country. Then we can say with truth and conviction that we move forward to ever better conditions for all of our people.

~ ~ ~

President Truman chose Eleanor Roosevelt to represent him and all Americans at the inauguration of a new president of Chile in Santiago. She was proud to go and was eager to make contact with some of the numerous Roosevelt family whose ancestors (on the Delano side) had settled there after emigrating from the Netherlands. The Chileans held former President Franklin Roosevelt in high esteem.

SANTIAGO, NOVEMBER 10—What I shall take away with me as a never-to-be-forgotten remembrance, however, is the warmth with which everyone speaks of my husband. I think it would be a good thing for governments to realize that a man's philosophy, when it is given practical demonstration through what he does at home for the people of his own country, can be vastly important to the people of other nations. If people anywhere make gains in their rights as human beings, then other people everywhere take heart and hope that their day, too, will come. This understanding of my husband's philosophy of government— namely, that it must be an instrument of service to the people— accounts, of course, for the warm reception which the people have given me.

~ ~ ~

Eisenhower and Nixon swept the election in November, and with that news the great wheels of government began to turn in a different direction and at a new pace. Though cordial in their limited public contacts and respectful of one another in their comments to the press,

*the new President and Mrs. Roosevelt could never have been consid-
ered political allies. She was simply too far to the left to remain part of
the White House team as a delegate to the UN. She submitted her
resignation to the President-elect and hoped he might refuse to accept
it, but he did—with pressure from the likes of J. Edgar Hoover,
Director of the FBI, who believed that Eleanor Roosevelt's liberal
leanings were dangerous to the country. Thus one of the most
important jobs of Eleanor Roosevelt's life came to a hasty end, with
the Covenant of Human Rights still unfinished at the UN. She would
have the satisfaction soon, however, of seeing the Declaration of
Human Rights adopted by the General Assembly. (And, as we shall
see in the final volume of selections from "My Day," her UN-related
work was by no means over.)*

*There must have been nostalgia in Mrs. Roosevelt's heart as she
watched the changing of the guard at what was soon to become the
Eisenhower White House.*

NEW YORK, DECEMBER 3—I saw a picture of Mrs. Truman welcoming Mrs. Eisenhower at the door of the White House, and I could
not help recalling when I visited Mrs. Hoover. I certainly was not as
well-dressed as Mrs. Eisenhower was.

The White House today is in a great deal better condition than it
was when my husband and I entered it. Also, there is much more
room on the third floor. I see by the papers that Mrs. Eisenhower
missed visiting the kitchen, and I always felt that that was one of the
most important and interesting parts of the house. Perhaps Mrs.
Eisenhower felt there would be plenty of time in the future for that.

~ ~ ~

*The year slipped toward its conclusion with some items of dark news
holding the public's attention. The Supreme Court refused to stay the
death sentences of Julius and Ethel Rosenberg, convicted of espionage
on behalf of the Soviets. The liberal establishment lobbied hard for a
new trial or at least for the mercy of life imprisonment with some hope
of parole, for many believed the Rosenbergs had been framed. But it*

was to no avail. McCarthyism thrived on scapegoats, and rightly or wrongly, this is what the Rosenbergs had become in the national nightmare about Communist subversion. Mrs. Roosevelt's tack was not to pass judgment but to use the case as another occasion to express her disagreement with the whole idea of capital punishment.

NEW YORK, DECEMBER 11—I am getting a considerable number of letters, all Communist-inspired so far as I can see, from people urging me to do something to prevent the execution of Julius and Ethel Rosenberg, who are slated to die around January 12. They were found guilty of being members of an atom-bomb espionage ring.

This Communist-inspired campaign is certainly going to do the Rosenbergs more harm than good. Some of the writers try to make it appear that this sentence was imposed on the Rosenbergs because they are Jews and is intended to start anti-Jewish activities in this country. That is utter nonsense.

The question of civil liberties in this case has been carefully watched. It is odd that the Soviets should harp on this when they themselves have come out openly in an anti-Semitic campaign. Nevertheless, they have tried everything, as can be seen in the letters that are coming to my desk.

I don't believe in capital punishment, but we do have capital punishment in our country. I don't know if putting the Rosenbergs to death will do us more good than if they were under a sentence of life imprisonment, but this country operates under law and as long as we have laws we must live up to them, making sure that the law is fairly administered.

Without question, the authorities in our country have given careful consideration as to whether the security of the United States would be benefited by death or life imprisonment. Punishment of this kind is used as a deterrent for others who might be tempted to do likewise and that also must have been given careful consideration.

~　　~　　~

With throngs of family gathering around her at Hyde Park for the Christmas holidays (by now, she could count almost twenty grandchildren), we find Mrs. Roosevelt still linking arms with the lame duck President, Harry Truman, in the last gasp of a legislative fight for something they both believed in deeply: national health insurance. The operative phrase in this final "My Day" column selected for this volume is "basic human right." All her working life Eleanor Roosevelt campaigned tirelessly to promote and defend such rights, for all the people, wherever she found them threatened, misunderstood, or not yet fully realized.

NEW YORK, DECEMBER 24—I am particularly interested in the health plan that the President's 15-member commission has recommended. If it is to be put in operation, of course, the new administration will have to study it and decide whether it is the best way that we can be sure to give all our people, as a basic human right, health services—free if need be for a few, and for all at very moderate cost.

I gather that the Compulsory Health Insurance Plan, which the American Medical Association objected to, is no longer under discussion. The commission, however, felt that there was a vast need "of medical personnel, health educational facilities, health centers, hospitals and services, and also the organization of these facilities to make them more available."

It was estimated that the annual cost to the taxpayers in accepting the recommendations of the commission would be $1,750,000,000 in federal and state funds.

This is, of course, a tremendous sum of money. But when we look at the loss to industry on account of neglected illness and the loss to the country because of the neglect in the area of health among our children we realize that if this plan would actually meet the actual health needs of the country it would pay us many times to put it into operation. Many of our people are never able to contribute fully to the national economy because of illness and many more become complete charges on their communities.

A life as fast-moving as Eleanor Roosevelt's resists easy summary. And the practical considerations of making three separate volumes of selected columns from "My Day" need not mislead us into thinking that at any point Mrs. Roosevelt came to a full stop in her work or social activity. Even when FDR died in 1945, she carried on almost immediately with writing her newspaper column. It took her only a few weeks in 1953 to begin finding her way into new United Nations work and in the new political atmosphere of the Eisenhower presidency.

Eleanor Roosevelt had another decade of life ahead of her, and though she would turn sixty-nine in the new year (age enough for most people to slow down), in some respects the pace of her life was soon to pick up even more. Her "My Day" column would record the best of it. Going forward now without any official or family connection to the government for the first time since her husband had entered politics in the 1920s, she would be more free than ever to express her opinions candidly and colorfully, letting the chips fall where they might. The readership of "My Day" continued to grow as the transformation of Eleanor Roosevelt from First Lady of the United States to First Lady of the World became complete.

Index

O

P

R

S

$\mathcal{U}$

$\mathcal{U}$

$\mathcal{W}$

DATE		